Building Bamboo Fences

Isao Yoshikawa

Building Bamboo Fences

Published by Graphic-sha Publishing Co., Ltd.,
1-14-17, Kudan-kita, Chiyoda-ku, Tokyo 102-0073, Japan
Tel: +81-(0)3-3263-4318 Fax: +81-(0)3-3263-5297

English translation: Língua fránca, Inc.

Distributed by Japan Publications Trading Co., Ltd.,
1-2-1, Sarugaku-cho, Chiyoda-ku, Tokyo 101-0064 Japan
Tel: +81-(0)3-3292-3751 Fax: +81-(0)3-3292-0410

Distributors:
United States: Kodansha America, Inc. through Oxford University Press,
198 Madison Avenue, New York, NY 10016.
Canada: Fitzhenry & Whiteside Ltd.,
195 Allstate Parkway, Markham, Ontario L3R 4T8.
United Kingdom and Europe: Premier Book Marketing Ltd.,
Clarendon House, 52 Cornmarket Street, Oxford OX1 3 HJ, United Kingdom.
Australia and New Zealand: Bookwise International Pty. LTD.,
174 Cormack Road, Wingfield, South Australia 5013, Australia
Asia and Japan: Japan Publications Trading Co., Ltd.,
1-2-1, Sarugaku-cho, Chiyoda-ku, Tokyo 101-0064 Japan

First printing: October 2001
Second printing: August 2003

ISBN4-88996-080-5

Printed and bound by Everbest Printing Co., Ltd. in China

Contents

Preface

A scene with a fresh green bamboo grove is symbolic of the natural beauty of Japan. Many species of bamboo grow not only in Japan but also in China and Southeast Asian countries, where bamboo has been traditionally used to make various household utensils, or used as a building material. Bamboo, in fact, has many more uses than wood.

Some of the most notable characteristics of bamboo are that it is hollow and has joints, and that its flesh is thin and easy to cut, yet rather strong. These characteristics support bamboo's surprisingly wide applications.

Japan has its native species of bamboo such as ma-dake and hachiku, which are not found in China or Southeast Asia. Ma-dake is an especially high-quality species with a stout stalk and relatively thin flesh, and is suitable for delicate working. This species has made a great contribution to the development of the art of bamboo fence building in Japan. The fact that there are so many type variations and that each design is sophisticated to such a high degree reflects the typical aesthetic sense and sensitivity of the Japanese people.

Today, however, bamboo fences are not seen as often as before. Even in Kyoto, the home of genuine bamboo fences, the number of bamboo fences is decreasing, and there are more and more plastic-made "bamboo fences." These artificial bamboo fences are, of course, not as valuable as genuine ones, although they are at times useful if placed at an inconspicuous location. It is sad, however, to see artificial bamboo fences in a Japanese-style garden. Artificial ones are used mainly for economical reasons.

Real bamboo begins to deteriorate within five years or so, and people nowadays tend to prefer artificial materials that are more durable. Using an artificial bamboo fence in a tea ceremony garden, however, conflicts with the philosophy of "chanoyu", the art of ceremonial tea making. The life of a bamboo fence consists of a short "green" period, followed by a long "light brown" period, and then decay and death–an existence that eventually vanishes, in which one finds the taste of Japanese wabi (austerity).I sincerely hope that authentic bamboo fences will never die out from Japanese culture.

This book showcases, with diagrams, the detailed designs of Japanese traditional bamboo fences, which have been developed by garden designers, and basic techniques for building them. It is the first book ever published that shows ordinary people how to build various bamboo fences by themselves.

Although this is an introductory book as far as bamboo fence building techniques is concerned, I am sure that those who wish to become professional garden designers will find it useful.

All the photos, detailed diagrams, and other explanatory illustrations are my own. Two illustrators, Mr. Makio Suzuki and Mr. Kazuaki Kometani, transformed my draft procedure illustrations into easy-to-understand diagrams. I would like to extend my sincere gratitude to them.

Isao Yoshikawa

History

Origin of Bamboo Fences

It is impossible to know exactly how old the history of bamboo fences is. One can only take a guess, since there is no extant ancient bamboo fence.

If a bamboo fence means any fence using bamboo, it is not hard to imagine that simply made "bamboo fences" did exist in ancient times.

In countries with warm climates where bamboo grows, people must have used it for various purposes from early days.

Early-stage primitive bamboo fences, which were popular in Southeast Asia, China, Japan, etc. from early days, can be regarded as a useful tool.

Different from wood, the convenience of bamboo must have been very useful for ancient people. It is the fastest growing plant, it is strong, and it is easy to obtain many bamboos of the same thickness. These characteristics make bamboo an ideal material for building fences.

Furthermore, it is assumed that simple brushwood fences (shiba-gaki), with vertical poles made of tree branches standing on the ground held between horizontal support poles made of bamboo, date back to ancient times.

In my opinion, the evolution from simple bamboo fences to more sophisticated ones involves the addition of some sort of formal beauty. Compared to the primitive structure in which round bamboos were combined and tied to each other, a more advanced structure in which split bamboos were woven must have been more beautiful, even if this was not recognized by the people who invented them.

A Brief History of Bamboo Fences in China

In recent years I have had the chance to study quite a few Chinese historical paintings closely. As a result, I have reached the conclusion, with confidence, that people in ancient China also built bamboo fences.

Historical picture scrolls indicate that Japanese bamboo fences were rapidly developed during the Heian and Kamakura periods, while in China, too, a similar development must have taken place during the Tang period. Therefore, at this point, I do not deny the possibility that early forms of bamboo fences found in Japan were not uniquely of Japanese origin, but that they came from ancient China.

The oldest forms of bamboo fences found in China include not only the most primitive ones, but also more advanced brushwood fences (shiba-gaki), stockade fences (yarai-gaki), ajiro-gaki, kenninji-gaki, and so on. The situation was very similar in Japan. Among the diverse forms of old bamboo fences, the one that appears most frequently in paintings is the ajiro-gaki.

For instance, in <Shikyô-shônan-hachihenzu> (owned by the Shanghai Museum) painted by Ma He Chi, an artist who served Emperor Kao Zong in the early Southern Sung period, a three-tiered ajiro-gaki, whose weaving method is similar to that of the Japanese numazu-gaki, can be clearly seen. During the Sung period, there were also simply made bamboo fences, brushwood fences (shiba-gaki), and stockade fences (yarai-gaki).

In the following period, the era of the Ming dynasty, bamboo fences were most popular, but their types and forms did not change much from the ones in the previous period. The majority were ajiro-gaki, which are seen in <Teijudô-zu> (owned by the Gu Gong Museum, Fig. 1) by Tang Yin (1470-1523), <Rinsha-sencha-zu> (owned by the Tienjin Art Museum) by Wen Cheng Ming (1470-1559), and many other works of the day.

There were also simple fences that looked like the kenninji-gaki, a typical example of which is seen in Wen's <Sekiheki-hikô-zu> (owned by the Shanghai Museum, Fig. 2).

In the Ching period, bamboo fences were even more often used as objects for paintings. There are so many

Fig. 1 An amishiro-gaki seen in an old Chinese painting <Teijudô-zu> (by Tang Yin, Ming period)

Fig. 2 A kenninji-gaki seen in an old Chinese painting <Sekiheki-hiko-zu> (by Wen Cheng Ming, Ming period)

examples that it is impossible to introduce all of them here. One important example, in which a three-tiered ajiro-gaki is described in subtle details, is <Sôjushii-zu> (owned by the Su Chou Museum) by Hua Yan (1682-1756), who was one of the leading artists of the early Ching period. Chien Du (1764-1844), an artist who lived during the second half of the Ching period, painted a large bamboo fence, probably a stockade fence (yarai-gaki), in his <Jinbutsu-sansui-zu> (Fig. 3).

All examples of Chinese paintings with bamboo fences have a definite common characteristic: they do not appear with grand buildings like palaces.

In many cases, bamboo fences belong to a scene with a simple thatched cottage, or the like, built in a rustic scenic location. From this fact, we know that the Chinese people of the day longed for a hermitic life in the mountains, and that such an environment is the ideal setting for bamboo fences.

Being one of the most easily obtained materials, bamboo was no doubt widely used as an inexpensive material for building simple enclosures. Artists of the time preferred to portray such ascetic life in their paintings–many paintings with bamboo fences were thus created.

In China today, however, due to the drastic change in the social system, there are few people who lead a hermitic life, and we do not usually find bamboo fences around ordinary houses or buildings.

In some of the famous Chinese style gardens with a forest, however, unique bamboo fences can be seen even today.

With their typical splendor, Chinese bamboo fences seem to have followed a different path from their sober Japanese counterparts. Especially interesting are bamboo fences which are similar to "dragon fences" (Chinese walls with a curved top).

A Brief History of Bamboo Fences in Japan

Early bamboo fences in Japan had much in common with their Chinese counterparts. Initially, simple brushwood fences (shiba-gaki) with vertical poles of tree branches held between bamboo-made horizontal poles were probably the most popular form of "bamboo fence." In Kojiki, there is mention of a "beautiful green brushwood fence," which is probably poetic term for a plain brushwood fence. In Emperor Seinei's chapter of Kojiki is a poem that reads:

My master has not made up his mind yet. He cannot get inside my firmly built brushwood fence (shiba-gaki).

Also, in Princess Hashi's chapter of The Tale of Genji, we read:

Because it would be troublesome if people in the neighborhood were to wake up, he does not even allow the guides to make any noise. Advancing on a path between shiba-no-kaki (brushwood fences), we only hear our horses stepping on the water of some streams running in the dark.

"Shiba-no-kaki" means the same as shiba-gaki.

From old picture scrolls we know that there were perhaps three types of brushwood fences in those days: one with a single row of vertically arranged tree branches; one with bundles of vertically arranged tree branches held between horizontal support poles, and one with multiple rows of tree branches diagonally arranged with the upper ends intersecting. Here, I want to show the cross-type brushwood fence seen in a Kamakura-period picture scroll <Boki-ekotoba> (owned by the Nishi-honganji Temple)(Fig.4).

In the Heian period, brushwood fences were regarded as something of the countryside scenery, and people of the day who preferred simple and quiet taste were attracted to them. This taste has something in common with the ancient Chinese people's yearning for a hermitic life, as well as the later sense of wabi (austerity).

In many pieces of Heian-period literature, there is

Fig. 3 A stockade fence seen in an old Chinese painting <Jinbutsu-sansui-zu> (by Chien Du, Ching period)

Fig. 4 A cross-type brushwood fence seen in a picture scroll of the Kamakura period <Boki-ekotoba>

mention of the "suigai" (transparent fence), which is different from the sukashi-gaki (see-through fence), a term used to indicate one of the major categories of Japanese bamboo fences. Suigai is a fence usually constructed with wooden plates fixed with slits between them (Fig. 5). Therefore, they do not usually belong to the bamboo fence family, although some of them were made by weaving bamboo slats. In Princess Hashi's chapter of The Tale of Genji, there is a mention of bamboo-woven suigai. This is a form of fence for which the ajiro-gaki building method is used.

There was another form of fence called tatejitomi. In The Pillow Book we read:

> Spiteful are the servants who stand by tatejitomi or sukashi-gaki and say, "It's going to rain soon," meaning it to be heard by their master.

From this statement, the tatejitomi can be interpreted as something different from suigai, but they seem to have shared some common characteristics. A tatejitomi usually meant a screen-like moving fence made of thin strips of Japanese cypress (hinoki) using the ajiro-weaving method.

There were also tatejitomi made of woven bamboo slats. In a picture scroll <Kôbôdaishi-gyôjô-emaki> (owned by the Tôji Temple) made during the Period of the Northern and Southern Dynasties, a tatejitomi with very thick green bamboos used as the oyabashiras is shown (Fig. 6).

Apart from tatejitomi, there was a form of fence called hinoki-gaki (Japanese cypress fence) (Fig. 7). In Tales of Ages Ago we read:

> There was a large mansion enclosed with a long cypress fence (hinoki-gaki).

From this statement we know that hinoki-gaki were built around mansion just as ajiro-gaki were.

Although the suigai, the tatejitomi, and the hinoki-gaki had some variations in style, they all belonged to the ajiro-gaki category, with the basic structure made of thin Japanese cypress strips or split bamboos woven in the ajiro pattern.

Among different varieties, the hinoki-gaki and the ajiro-gaki were almost the same in ancient times. Based on the modern classification, however, any fences made of split bamboos woven in the ajiro pattern are called ajiro-gaki.

There were also other variations with different structures, from which the kenninji-gaki and the ôtsu-gaki developed. They will be referred to in a later chapter where the general bamboo fence classification is explained.

From the Heian period through the Kamakura and Muromachi periods, there was no remarkable change in the design and variety of bamboo fences. It was after "chanoyu," the art of ceremonial tea making, was established in the Momoyama period that bamboo fences were reevaluated.

The "Roji", the garden adjacent to a tea arbor with stepping stones and a stone washbowl, is thought to be a spiritual space indispensable in the art of chanoyu, and bamboo fences became an essential part of roji as barriers, partitions, and decorative objects.

While in the roji, the people participating in the tea ceremony were required to have the "wabi" spirit, so sturdily built, heavy-looking plaster or wooden walls were not appropriate. Bamboo fences, with their plain and sophisticated taste, however, were ideal.

Used as decorative objects in the roji, bamboo fences developed greatly. Simple fences like short sode-gaki were given a certain importance, but sukashi-gaki such as four-eyed fences constructed on both sides of the intermediate gate as partitions between the outer and inner roji were especially popular.

It was, however, not until the Edo period that bamboo fences gained the variety and sophistication seen today.

In the Edo period, the elements that were originally unique to the roji, such as stepping stones, pavement, stone lanterns, and a stone washbowl, began to be placed in traditional Japanese gardens. Consequently, bamboo fences, which were by then popular elements in roji, were also used for ordinary gardens. Bamboo fences, with their elegance,

Fig. 5 A suigai seen in a picture from <Kegon-engi> (owned by the Kôzanji Temple, Kamakura period)

Fig. 6 A tatejitomi seen in a picture scroll <Kôbôdaishi-gyôjô-emaki> (Period of the Northern and Southern Dynasties)

Fig. 7 A hinoki-gaki seen in a picture scroll <Kôbôdaishi-gyôjô-emaki> (Period of the Northern and Southern Dynasties)

seemed to be popular especially in the early Edo period when many excellent paintings of bamboo fences on sliding partitions (fusuma-e) were produced.

The fusuma-e of a shino-gaki (painted in the early Edo period) owned by the Tenkyû-in of the Myôshinji Temple in Kyoto is especially famous. Here, however, I want to show the wonderful fusuma-e of a brushwood fence (painted in the early Edo period) which is owned by the Seianji Temple in the city of Ôtsu (Fig. 8).

In the early Edo period, "Kokin-sadô-zensho" (published in 1694) was completed with descriptive drawings of famous roji of the day. From those simple drawings in this book, it is known that a wide variety of bamboo fences already existed. Let me show below an example of a brushwood fence, with brushwood branches standing in a row, as portrayed in a drawing entitled <Roku jô-ô-no-sashizu-hirano-roji> (Fig. 9).

After the mid-Edo period, many books on the art of garden design were published, some of which directly referred to bamboo fences. Also, many paintings and drawings of famous gardens, in which various forms of bamboo fences can be seen, were published.

In addition to the ordinary " 垣 " there are other Chinese characters used to indicate a bamboo fence, such as " 籬 ", " 牆 ", " 墻 " and " 屏 ".

One of the early books on garden design <Tsukiyama-teizô-den> (published in 1735) by Enkin Kitamura carries many drawings of gardens with some varieties of bamboo fences.

Among such books, <Tsukiyama-senshiroku> (published in 1797), handwritten by a Buddhist priest, Tôboku, was one of the first books to refer specifically bamboo fences. In the second volume of this book is a chapter called "Bamboo Fences," in which the following thirteen varieties of bamboo fences are introduced with simple explanations.
Daimyô-gaki, shoin-gaki (study fence), teppô-gaki (rifle barrel fence), rikyû-gaki, chasen-gaki, ikô-gaki, fusei-gaki, sui-gaki, nidan-gaki (two-tiered fence), sandan-gaki (three-tiered fence), rachi-gaki, nanzenji-gaki, and myôshinji-gaki. These names are rather different from the ones we know today, and some of them, in fact, do not make sense. Further research is necessary.

Two years after the publication of <Tsukiyama-senshiroku> <Miyako-rinsen-meishô-zue> by Akisato Ritôken was published in 1799. This book contains many paintings of famous gardens in Kyoto, in which a wide variety of bamboo fences can be seen. Shown below is the bamboo fence portrayed in the painting of the garden of the Sôkokuji Temple's Rinkôin, included in the first volume (Fig. 10).

Thirty years later, Ritôken published his <Ishigumi-sono-yaegaki-den> (1827) and <Tsukiyama-teizô-den Part Two> (1828). The former, especially, contains many drawings of bamboo fences with rather detailed explanations. The names of bamboo fence varieties as known today originated in this book, which introduced thirty-seven types of bamboo fences as well as fourteen kinds of wooden and other doors. The latter has illustrated examples showing how those bamboo fences should be used in gardens.

We have seen the long tradition of the art of bamboo fence building from the Heian period till today. Japanese bamboo fences are unique in the fact that they have a large variety and delicate structures and designs. This is because the development of Japanese bamboo fences was closely linked with the roji in chanoyu, while also Japanese native ma-dake served as an ideal material for elaborate working.

Fig. 8 A brushwood fence seen in a fusuma-e of the Edo period (owned by the Seianji Temple, Ôtsu)

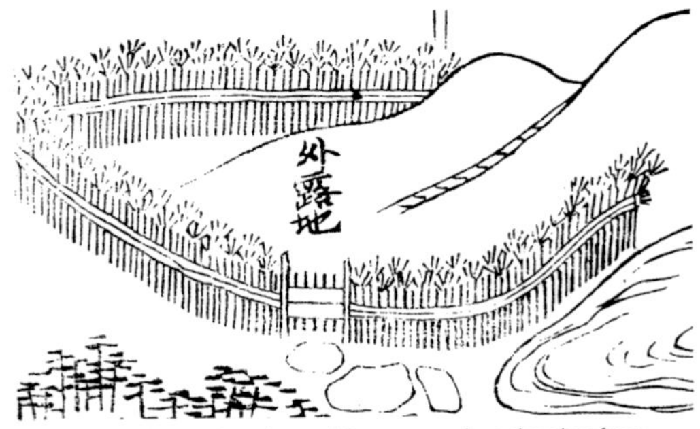

Fig. 9 A single-row brushwood fence seen in a drawing from <Kokin-sadô-zensho>

Fig. 10 A kenninji-gaki style fence and an ajiro-gaki seen in a picture from <Miyako-rinsen-meishô-zue>

Classification

Kenninji-gaki

The first bamboo fence of this style is said to be the one located at the Kenninji Temple, an old Rinzai Zen temple in Kyoto, hence the name. It is the most common variety of the shahei-gaki (screening fence) today.

The kenninji-gaki presumably obtained its name during the Edo period, and one of the oldest mention of this fence in literature was made in <Ishigumi-sono-yaegaki-den> with an explanatory note and diagram (Fig. 11). There is also a design diagram for a five-tiered fence with the following explanatory statement.

"If the height is six shaku (approx. six ft.), it would be best to use this ratio. Use quarter-split bamboo for the rear side of this fence. Arrange a single layer of yarai-omote, but the posts are not to be seen from the front side. Horizontal support poles are attached on the front side."

On later pages, there is a structural diagram of the sô-kenninji-gaki with an explanatory note.

Also, in <Kiyû-shôran> (published in 1830) is a statement that reads:

"Among the many fences made of bamboo or bush clover, fences using quarter-split stout bamboo canes, which are now popular in Edo, are called kenninji-gaki. From the fact that fences like this are not referred to in any of the existing literature, we know that they were invented only recently. Originally, bamboo of high quality grew at this temple...."

From this we learn that the kenninji-gaki was very popular in Edo.

We also know however, from <Hônen-shônin-eden> (Kamakura period, owned by the Chion-in Temple), that the original form of the kenninji-gaki already existed in the Kamakura period. Similar bamboo fences were also built in ancient China.

The exact design of the "original" kenninji-gaki is not known yet. Some scholars say its prototype is the toba-gaki, a fence arranged with a row of old toba, while others say it used to be called kajiwara-gaki in ancient times. There is still another theory which says that the tateko-gaki, meaning "vertical pole fence," later developed to the kenninji-gaki.

A very interesting fact is that, in Tokyo today, there are many people who pronounce it as "kennenji-gaki."

From this fact, some people conclude that the name of the fence comes from a temple called Kennenji. This is, however, totally wrong. It is one of the most typical characteristics of the Edo dialect to pronounce "nin" as "nen."

The basic structure of this variety is characterized by the use of split bamboos (Fig. 12). The kenninji-gaki has three styles in design— shin, gyô, and sô. For structural details, please refer to the explanatory note with the basic diagram in later pages.

Ginkakuji-gaki

The original ginkakuji-gaki is located on the east side of the approach to the main building of the Jishôji Temple (commonly called Ginkakuji), a well-known Zen temple in Kyoto. The long bamboo fence constructed along the approach and the green of the hedge of beautifully trimmed camellia and other plants almost hanging over the fence together create a wonderful harmony and give a unique atmosphere to the temple's front garden.

This bamboo fence resembles a kenninji-gaki, but its height is only one meter or so. The main characteristics of the ginkakuji-gaki are that it is built atop a stone wall, that half-cut stout bamboos are used for vertical poles (tateko), and that especially thick horizontal support poles (oshibuchi) are fixed at two levels–one at the bottom, and the other in the middle.

The original fence at the Jishôji Temple used to have thick-stemmed bamboos for horizontal support poles, but now ma-dake is used.

Strictly speaking, a ginkakuji-gaki must have half-cut thick bamboos as vertical pieces, although today any low bamboo fences using kenninji-gaki style split-bamboo vertical pieces with two tiers of horizontal support poles are customarily called ginkakuji-gaki. There are many cases in which a ginkakuji-gaki is not built upon a stone wall, but since it is a low fence, the best way is to build one on top of a stone wall or a bank.

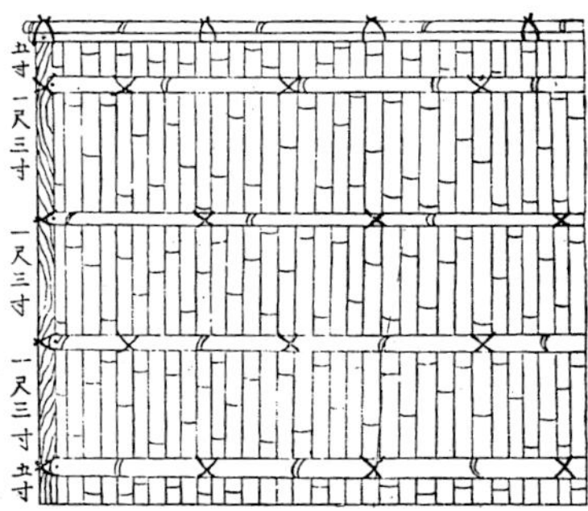

Fig. 11 A picture of kenninji-gaki from <Ishigumi-sono-yaegaki-den>

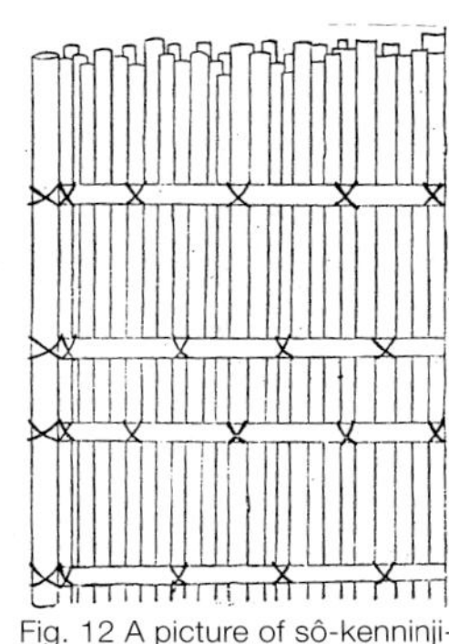
Fig. 12 A picture of sô-kenninji-gaki from <Ishigumi-sono-yaegaki-den>

Shimizu-gaki (shino-gaki, sarashi-gaki)

In the original form of the shimizu-gaki, thin shimizu-dake were used for vertical pieces (tateko). Today, however, the name is used only to indicate the variety of fence. Any bamboo fence using any small bamboos, even if they are not shimizu-dake, is generally called shimizu-gaki.

Precisely speaking, in this category a fence made of shino-dake should be called a shino-gaki, and one made of sarashi-dake, a sarashi-gaki. There is also a variety that uses gara-dake (Chinese bamboos) for vertical pieces which are usually used to build yotsume-gaki (four-eyed fences).

Shimizu-dake is the generic name for processed shino-dake, which is any thin species in the me-dake family. Their hulls are removed, surfaces polished, oil removed, bends straightened, and they are sorted out by thickness and length. The same process is applied to prepare sarashi-dake, which is made from small gara-dake or black bamboo.

Shino-gaki, on the other hand, means a bamboo fence made of unprocessed shino-dake. Historically, the shino-gaki is older than the sarashi-gaki. The beautiful picture of a shino-gaki with a window in one of the fusuma-e at Tenkyû-in of Myôshinji Temple from the early Edo period is well known.

The main characteristic of these varieties of bamboo fence is that the vertical pieces (tateko) are held by support poles (oshibuchi) without horizontal frame poles (dôbuchi). This way, the fence looks the same on either side, which is the greatest advantage of these varieties. The disadvantage, however, is that they are not very strong. Because it is a processed product and has a soft surface, shimizu-dake is vulnerable against wind, rain, and strong sunlight.

A shimizu-gaki is, therefore, usually built with a roof, located under eaves, or built as a sleeve fence (sode-gaki).

With shimizu-dake used for vertical pieces, it is difficult to get a smooth fence surface. To obtain the best result possible, many support poles are required. For the structural details, please see the explanatory diagram shown later.

Misu-gaki (bamboo screening fence)

A misu is a kind of hanging screen that was used in a noble man's residence in ancient times. The emperor, aristocrats, or the Shôgun, when they met someone who was below them in rank, would speak through a misu.

The misu-gaki was so named because of its resemblance to misu. It is also called sudarė-gaki (meaning the same).

It has a relatively simple structure with horizontal frets (kumiko) fixed into the vertical groove made on the inner side of each oyabashira (oyabashira). The most significant characteristic of this variety is that vertical support poles (oshibuchi) are attached on both sides. Since this is similar to the case of the katsura-gaki, the misu-gaki might have been invented as a simplified form of the katsura-gaki. Unlike the katsura-gaki, however, the fushidome method is used for the top ends of tateko instead of cutting them diagonally.

In some cases, small round bamboos are used for support poles instead of split bamboos. Sarashi-dake is most often used for frets, but because it is not very durable against moisture, it should be used where it does not get wet from the rain. There is a variety in which frets are made of split bamboos. For the structural details, please see the explanatory diagram shown later.

Ôtsu-gaki

There are many theories about the origin of this variety. According to a legend, when the Korean delegation moved from Kyoto to Edo in 1711 (Edo period), bamboo fences of this style were built in Ôtsu along their route— hence this name. A descriptive illustration of this original ôtsu-gaki (Fig. 13) is included in <Ishigumi-sono-yaegaki-den> with the following explanation.

> " This fence is also called chosen-yarai, ôtsu-gaki, or kumi-kakine....It uses quarter-split thick bamboo canes and is constructed in a way that is similar to the kenninji-gaki, with rear side of the kenninji-gaki at the front."

The word " 馬行 "(yarai) is not correct; the correct spelling should be " 行馬 "and it is pronounced koba. This word means a horse fence or the like. The aforementioned illustration shows that the original ôtsu-gaki was exactly the same as ones that are normally constructed today. Vertical pieces (tateko) are alternately inserted through horizontal

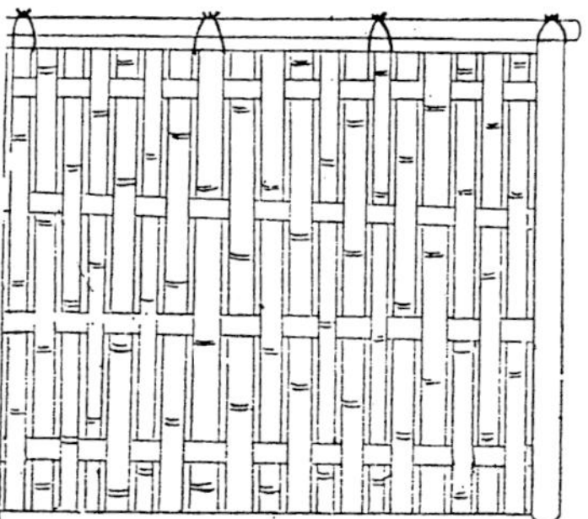

Fig. 13 An illustration of ôtsu-gaki from <Ishigumi-sono-yaegaki-den>

frame poles (dôbuchi) made of split bamboo canes. This style is totally different from the yarai-gaki, and clearly belongs to the ajiro-gaki family judging from the fact that a weaving method is used. Therefore, it is wrong to call this type of fence a yarai-gaki.

This structural pattern must have been popular in ancient times. A picture of a similar bamboo fence appears in <Boki-ekotoba> owned by the Nishi-honganji Temple (Kamakura period, Fig. 14). Normally, an ôtsu-gaki does not use a central support pole, but there are exceptions. The advantage of this fence is that it can be built rapidly with split bamboo canes, although this means the fence has a definite front and back. For the structural details, please see the explanatory diagram later.

Teppô-gaki (rifle barrel fence)

The teppô-gaki is a very special fence, and there are many theories about the origin of its name. The name "teppô" comes from "teppô-zuke," the name of the structure in which vertical pieces (tateko) are attached to the horizontal frame poles (dôbuchi) on the front and back sides alternately. It is said that the name has its origin in the way soldiers put their rifles (teppô) in a row on ancient battlefields.

In terms of structure, the yotsume-gaki (four-eyed fence) was originally a kind of teppô-gaki. What is special about the teppô-gaki is that they are made both as screening fences and see-through fences. When built as a screening fence, a certain degree of transparency is often maintained if seen at an angle. Another characteristic is that it is mostly used as a sleeve fence (sode-gaki).

Usually, vertical bamboo canes are attached on the front and backsides of the horizontal frame poles alternately. When made as a sode-gaki (sleeve fence), it is not unusual for various maki-tateko (twining vertical poles) to be used.

Some people think that there should be another name for teppô-gaki with maki-tateko, but in my opinion, what kind of vertical poles are used should not matter. In <Ishigumi-sono-yaegaki-den> there is an illustrated explanation of a teppô-gaki built as a sleeve fence (Fig. 15) together with a structural diagram. The explanation reads:

In building a Teppô-gaki, tateko of two different heights are attached to the dôbuchi; long ones on the front side, and short ones on the rear side, as shown in the illustration. They are made of scorched logs, stout bamboo canes, or yagara-dake. They can also be built using bush clover and thick bamboo canes. Any material such as reeds, thick bamboo canes, scorched logs, etc. can be used.

Here, the term "teppô-gaki" is used regardless the type of vertical poles (tateko). There is a variety of the teppô-gaki called ô-dake-teppô-gaki that uses especially stout bamboo canes for vertical poles. For the structural details, please see the explanatory diagram later.

Tokusa-gaki (Dutch rush fence)

This variety is named from the plant called tokusa (Dutch rush). Tokusa is a perennial, evergreen plant, which is relatively short but grows well even where there is little sunlight. Hollow and with joints, the plant looks as if it was a miniature version of the regular bamboo. From old times, tokusa was used to fine-sand the surface of woodwork. There are books that refer to the tokusa-gaki as a fence actually made of the tokusa plant. This is a serious mistake.

A tokusa-gaki is not a fence made of tokusa, but it was named from the fact that the row of split-bamboo vertical poles (tateko) of the tokusa-gaki reminds people of the plant. This form of bamboo fence with vertically arranged split bamboos attached is called tokusa-bari. The same method is often used for building the type of wall called tokusa-bei. The tokusa-gaki is characterized by the lack of horizontal support poles (oshibuchi). The vertical pieces (tateko) are either nailed to the wooden frame poles (dôbuchi), or, if the frame poles are made of bamboo, firmly tied to them using dyed ropes. In fact, the beautiful appearance of the specially knotted ropes is one of the outstanding characteristics of the tokusa-gaki. For the structural details and the standard methods of rope tying, please see the explanatory diagram later.

Takeho-gaki (bamboo branch fence)

"Takeho" means a bamboo branch, and any fences made of bamboo branches are generally called takeho-gaki.

Fig. 14 A picture of ôtsu-gaki style fence of the Kamakura period from <Boki-ekotoba>

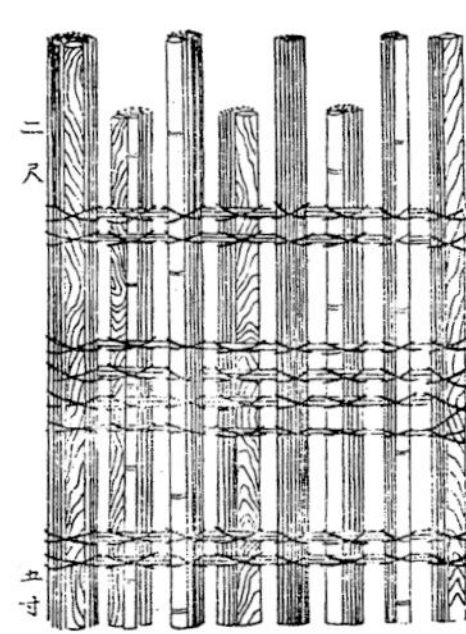

Fig. 15 An illustration of a teppô-gaki seen in <Ishigumi-sono-yaegaki-den>

Sometimes they are called ho-gaki (meaning the same). The takeho-gaki vary greatly in form and design, and many of its varieties are called other names. Putting such varieties aside, here we want to define takeho-gaki as a bamboo fence that uses, in a normal way, bamboo branches as its vertical pieces (tateko) (Fig. 16).

Bamboo branches can be classified into two categories: "white" branches and "black" branches. The "white" category includes branches of such species as hachiku, môsôchiku, ma-dake, etc., whose color is pale brown. The "black" category, on the other hand, means branches of the kurochiku plant; ones produced in Kôchi Pref. are regarded to have the best color and quality.

The following statement about bamboo branches is an excerpt from <Tsukiyama-teizô-den>, in which the term "ho-gaki" is used.

Bamboo branches used for ho-gaki (branch fence) must be ones in season, and must be dipped in hot water before use.

Roughly speaking, there are three forms of takeho-gaki. One is the form in which many bamboo branches are used as vertical pieces in the same way as brushwood is used for shiba-gaki. Another is the form in which small bamboo branches are used as a core and thicker branches are arranged around it as vertical pieces held in place with horizontal support poles. The other is the form in which small, short branches are arranged in a number of tiers. The first two forms are popular in the Kansai area while the third is often seen in the Kantô area. For the structural details of this "black" variety, please see the explanatory diagram later.

Also, there are a few cases of ancient-style takeho-gaki, in which bundled bamboo branches are diagonally arranged crosswise and alternately tied to one horizontal frame pole on both sides. Many fences of this style were built as a kind of shiba-gaki (brushwood fence) during the Heian and Kamakura periods. A picture of this type of fence built as a takeho-gaki can be seen in <Hônen-shônin-eden>, etc.

Most of Kansai style takeho-gaki fences do not have a top molding (tamabuchi) and their tops are left uncovered in their natural shape. A fence which has end post (oyabashira) with especially large tops is called chasen-gaki (Fig. 17), since it looks like a chasen, or a bamboo whisk used in ceremonial tea making.

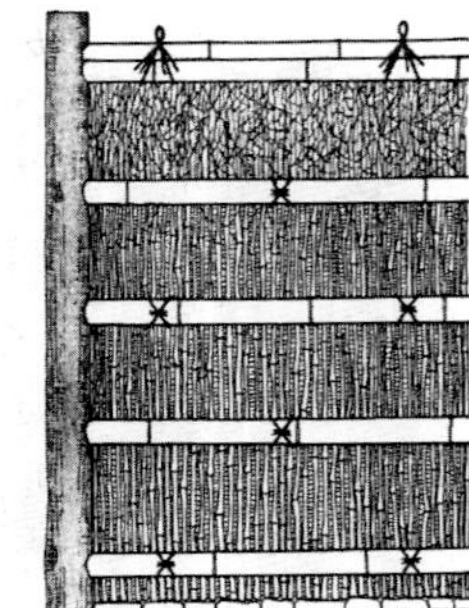

Fig. 16 A picture of a takeho-gaki with a molding at the top (from <The Bamboo Fences of Japan> by Isao Yoshikawa)

Mino-gaki (raincoat fence)

This variety was so named because its outer appearance looks like that of a mino, a traditional straw raincoat. Most mino-gaki today are made of bamboo branches, and ones using "black" branches (kurochiku) are especially popular in the Kantô area. In the old days, however, branches of trees or the hagi plant (Japanese bush clover) were normally used instead of bamboo branches. In constructing a mino-gaki, bamboo branches are arranged upside down, just like those for straw raincoat, and the fence top is covered by a decorative molding called tamabuchi, but horizontal support poles (oshibuchi) are not ordinarily used. Long mino-gaki are rarely seen, and they are usually built as small sleeve fences (sode-gaki). There are cases in which the lower half of a mino-gaki is made as a kenninji-gaki, yotsume-gaki, or tokusa-gaki. Those with the upper half made as mino-gaki are called han-mino-gaki (half mino-gaki), and those with the branches for the lower half deliberately left unaligned are called yabure-mino-gaki (broken mino-gaki). A variety which has a number of horizontal tiers over the surface, called yoroi-gaki, also belongs to the mino-gaki category. For the structural details, please see the explanatory diagram later.

Katsura-gaki

The original katsura-gaki is the long, massive fence situated near the main gate of Katsura Detached Palace in Kyoto: The katsura-gaki was constructed as its outer fence during the Meiji period when it became a detached palace. The katsura-gaki is probably the most labor-intensive, and therefore the most expensive variety of bamboo fence. Katsura-gaki was preciously the name that the hachiku hedge built along the Katsura River, which still exists today, was called. Bamboo Fences like this used to be called ho-gaki, katsura-ho-gaki, rikyû-gaki, etc., but today any bamboo branch fence of this style is commonly called katsura-gaki.

In the original katsura-gaki construction method, the core consists of small bamboo branches, and thicker branches are used as horizontal frets (kumiko) on the surface. The twigs of the branches for horizontal frets are not removed, so that they can be arranged to produce a checkered pattern at

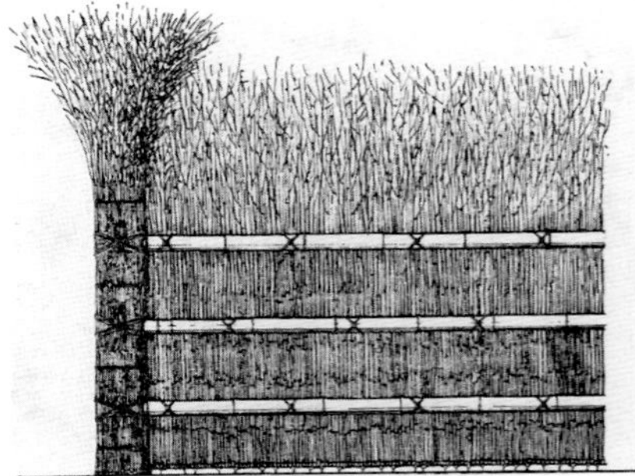

Fig. 17 A picture of a variety of takeho-gaki called chasen-gaki (from <The Bamboo Fences of Japan> by Isao Yoshikawa)

intervals of six feet. Except for the original fence, however, this is rarely seen. The main characteristic of the katsura-gaki is that split stout bamboo canes with their protruded top ends cut diagonally are used as vertical support poles (oshibuchi). A horizontal support pole (oshibuchi) is attached on top of the vertical support poles.

Since it requires so much labor and money to build a katsura-gaki in the original style (Fig. 18), authentic katsura-gaki are rarely seen. Instead, many of the existing katsura-gaki use twig-less branches, or use split bamboo slats or shino-dake instead of bamboo branches for frets (kumiko). The misu-gaki can be regarded as a simplified form of the katsura-gaki.

Nanzenji-gaki

The original fence is found at the Nanzenji temple, a famous Rinzai Zen temple in Kyoto.

As I mentioned in the section "A Brief History of Bamboo Fences in Japan," the term "nanzenji-gaki (or nanzenji-dake)" appears in <Tsukiyama-senshiroku>, an old book on the art of garden design, but since there is no further explanation, it is not known what its design was exactly like. How it was related to the present original fence is also unknown, but the present one was probably constructed at a later time.

In the present original nanzenji-gaki, horizontal frame poles (dôbuchi) made of half-split bamboo canes extend between the end post (oyabashira) at three height levels— center, upper, and lower— with vertical slats (tateko) alternately inserted through them.

The outstanding feature of this variety is that vertical pieces made of hagi (Japanese bush clover) are arranged at certain intervals. Earlier nanzenji-gaki had their central horizontal frame pole uncovered, but recent ones have a half-split bamboo cane over the central frame pole as a support pole. I do not know which way the real original was built, but, in my opinion, the earlier one looks more appropriate.

Normally, nanzenji-gaki using hagi are not built. Most of nanzenji-gaki built today are like ordinary kenninji-gaki with bamboo branches.

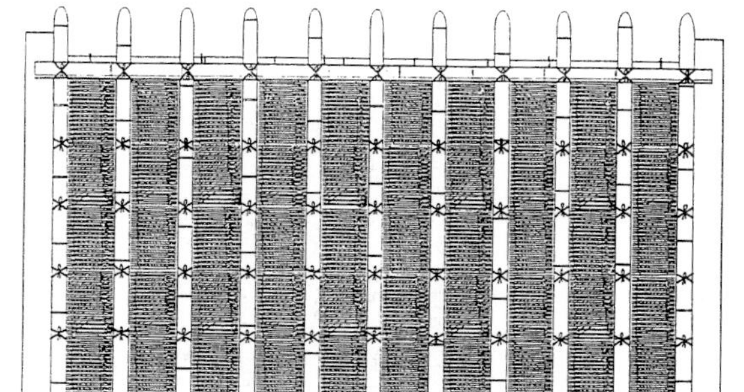

Fig. 18 An illustration of the katsura-gaki (by Isao Yoshikawa)

Kuromoji-gaki (spicebush fence)

Kuromoji-gaki is the general name for any fences built using branches of kuromoji (spicebush), a deciduous shrub of the camphor family which naturally grows in low mountains. The branches of this plant are strong and give out a good scent, and therefore are a popular material for toothpicks, which are made by peeling off the bark and cutting them thinly. A fence with kuromoji branches used as vertical pieces (tateko) is called a kuromoji-gaki, but according to a wider classification, the kuromoji-gaki belongs to the shiba-gaki (brushwood fence) category.

Vertical pieces are made of relatively long kuromoji branches which have been dried in the shade and straightened. This process requires a lot of labor and time, making the products very expensive, although they are often used even today for sode-gaki (sleeve fences), etc. because of their durability.

In <Ishigumi-sono-yaegaki-den>, the kuromoji-gaki is not directly referred to, but a picture of a similar fence called uguisu-gaki (Fig. 19) is included with the following explanatory note.

> It is a shiba-gaki (brushwood fence) built with spicebush branches. The style in which horizontal frame poles of especially thick bamboo and ropes made of twisted catalpa are used is called the kikori-musubi (woodcutter tie), which is regarded as one of the best quality for use in a tea garden.

The original pronunciation of the Chinese character "梢" is "sho," and its meaning is bamboo whisk. But here, the character is incorrectly used to indicate a fence.

This uguisu-gaki is a variety of kuromoji-gaki, and with the tops of the vertically arranged kuromoji branches varied in height to look natural; they have more of a wabi taste. The main characteristic of kuromoji-gaki is that they do not usually have a top molding (tamabuchi).

Hagi-gaki (bush clover fence)

This is also a kind of brushwood fence (shiba-gaki), which uses branches of hagi, Japanese bush clover. With its thin branches and small twigs, the hagi-gaki looks extremely

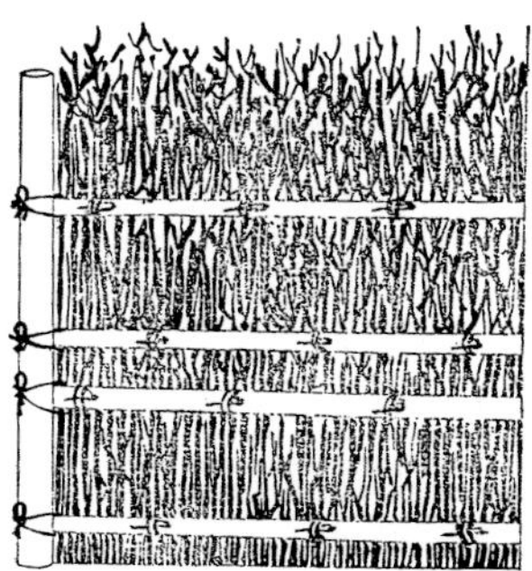

Fig. 19 A picture of an uguisu-gaki, a kind of kuromoji-gaki, included in <Ishigumi-sono-yaegaki-den>

delicate, elegant, and graceful. Hagi has more applications than kuromoji, and is used for details of fences in various ways. It is a material indispensable in building sleeve fences (sode-gaki).

One of the first mentions of the term "hagi-gaki" was made in the following statement, in <Tsukiyama-teizô-den>, a book on the art of garden design.

> Bush clover used for hagi-gaki should be harvested in July or August, before the leaves fall. Brushwood used for shiba-gaki should be harvested in October, November, or December, after the leaves fall.

The hagi-gaki, which uses hagi branches as vertical pieces (tateko), is used in the same way as the kuromoji-gaki. Fences using hagi branches in different way, such as maki-tateko (twining vertical pieces), for example, have different names.

There are statements in <Ishigumi-sono-yaegaki-den>, et.al. are statements about how hagi is used for the details of other style fences.

Ajiro-gaki, numazu-gaki

The ajiro-gaki is the oldest form of bamboo fence. As I already mentioned in the chapter "History," they began to be built before the Sung period in China. In Japan, they were used as hinoki-gaki during the Heian and Kamakura periods.

While the hinoki-gaki uses thin plates of hinoki or some other similar plant, the ajiro-gaki uses frets made of bamboo woven in the ajiro pattern.

Numazu-gaki is a kind of ajiro-gaki, whose main characteristic is that it is made of shino-dake branches which are woven crosswise diagonally. It was so named because fences made of woven hakone-dake slats once became very popular in Numazu, Shizuoka Pref. In <Ishigumi-sono-yaegaki-den> there is a picture of a numazu-gaki (Fig. 20) with the following note.

> The numazu-gaki is constructed by weaving slats of stout bamboo in the ajiro pattern, as shown in the diagram. The original form of numazu-gaki requires the use of yagara-dake and of round hakone-dake for posts and frames.

According to this note, fences made by weaving split bamboo canes can also be called numazu-gaki, and there have been many numazu-gaki built this way.

The disadvantage of using split bamboos is that the appearance of one side of the fence will be different from that of the other, which is the reason why shino-dake is preferred. Split bamboos can, however, be woven in such a way that outside-surfaced and inside-surfaced slats alternate. The problem with this method is that the inside surface tends to change its color sooner than the outside surface. Any ajiro-gaki style fence, which is made by weaving small and thin bamboos, tends to become fat in the center. To correct this, a number of support poles (oshibuchi) are horizontally placed.

Yotsume-gaki (four-eyed fence)

Literally meaning "four-eyed fence," this is the most popular kind of sukashi-gaki (see-through fence), and one of the most common varieties of bamboo fence using gara-dake. The origin of its name, according to one theory, is in the fact that the fence has four "eyes" in each vertical row divided by the four horizontal frame poles (dôbuchi), or according to another theory, that the pattern resembles the family emblem called yotsume. The former theory is probably correct. The structure is quite simple: it is more of a barrier with the vertical poles (tateko) attached to the horizontal frame poles using the teppô-zuke method.

Because similar fences are described in Heian and Kamakura period picture scrolls, etc., we know that the yotsume-gaki already existed in ancient times.

In <Ishigumi-sono-yaegaki-den> there are pictures of shin-yotsume-gaki, yuikomi-yotsume-gaki, and sô-no-yotsume-gaki with explanatory notes. The following is part of the explanation which the picture of the shin-yotsume-gaki (Fig. 21) is furnished with.

> It is five shaku (approx. five ft.) tall. The difference between the long and short poles used as tateko is one shaku (approx. one ft.). The interval between each two tateko is also one shaku. It is needless to explain how the tateko should be fixed to the dôbuchi.

The shin-yotsume-gaki described in this picture is built in a special way using a wooden plate for the central horizontal

Fig. 20 A picture of numazu-gaki included in <Ishigumi-sono-yaegaki-den>

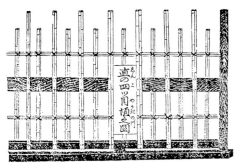

Fig. 21 A picture of a shin-yotsume-gaki from <Ishigumi-sono-yaegaki-den>

support pole, and with the fence bottom not fixed in the ground, so that the fence is movable. The other two varieties, which have four horizontal frame poles with the two in the middle placed close to each other (fukiyose), are almost the same as the modern yotsume-gaki.

Nowadays, it has become popular, especially in the Kantô area, to use three horizontal frame poles. In the Kansai area, however, the original method of using four poles is most common. A yotsume-gaki is considered to be an indispensable element of the area of a roji near the intermediate gate. <Sadô-yoroku> edited by Sôhen Yamada (published during the early Edo period) includes the following statement.

1. Yotsume-gaki: A yotsume-gaki must be constructed if the gate is in the sarudo style. The height is about four shaku one sun (approx. four ft. one in.). Place four bamboo canes horizontally at intervals of six sun (approx. seven in.). When posts are used, make horizontal holes of the right size in each post, and insert the horizontal canes through them and nail them inside....

An example of a yotsume-gaki built in a roji is illustrated below (Fig. 22). For the structural details, please see the explanatory diagram later.

Kinkakuji-gaki

The original kinkakuji-gaki is situated at the Rokuonji Temple (commonly called Kinkakuji), a famous Rinzai Zen temple in Kyoto. The kinkakuji-gaki is known as a highly sophisticated form of ashimoto-gaki (foot-level fence). There are two kinkakuji-gaki style fences there, even today, between the famous Ryûmon-baku falls located in the north end of the Rasen and the tea-ceremony arbor, Sekka-tei. Fences built in a similar style already existed in the Edo period, but the modern style of kinkakuji-gaki was established and named after the Meiji period.

The outstanding characteristic of this variety is that it does not use horizontal frame poles (dôbuchi); low vertical poles (tateko) are lined in a single row between the oyabashiras (oyabashira); and that a molding (tamabuchi) made of especially stout half-split bamboos are placed at the top. There are two original methods of attaching the horizontal support poles (oshibuchi) depending on the height of the fence. For a low fence, a pair of stout half-split bamboo canes, which are of the same thickness as the one used for the top molding, is fixed at a low level to hold the oyabashiras and vertical poles in between. For a relatively high fence, two pairs of horizontal support poles made of gara-dake are used to hold the oyabashiras and vertical poles in between at two levels. For the structural details, please see the explanatory diagram later.

Yarai-gaki (stockade fence)

"Yarai" is a general term used to mean any barrier, and does not mean a bamboo fence only. The original (and correct) spelling for yarai is "遣い", meaning a fence used as a partition.

As I mentioned previously in the section about the ôtsu-gaki, yarai was spelled "馬行" in <Ishigumi-sono-yaegaki-den>. In the Chinese language, on the other hand, the spelling "行馬" is generally used, meaning any simple fence built at the roadside as a horse barrier. Consequently, some yarai-gaki are constructed with logs. Furthermore, the framework (kumiko), which is usually arranged crosswise diagonally, are sometimes built vertically and horizontally.

In another section of <Ishigumi-sono-yaegaki-den> there is a picture entitled "Saku-matawa-yarai" with the following explanatory note.

> They are built with logs of cedar or cypress. Ones in the koshisaki style are sometimes built in the shape of octagon, ax, etc. In days gone by, they used to be called hei-gaki (wall fence).

This picture shows a wooden yarai-gaki made of vertically and horizontally arranged logs.

The modern style yarai-gaki, however, are fences made of diagonally crosswise arranged bamboo canes. Some people say that these and the ôtsu-gaki style fences are the same but this is not the case.

In the yarai-gaki building method, bamboo canes are arranged crosswise diagonally and tied to the horizontal frame poles (dôbuchi), and not woven as in the ôtsu-gaki style. Easy to make and strong, the yarai-gaki style fences have been widely built as temporary fences. Even in the premises of daimyô mansions, yarai-gaki were often constructed (although not around the main gate). Take Toyama-sô, a villa owned by

Fig. 22 A picture of the two-tiered yotsume-gaki in the Shôden'in roji at the Kenninji Temple from <Miyako-rinsen-meishô-zue>

Fig. 23 A picture of a yarai-gaki built in a garden included in <Miyako-rinsen-meishô-zue>, by Gan'ami

the Tokugawa family, for instance: its ground was enclosed by double yarai fences, whose total length measured approximately 6,200 meters in 1801.

In earlier times, yarai-gaki also seemed to be popular as elements for ordinary Japanese-style gardens and gardens attached to ceremonial teahouses. A yarai-gaki is portrayed in the picture entitled <Onshû-fushimiyashiki-roji> in <Matsuya-nikki> published in 1641, as well as in various other pictures from the time (Fig. 23). For the structural details, please see the explanatory diagram shown later.

Ryôanji-gaki

The original of this ashimoto-gaki (foot-level fence) is the one constructed along the approach to the head priest's residence of the Ryôanji Temple, a famous Rinzai Zen temple. Another ryôanji-gaki, which was built on a much smaller scale, probably around the first year of the Showa period, is located in the roji of Zôroku-an, a tea arbor situated to the east of the Hôjô building.

The original ryôanji-gaki is built low with frets (kumiko) made of pairs of split bamboos arranged crosswise diagonally in a style similar to the yarai-gaki. It has a top molding (tamabuchi), which is made of thinner half-split bamboo canes, and a support pole (oshibuchi) at the bottom. The ends of the frets are not usually stuck into the ground, but are held above the ground with a bottom horizontal support pole. There are many varieties, however, whose frets are stuck in the ground. For the structural details, please see the explanatory diagram later.

Kôetsu-gaki

Also called Kôetsuji-gaki or Gagyû-gaki, the original fence of this style is situated at the Kôetsuji Temple in Rakuhoku-takagamine, Kyoto Pref. At this temple, Taikyoan, a tea-ceremony arbor noted in connection with Hon'ami Kôetsu, was reconstructed as a hermitage-like thatched cottage, and there are a number of new teahouses as well. The original kôetsu-gaki is constructed as a large-scale, winding partition between their gardens and the temple premises. With its total length measuring about eighteen meters, the fence is a stately looking sukashi-gaki (see-through fence). According to legend, the fence is said to have been designed by Kôetsu himself, but it is unknown whether or not this legend is true. The kôetsu-gaki is constructed in the same way as the yarai-gaki except that it has a thick top molding (tamabuchi), with one or both ends touching the ground.

From a picture in <Miyako-rinsen-meishô-zue> (Fig. 24), etc., it is known that fences of this style were already common in the Edo period. The kôetsu-gaki can be regarded as a developed variety of such style.

Today, there are many different varieties such as one with frets (kumiko) made of small, thin round bamboo canes. For the structural details, please refer to the explanatory diagram later.

Fig. 24 A picture in which a kôetsu-gaki style fence is seen in a garden attached to a residence (From <Miyako-rinsen-meishlô-zue>, painted by Shôami)

Nanako-gaki

"Nanako" is spelled "魚子", "斜子", or "七子". The term "nanako-ori" is used to refer to a kind of silk cloth, whose texture looks like fine fish roe.

Some people say that the nanako-gaki was so named because it looked like that texture, while others say, because it is also called "uroko-gaki" (fish scale fence), the name refers to the scale-like shape of the fence.

Among the diverse varieties of bamboo fence, this has perhaps the simple structure of all. Thin, long slats of bamboo of one to two centimeters width are bent into the shape of an arch and both ends are stuck in the ground.

The nanako-gaki is not peculiar to Japan, and is seen in every part of the world where bamboo grows. The nanako-gaki is used for public areas such as parks more often than for gardens or yards attached to residential houses. There is a variety of nanako-gaki which is movable with arch-shaped bamboo slats fixed to a base made of stout half-split bamboo canes.

In addition to the varieties described above, there are numerous other varieties with different names such as taimatsu-gaki (torch fence), tachiai-gaki, daitokuji-gaki, yoroi-gaki (armor fence), hiwada-gaki (cypress bark fence), hishigi-gaki, ôgi-gaki (fan fence), mase-gaki, tsuitate-gaki (screen fence), etc. There are also a large number of varieties in the sode-gaki family (Fig. 25).

Fig. 25 A picture of a nozoki-gaki, a kind of sode-gaki, from <Ishigumi-sono-yaegaki-den>

Kenninji-gaki

1. A massive kenninji-gaki constructed along a sloping road. The four oshibuchi on the exterior surface, with the molding at the top, are characteristic of the Kansai style (Kyoto).

2. A well-made Kansai-style kenninji-gaki matched with a low stone wall (Kyoto).

3. A kenninji-gaki with five slender oshibuchi, its upper edge lined with tiles (Sakurai).

4. A Kansai-style kenninji-gaki with tiles at the top separated slightly from the fence itself (Kyoto).

5. A kenninji-gaki having an upper edge lined with tiles and its topmost outer rail positioned slightly lower than usual (Uji).

6. This kenninji-gaki, with slender oshibuchi, is used to enclose a carport (Muroran).

7. A freshly built Kansai-style kenninji-gaki in a dry-landscape front garden. The space between the tamabuchi and first oshibuchi is extra-wide, and lining stones (sashi-ishi) have been placed between the slats and the ground (Tsurugaoka Hachiman-gu shrine, Kamakura).

8. A gyo-style kenninji-gaki, without a tamabuchi (Head priest's residence, Kennin-ji temple, Kyoto).

9. A kenninji-gaki with a lining board at the bottom and oshibuchi in the suhama style (Yamanashi prefecture).

10. A kenninji-gaki with "windows" at the top, allowing podocarpus branches to protrude through (Ichihara)

11. A "compressed" version of the kenninji-gaki atop a stone wall. This arrangement is known as a ginkakuji-gaki (Jisho-ji [Ginkaku-ji] temple, Kyoto).

12. A ginkakuji-gaki whose tateko have been cut in such a way as to just fit over the stone wall (Tokyo).

Shimizu-gaki

1. A short shimizu-gaki atop a stone wall, with tateko of fine bamboo and stout oshibuchi, reminiscent of a ginkakuji-gaki (Uwajima).

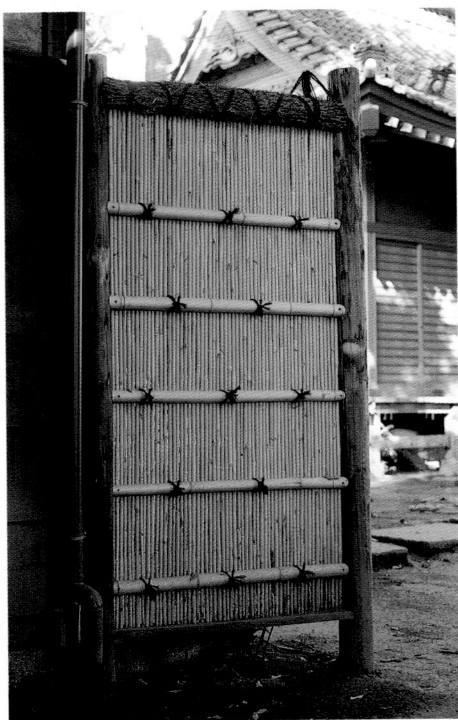

2. A shimizu sode-gaki, with tateko of fine bamboo (Chiba).

3. A shimizu-gaki made entirely with cured bamboo and paired oshibuchi (Hoya).

Misu-gaki (bamboo screening fence)

1. A beautiful misu-gaki built behind a dry-landscape garden (Shueiji Temple, Ichihara)

2. A misu-gaki with vertical oshibuchi, each consisting of a pair of sarashi-dake, built in a front garden (Tokyo)

3. A special style misu-gaki with windows in the middle and at the bottom (Nagano Pref.)

4. A misu-gaki, looking unique with horizontal narrow wooden plates as part of kumiko, enclosing the small garden of a private residence (Kurashiki)

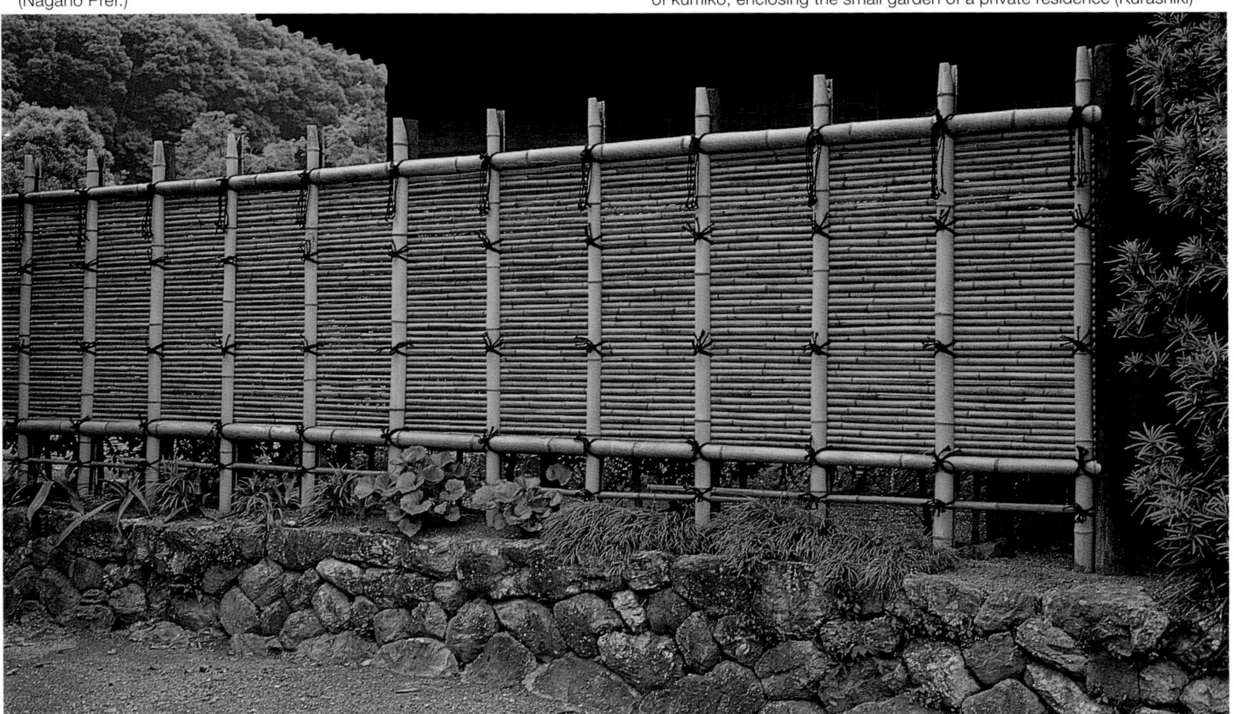

5. A misu-gaki built as a barrier between street and house. The tops of the vertical oshibuchi are cut at an angle. The upper horizontal oshibuchi is arranged in a style similar to that of the katsura-gaki. Thin round bamboos are placed between the lower horizontal oshibuchi and the ground for decoration.(Shizuoka Pref.)

Ôtsu-gaki

1. A four-tiered ôtsu-gaki with tateko woven into the dôbuchi (Ichihara)

2. A large-scale ôtsu-gaki with oshibuchi in the middle and at the bottom (Nanzenji Temple, Kyoto)

3. A four-tiered ôtsu-gaki with dôbuchi covered with oshibuchi of stout half-split bamboo canes. Built atop a stone wall, part of the fence is raised to a higher level along the slope. (Rinkyûji Temple, Kyoto)

Teppô-gaki (rifle barrel fence)

1. A large-scale five-tiered teppô-gaki made of stout bamboo canes atop stone masonry. The fence has front tateko in groups of three, and rear tateko in groups of six, which are fixed to the five dôbuchi of gara-dake. (Meishu-no-taki Park, Tokyo)

2. A four-tiered teppô-gaki with tateko in groups of three built in a front garden (Dairenji Temple, Urayasu)

3. A teppô-gaki with paired dôbuchi of gara-dake with the two in the middle wide apart (Former Shiba Detached Palace, Tokyo)

4. A gorgeous teppô-gaki with tateko of bamboo branches bound together in the shape of torches (Myôgenji Temple, Toyokawa)

5. A delicately constructed teppô-gaki with tateko made of bundles of bush clover (hagi) branches, used as a partition for a front garden (Nara Pref.)

Tokusa-gaki (Dutch rush fence)

1. The front of a typical tokusa-gaki with tateko arranged in such a way that they look like a group of tokusa plants. The lines created by the nails add to its lasting beauty (Kyoto)

2. One of the beauties of the tokusa-gaki is its rope ties (Kôfu)

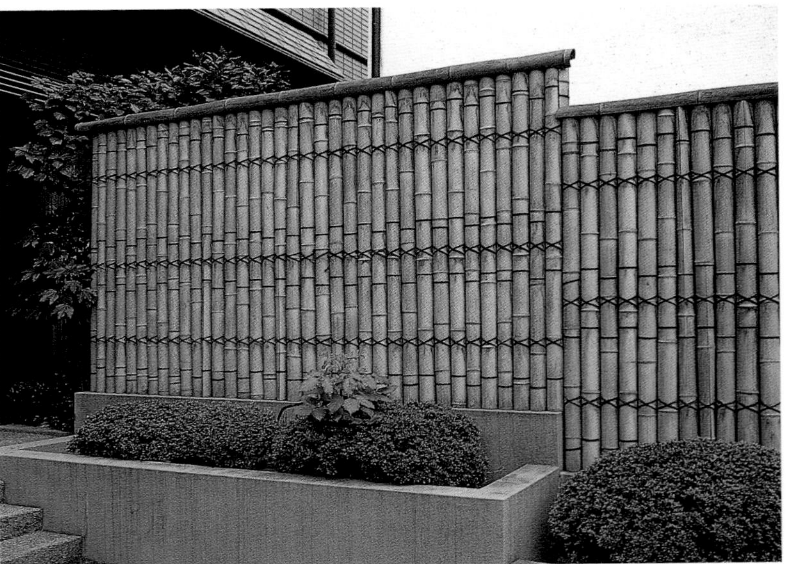

3. A two-leveled tokusa-gaki with tateko of stout bamboo canes and a kasa-dake molding at the top, built as a partition (Saitama Pref.)

Takeho-gaki (bamboo branch fence)

1. A three-tiered takeho-gaki with a supplementary support pole of gara-dake near its top. The tip of the tateko is left unheld by a furedome, and looks natural. The oyabashiras, which are made of bundled bamboo branches, are built using the makibashira (bound-branch post) method. (Rokuonji Temple, Kyoto)

2. A takeho-gaki constructed on top of a stone wall, topped with a roof made of fired cedar. The basic structure is the same as the one in the upper photograph, but the arrangement of small branches inside the fence is more beautiful. (Kyoto)

3. A four-tiered takeho-gaki with dôbuchi of stout bamboo and a roof made of cedar bark (Kyoto)

4. A four-tiered takeho-gaki with two dôbuchi in the middle attached using the suhama method and small bamboo branches used to hold the tateko in place near the top (Kyoto)

5. A two-stage takeho-gaki of elaborate workmanship, which looks like a standing screen (Kyoto)

6. A common style of takeho-gaki with the corner post built in the makibashira (bound-branch post) method (Kyoto)

7. A rustic takeho-gaki having the kenninji-gaki structure, with some leafed branches used for tateko and the branches in the uppermost tier arranged upside down (Kôzenji Temple, Yamagata)

8. A four-tiered takeho-gaki used as a sleeve fence (Dairenji, Urayasu)

9. A primitive style takeho-gaki, a type often mentioned in ancient literature, with wild top twigs (Ichihara)

10. A takeho-gaki built in an indoor garden, with a stately oshibuchi made of stout bamboo (Tokyo)

11. A takeho-gaki with beautifully arranged tateko and joints lined evenly, used as a screening fence (Kyoto)

12. A typical Kantô-style takeho-gaki with tateko made of kurochiku. The arrangement of the oshibuchi is beautifully designed. (Tokyo)

13. A three-tiered takeho-gaki of kurochiku branches built on top of an ôyaishi stone wall (Tokyo)

Mino-gaki (raincoat fence)

1. A kind of mino-gaki in a front garden. With the lower half built in the kenninji-gaki style, this fence is called a han-mino-gaki (half mino-gaki). A mino-gaki with rows of tateko is also called yoroi-gaki (armor fence) (Saitama Pref.)

2. A mino-gaki with a yarai-gaki at the bottom (Narita)

3. A typical yoroi-gaki (armor fence) with five rows of tateko made of bamboo branches. Today, the mino-gaki is rarely built in this style. (Saitama Pref.)

Unclassified Fences

1. One of the most common unclassified fences with Chinese characters ("四神" meaning "four gods") on the front surface (Sekizôji Temple, Hyogo Pref.)

2. A typical unclassified fence called aboshi-gaki, representing a net (Tokyo)

3. An unclassified fence with the kumiko of the upper part made in the kenninji-gaki style and uniquely arranged horizontal oshibuchi (Kyoto)

4. An unclassified fence with a boldly slanted tamabuchi and a see-through top of tateko (Kyoto)

5. An unclassified fence built on a wall, constructed as the background fence of a dry-landscape garden. The twelve sections divided by vertical oshibuchi have kumiko of bamboo canes arranged at different angles (Fukuchiyama)

Yotsume-gaki (four-eyed fence)

1. A low three-tiered yotsume-gaki with front tateko of a single pole and rear tateko of paired poles. The fence and the bamboo thicket create a beautiful harmony (Tenshaen, Uwajima)

2. A four-tiered yotsume-gaki built on both wings of the intermediate gate in a tea garden. The uppermost dôbuchi is attached well below the top of the tateko poles. (Hanshoan, Tokyo)

3. A standard three-tiered yotsume-gaki used as a partition (Gôtokuji, Tokyo)

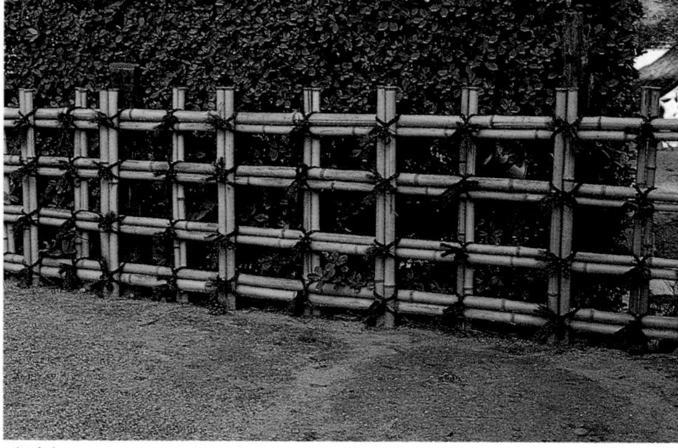

4. A low yotsume-gaki with the tateko and dôbuchi made of paired bamboo canes (Tamamo Park, Takamatsu)

5. A long three-tiered yotsume-gaki constructed along a path in a garden (Sapporo)

6. An unusual yotsume-gaki with multiple horizontal poles tied together at the bottom, built as the enclosing wall of a residence (Tokyo)

7. A four-tiered yotsume-gaki with front and rear tateko made of single and paired poles alternately arranged. While ordinary yotsume-gaki are made from gara-dake of ma-dake, was used for this fence, hachiku (Yamanashi Pref.)

Kinkakuji-gaki

1. A kinkakuji-gaki with tateko of slender canes, and horizontal oshibuchi and the tamabuchi of stout canes (Kyoto)

2. A kinkakuji-gaki with two tiers of oshibuchi made of gara-dake (Former Shiba Detached Palace, Tokyo)

3. An especially short kinkakuji-gaki constructed as a decorative fence in a garden (Tokyo)

4. A rather low kinkakuji-gaki used as a partition between main and intermediate gardens (Ichihara)

5. A low kinkakuji-gaki harmonizing well with the stone and other elements of the garden located in front of the main gate. Slender gara-dake is used for the tateko, and the oshibuchi are fixed to the posts. (Kyoto)

6. A long straight kinkakuji-gaki constructed by the pavement of a front garden. Relatively stout canes are used for tateko with oshibuchi of stout half-split bamboo attached on both sides of the fence. (Yamanashi Pref.)

7. A relatively tall two-tiered kinkakuji-gaki built atop a stone wall (Kagetsutei, Shimoda)

8. A kinkakuji-gaki matching well with the garden elements such as the stones and stone lantern (Ichihara)

Yarai-gaki (stockade fence)

1. A yarai-gaki using stout bamboo canes, built on top of a stone wall in front of a main gate. This style of low yarai-gaki, in which horizontal oshibuchi poles are tied to the intersections of kumiko, is especially popular in the Kansai area. (Kohôan, Kyoto)

2. A simply structured low yarai-gaki with square posts (Kanazawa)

3. A beautifully constructed yarai-gaki built atop a bank in a front garden (Kohôan, Kyoto)

4. A Kansai-style yarai-gaki using stout bamboo, built as the enclosing wall of a residence house (Nara)

5. A yarai-gaki constructed on top of a wall with the rear kumiko showing the inside surface (Kyoto)

6. The most common type of two-tiered yarai-gaki with dôbuchi made of gara-dake (Ritsurin Park, Takamatsu)

7. A relatively tall yarai-gaki with kumiko of split bamboo and a tamabuchi at the top (Sakura)

8. A three-tiered large eyed yarai-gaki built as the sleeve (sode) of a garden gate (Yamanashi Pref.)

9. A yarai-gaki with dôbuchi of gara-dake and kumiko poles arranged at close intervals (Myôgenji Temple, Toyokawa)

10. A yarai-gaki using split bamboo for kumiko, built as a barrier. The kumiko slats are arranged at about forty-five degrees so that each eye is almost a square. (Ôdate)

Ryôanji-gaki

1. An original-style ryôanji-gaki built as a partition in the precincts of the Ryôanji Temple. The eyes of the kumiko are made in the shape of horizontal diamonds. (Ryôanji Temple, Kyoto)

2. A ryôanji-gaki constructed along the side of the stone stairway leading to the head priest's residence (Ryôanji, Kyoto)

3. A ryôanji-gaki with eyes in the shape of vertical diamonds (Nagano Pref.)

4. A ryôanji-gaki enclosing the front garden of Kikugetsutei (Ritsurin Park, Takamatsu)

5. A ryôanji-gaki with kumiko of gara-dake and a thick intermediate post (Former Shiba Detached Palace, Tokyo)

Kôetsu-gaki

1. A traditional kôetsu-gaki located between a front garden and main garden (Tsukuba)

2. A small kôetsu-gaki used for decoration in a garden (Chiba)

3. An unusual kôetsu-gaki with its tamabuchi and bottom frame pole made of bound spicebush branches (Kyoto)

4. A modern style kôetsu-gaki with curved tamabuchi and kumiko arranged in the midare style (Nagano Pref.)

5. The original kôetsu-gaki at the Kôetsuji Temple. The fence is bent in a long curve, with kumiko of paired split bamboo and the eyes slightly elongated height-wise (Kôetsuji Temple, Kyoto)

Other Fences

Katsura-gaki

1. A large-scale katsura-gaki constructed in a style of takeho-gaki, located near the main gate of famous Katsura Detached Palace garden. The horizontal bamboo branches are arranged to produce a checkered pattern. (Katsura Detached Palace, Kyoto)

2. A katsura-gaki with surface kumiko of relatively thick bamboo branches (Sankeien, Yokohama)

3. A double-faced katsura-gaki constructed to enclose a dry-landscape garden (Tsurugaoka-hachimangû, Kamakura)

4. A katsura-gaki with a roof, built as a partition in a tea-garden style Japanese garden (Ibaraki Pref.)

5. Katsura-gaki matching well with the stones and hair moss of a garden. Stout bamboos are used for the vertical oshibuchi, and another for the horizontal oshibuchi at the top. (Tsurugaoka-hachimangû, Kamakura)

6. A beautiful katsura-gaki with kumiko of elaborately arranged branches, built as a sode-gaki (Kyoto)

7. A variation of katsura-gaki with a roof, built in a form of katsura-gaki as the enclosure of precincts (Kyoto)

8. A variation of katsura-gaki with kumiko of split bamboos instead of bamboo branches (Kyoto)

Nanzenji-gaki

1. A nanzenji-gaki blending in well with an autumn garden. Tateko made of bush clover are arranged at intervals (Main building of the Nanzenji Temple, Kyoto)

2. An original nanzenji-gaki with tateko of split bamboos arranged in the ôtsu-gaki style (same as above)

3. A fence using the kenninji-gaki structure, with kuroho branches arranged in a nanzenji-gaki style (Nagano Pref.)

Kuromoji-gaki (spicebush fence)

1. A three-tiered kuromoji-gaki with especially stout split bamboo canes used for horizontal oshibuchi and spicebush branches for tateko. The top of the tateko are well above the uppermost oshibuchi, with a horizontal support made of spicebush branches attached near the tip. (Kyoto)

2. A kuromoji-gaki with a roof, built on top of a low wall (Kyoto)

3. A kuromoji-gaki with unusual oshibuchi, built in front of a main gate as a partition (Kyoto)

Ajiro-gaki

1. An ajiro-gaki with a roof with kumiko of woven split bamboo slats, built as the screen of a carport (Nagano Pref.)

2. An ajiro-gaki made of woven shino-dake, built behind an iron washbowl (Korakuen, Tokyo)

3. A tall ajiro-gaki with the upper part made of split bamboo slats woven in the ajiro pattern and the lower part with tateko and oshibuchi (Chiba Pref.)

Nanako-gaki

1. A nanako-gaki is the simplest form of bamboo fence. These nanako-gaki, using slender split bamboo slats, are built on both sides of a walk in a park. The two fences are different in style. (Ritsurin Park, Takamatsu)

2. A nanako-gaki with bamboo slats overlapping each other and tied using dyed ropes (same as above)

3. A movable nanako-gaki with the ends of the curved bamboo slats inserted into holes made in a half-split stout bamboo cane (Yamanashi Pref.)

Hagi-gaki (bush clover fence): A three-tiered hagi-gaki with dried bush clover branches used for the tateko, and paired thin round bamboo canes to hold the tateko in place near the top (Ryōanji Temple, Kyoto)

Sugikawa-gaki (cedar bark fence): An elegant sugikawa-gaki with fine tiled roofs and tasteful slender bamboo oshibuchi, constructed on both sides of a garden gate (Fukuchiyama)

Chasen-gaki (tea whisk fence): A unique chasen-gaki with bundled bamboo branches fixed to the dôbuchi (Kyoto)

Original fence: A fence using opened bamboo canes (hishigi-dake) for the tateko (Kyoto)

Original fence: A fence with see-through tateko of split bamboo and oshibuchi (Urayasu)

Original fence: A combination of a yarai-gaki and a takeho-gaki (Uji)

Original fence: One yotsume-gaki on top of another (Okayama)

Original fence: A low sukashi-gaki with gara-dake arranged crosswise vertically and horizontally (Tokyo)

Kekkai: A plain barrier made of stout bamboo canes— the most primitive form of bamboo fence (Kyoto)

Sode-gaki (sleeve fence)

1. A sode-gaki with a round window, using black bamboo branches (kuroho) for the tateko (Muroran)

2. A two-stage short sode-gaki with tateko of bamboo branches (Kyoto)

3. An elaborately designed sode-gaki of bamboo branches built as a screen (Kyoto)

4. A three-tiered sode-gaki with delicately arranged bamboo branches. A furedome of split bamboo is attached near the top to hold the tateko in place. (Kyoto)

5. A gorgeous movable tsuitate-gaki, resembling a regular sode-gaki, with a base at the bottom of each oyabashira (Kyoto)

6. A sode-gaki with the upper half made in the mino-gaki style, with the lower tips of branches cut in a curve, and the lower half with tateko of shino-dake, built by the entrance of a house (Matsudo)

7. A four-tiered sode-gaki constructed in the kenninji-gaki style and made of môsôchiku (Makayaji Temple, Shizuoka Pref.)

8. A sode-gaki made of bamboo branches with a latticed window at the top (Kyoto)

9. A sode-gaki made mostly of bush clover with oshibuchi of stout split-bamboo canes (Shiga Pref.)

10. A sode-gaki in the teppô-gaki style using bamboo canes and branches (Kamakura)

11. A teppô-gaki used a sode-gaki made of slender gara-dake (Ichihara)

14. A sode-gaki using spicebush and shino-dake together (Hyogo Pref.)

17. A sode-gaki with bundled black branches and latticed sarashi-dake (Chiba Pref.)

12. A very short sode-gaki with bundled bamboo branches and latticed split bamboo slats (Kyoto)

15. An arch-shaped sode-gaki made of bush clover and bamboo (Ehime Pref.)

18. A sode-gaki with parts built in different styles (Toyohashi)

13. A sode-gaki in the yotsume-gaki style built at the entrance of a tea arbor (Tokyo)

16. A sode-gaki made solely of spicebush (Kyoto)

19. A sode-gaki with ajiro-gaki style kumiko and latticework kumiko put together (Shimane Pref.)

Basic Techniques and Procedures for Building Bamboo Fences

Illustrated Explanations of Bamboo Fence Terms

Oshibuchi

A piece of bamboo placed over tateko, etc. to hold it firmly in place.

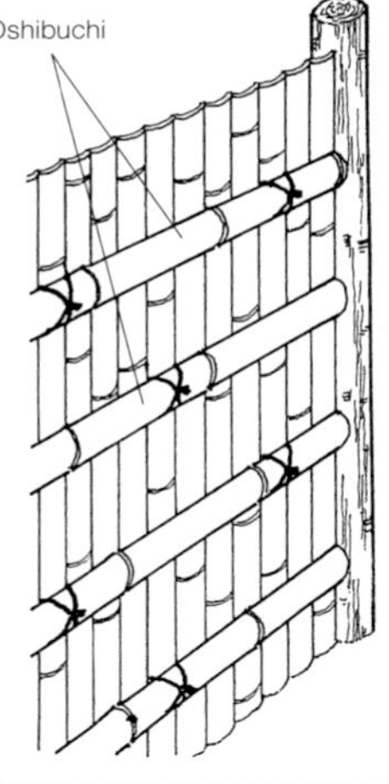

Kumiko

Any bamboo pieces that constitute the main parts of the fence surface. Those arranged vertically are called tateko.

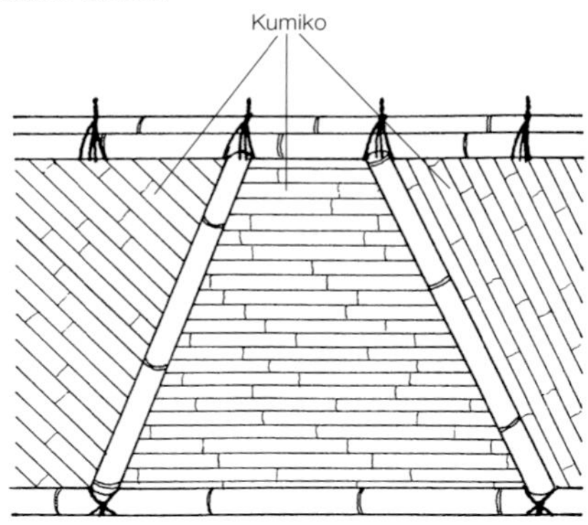

Oyabashira

A stout post, which provides the fundamental support for the fence structure, positioned at the end of a fence. It is also called tomebashira.

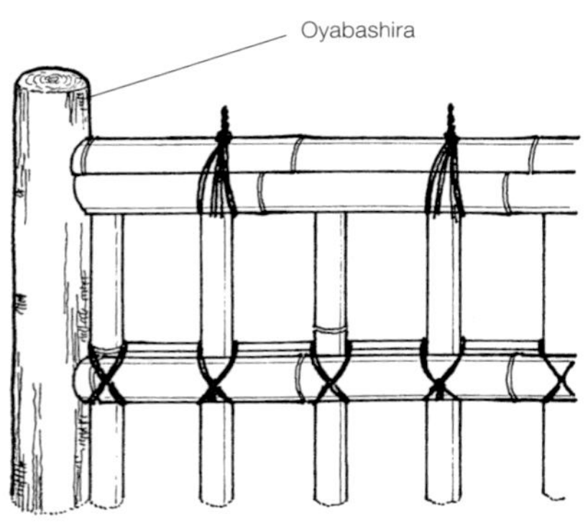

Shinobi-dake

A slender piece of bamboo, usually split, used as an invisible support to hold tateko or kumiko in place, always covered with oshibuchi.

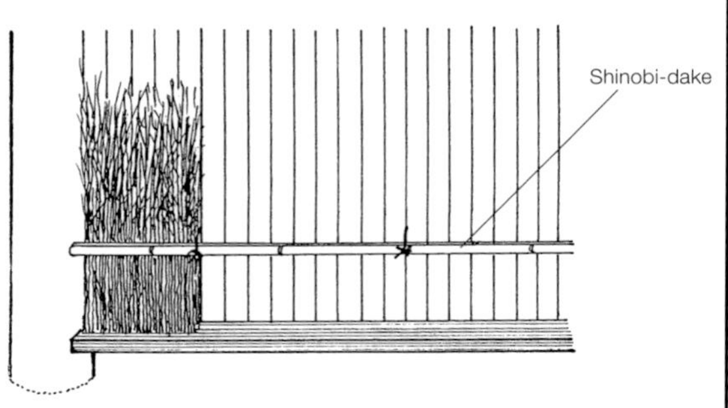

Kasa-dake

A half-split bamboo placed at the top of a bamboo fence.

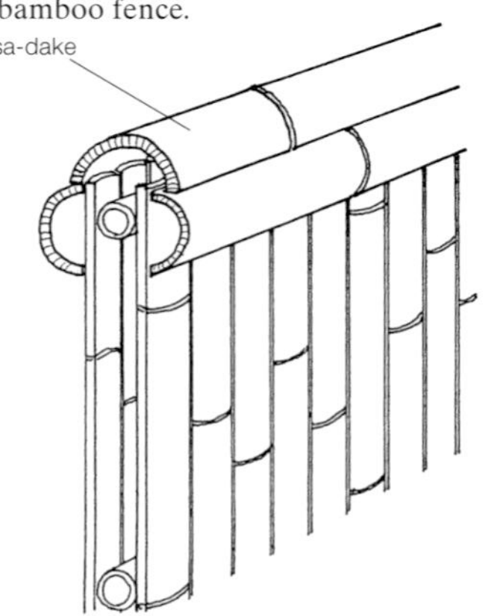

Shahei-gaki

Any bamboo fence that is used as a screen.

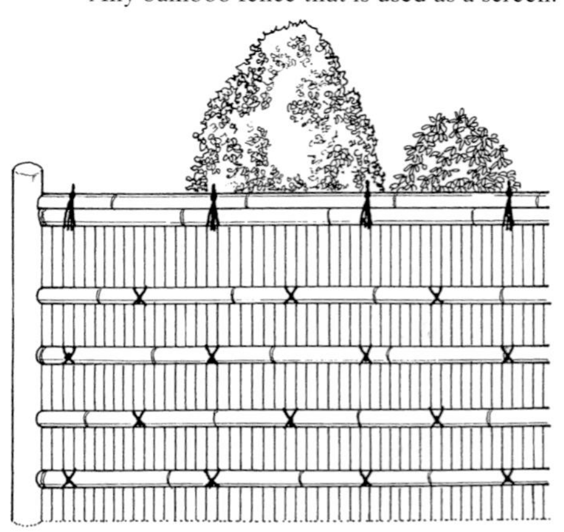

Sukashi-gaki

Any bamboo fence that can be seen through.

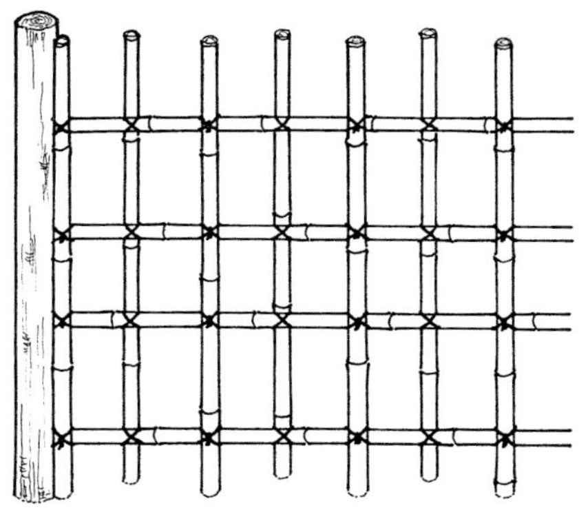

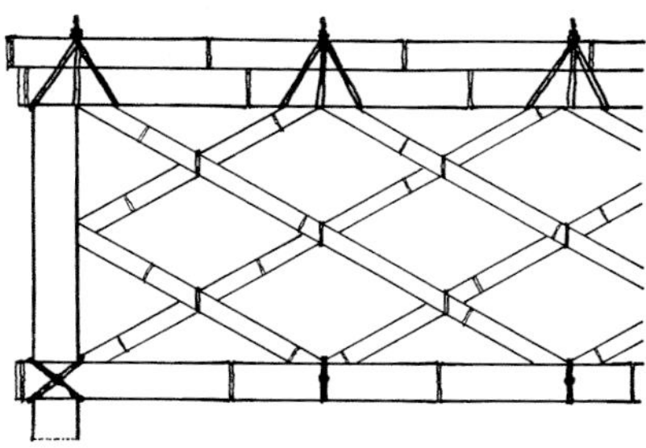

Sode-gaki

A small bamboo fence built against a building; so called because it resembles the sleeve (sode) of a kimono.

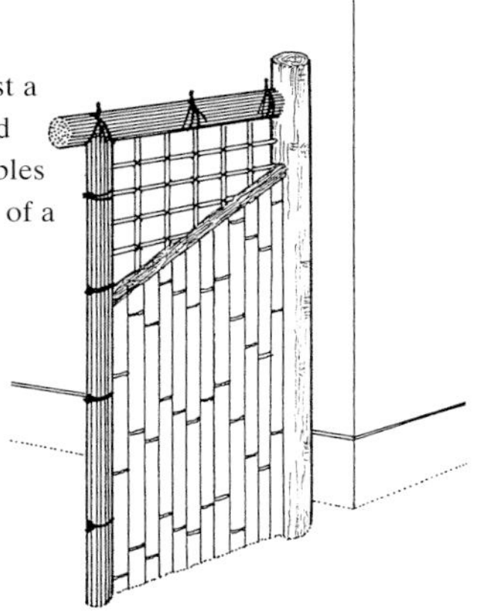

Tateko

Vertically arranged kumiko

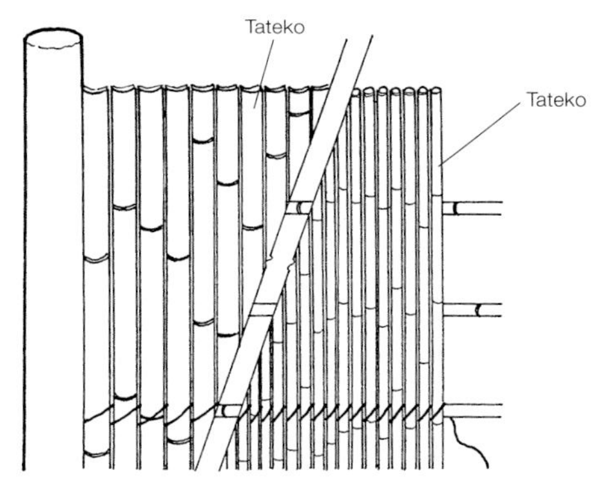

Takeho

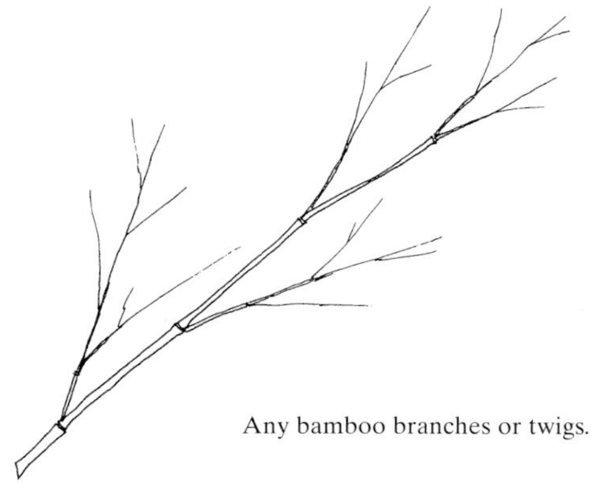

Any bamboo branches or twigs.

Tamabuchi

Any molding that covers the top of a bamboo fence. Tamabuchi usually includes the uppermost oshibuchi and the kasa-dake on top of it.

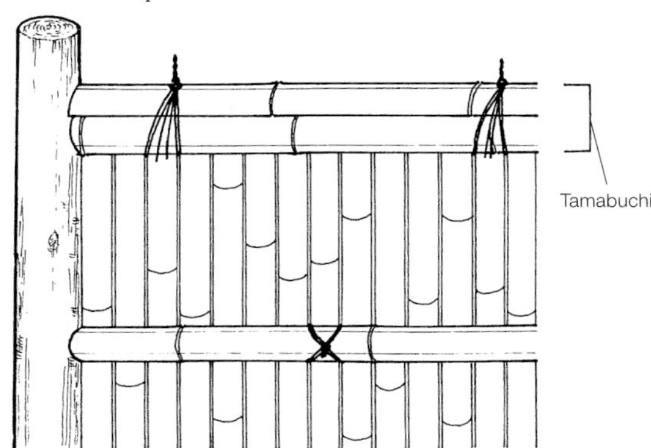

Dôbuchi

A piece of bamboo or a rafter extending between oyabashira, on which kumiko, etc. are attached.

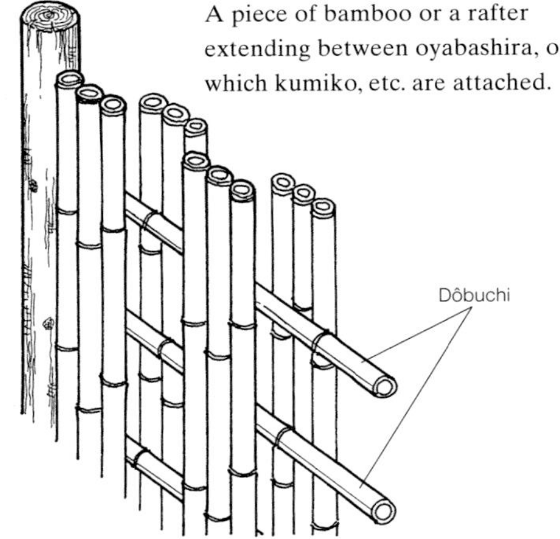

Fushidome

Cutting a bamboo cane just above a joint.

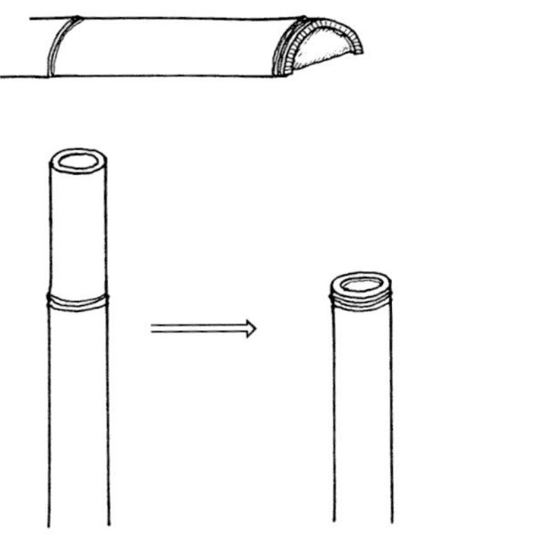

Mumeita

A narrow supporting board near the bottom of a fence to hold tateko, etc. off the ground.

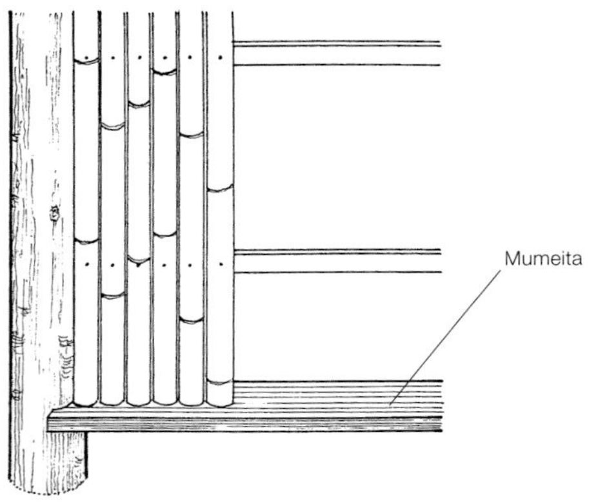

Makibashira

A post wrapped with pieces of different material for decorative effect.

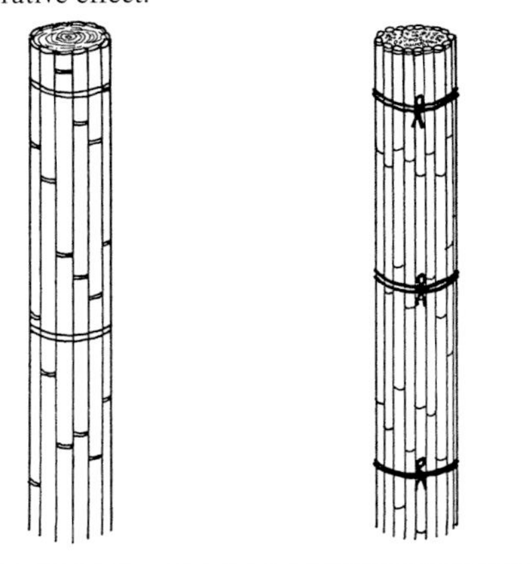

Mabashira

A vertical supporting post, which is less thick than an oyabashira, positioned in the middle of a fence. An intermediate post.

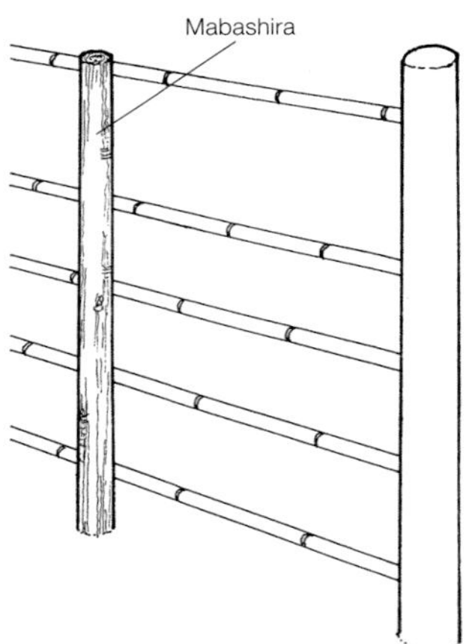

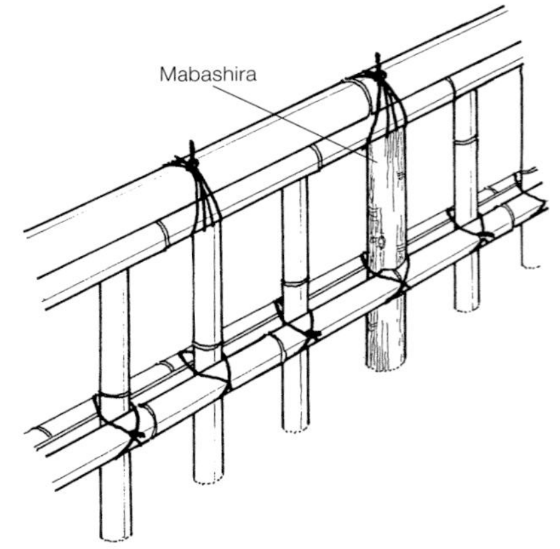

Basic Techniques

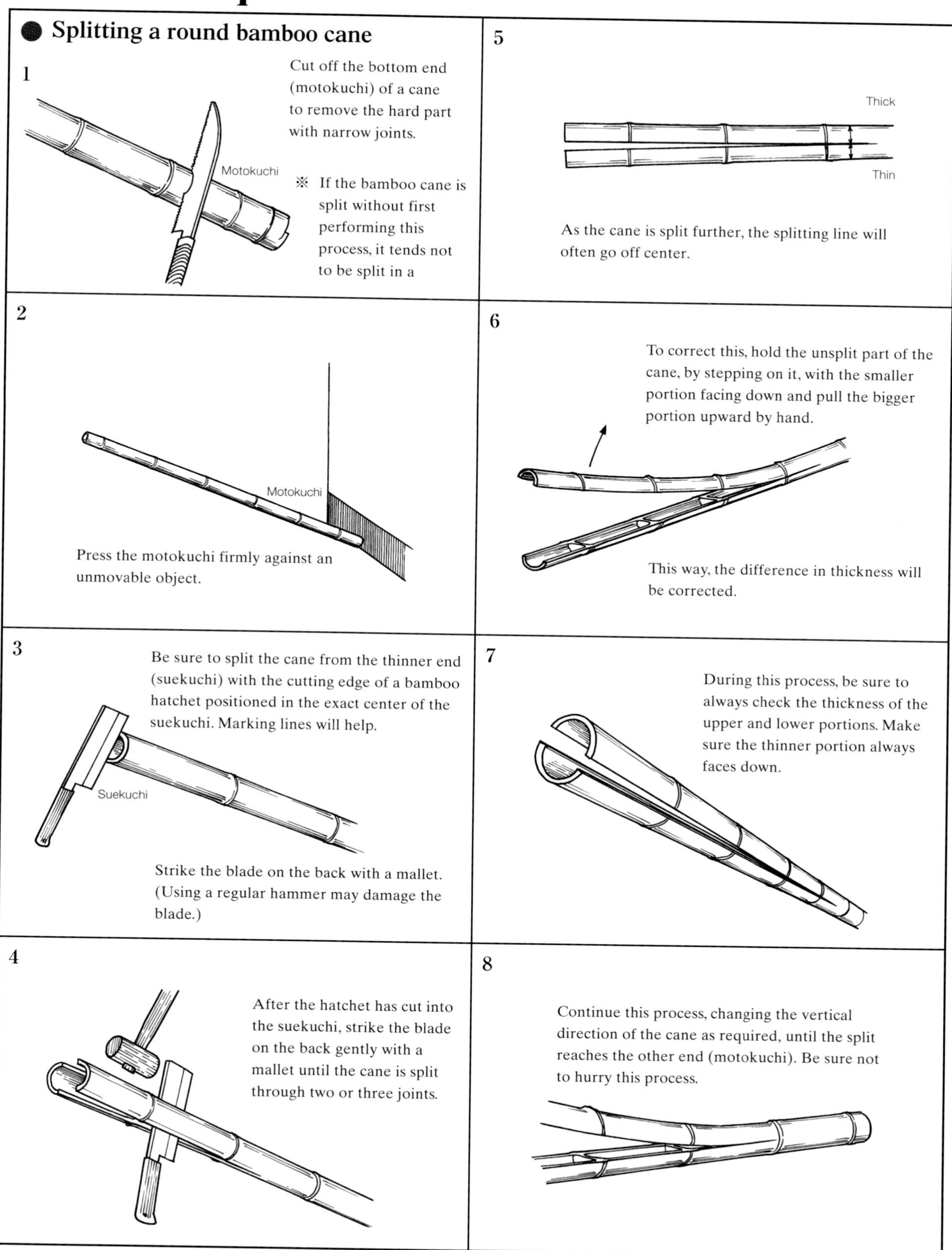

● Splitting a round bamboo cane
1
Cut off the bottom end (motokuchi) of a cane to remove the hard part with narrow joints.
Motokuchi
※ If the bamboo cane is split without first performing this process, it tends not to be split in a
2
Motokuchi
Press the motokuchi firmly against an unmovable object.
3
Be sure to split the cane from the thinner end (suekuchi) with the cutting edge of a bamboo hatchet positioned in the exact center of the suekuchi. Marking lines will help.
Suekuchi
Strike the blade on the back with a mallet. (Using a regular hammer may damage the blade.)
4
After the hatchet has cut into the suekuchi, strike the blade on the back gently with a mallet until the cane is split through two or three joints.
5
Thick
Thin
As the cane is split further, the splitting line will often go off center.
6
To correct this, hold the unsplit part of the cane, by stepping on it, with the smaller portion facing down and pull the bigger portion upward by hand.
This way, the difference in thickness will be corrected.
7
During this process, be sure to always check the thickness of the upper and lower portions. Make sure the thinner portion always faces down.
8
Continue this process, changing the vertical direction of the cane as required, until the split reaches the other end (motokuchi). Be sure not to hurry this process.

9

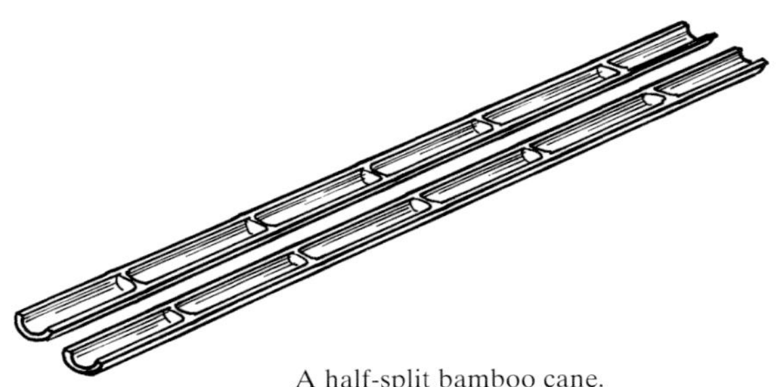

A half-split bamboo cane.

Bends of round bamboo cane

A round bamboo looks straight or nearly straight when viewed from the branched side.

When viewed at an angle of ninety degrees, however, the bamboo cane looks bent at each joint.

Splitting a bamboo cane to be used for oshibuchi

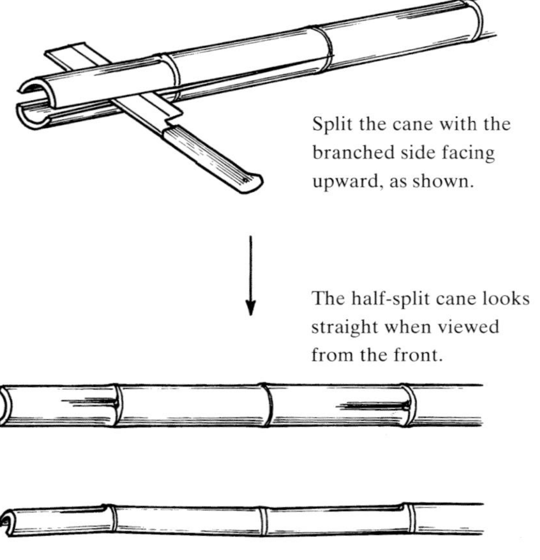

Split the cane with the branched side facing upward, as shown.

The half-split cane looks straight when viewed from the front.

The cut surface has bents at the joints.

Splitting a bamboo cane to be used for kasa-dake

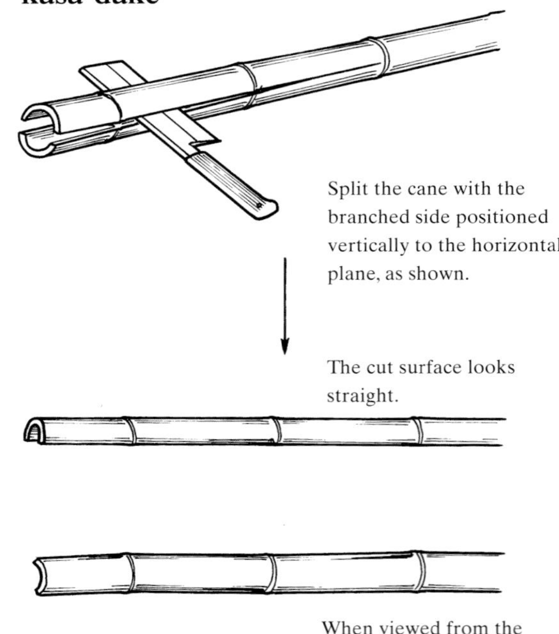

Split the cane with the branched side positioned vertically to the horizontal plane, as shown.

The cut surface looks straight.

When viewed from the front, the half-split cane has bents at the joints.

Correcting the bend of split bamboo

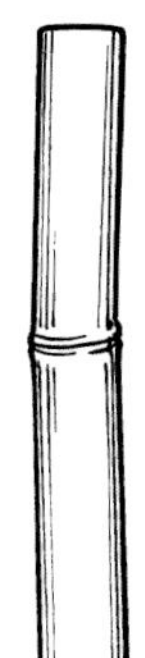

A bend in split bamboo can be corrected with a cut.

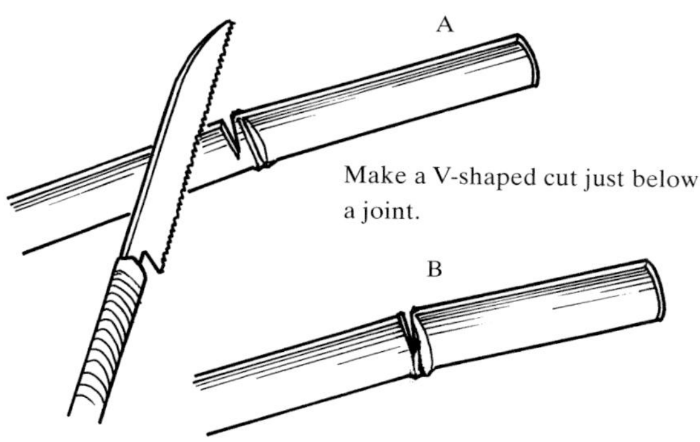

Make a V-shaped cut just below a joint.

Make a V-shaped cut at a joint. Make a relatively narrow cut depending on the bend, and cut as deep as two-thirds of the diameter so that the bend can be corrected appropriately.

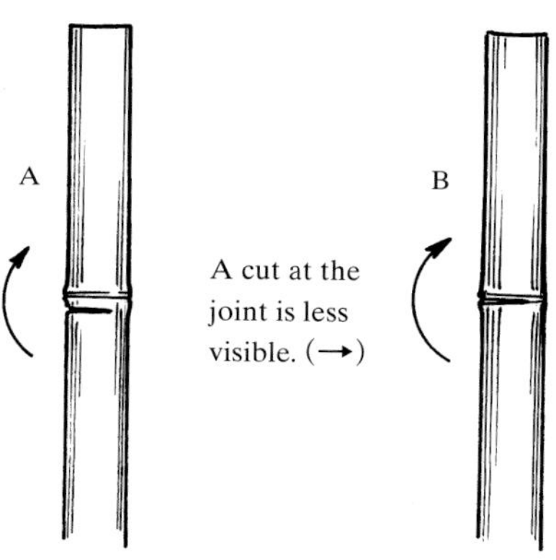

A cut at the joint is less visible. (→)

Joining two split bamboo canes

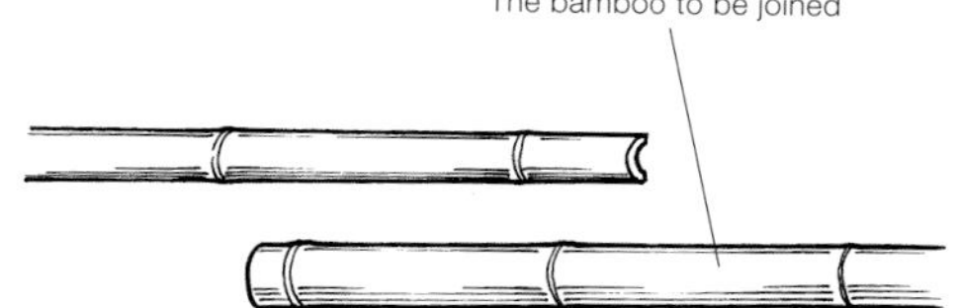

Select a bamboo cane of appropriate thickness.

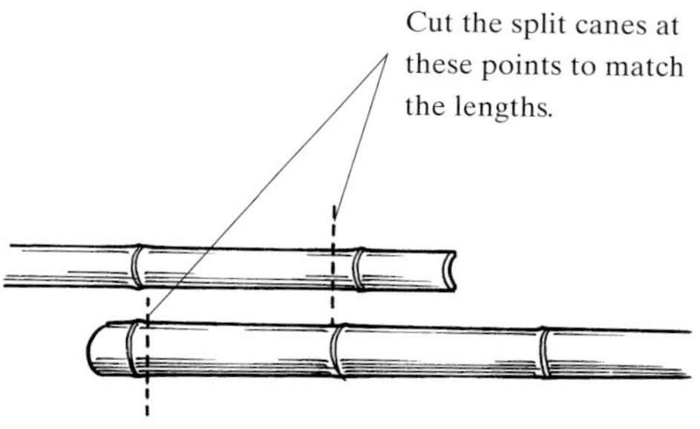

Cut the split canes at these points to match the lengths.

Two split canes when joined, viewed from the outside.

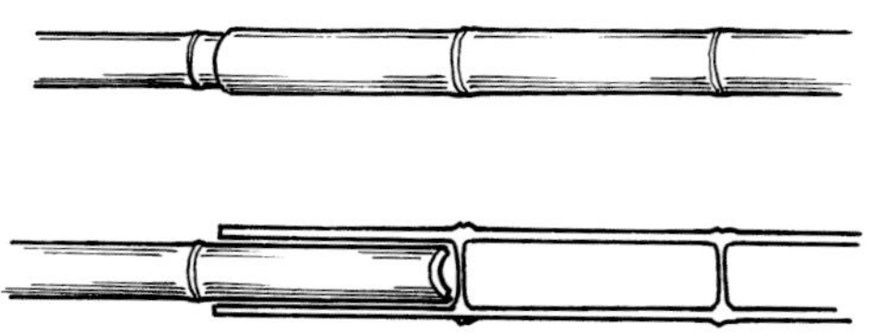

Same as above, viewed from the inside.

※ This joining method is used for tamabuchi and garadake as well.

Matching a tateko with a log-made oyabashira

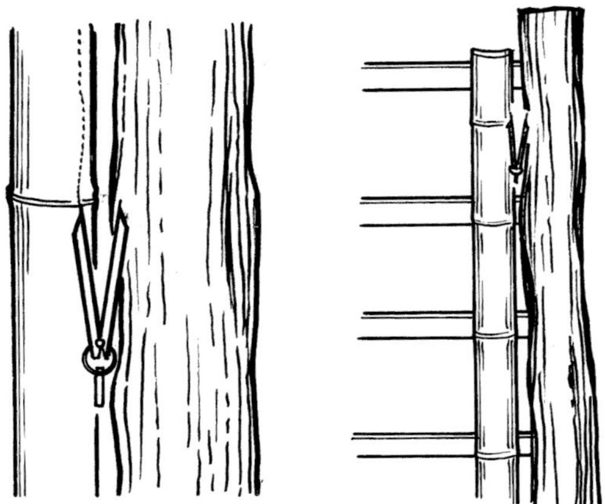

Draw a line on the tateko to match the inside surface of the post, using a pair of compasses.

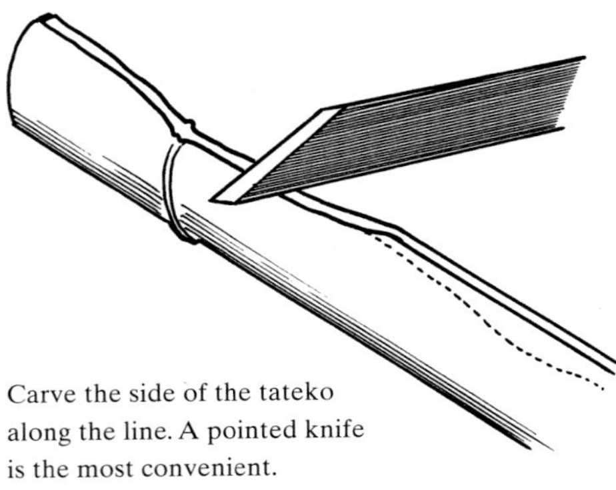

Carve the side of the tateko along the line. A pointed knife is the most convenient.

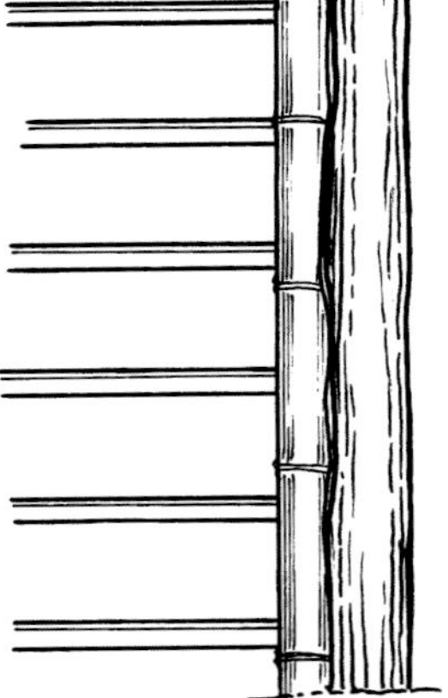

This way, the carved side of the tateko will precisely match the inside surface of the oyabashira.

Connecting a bamboo cane perpendicularly to a half-split bamboo

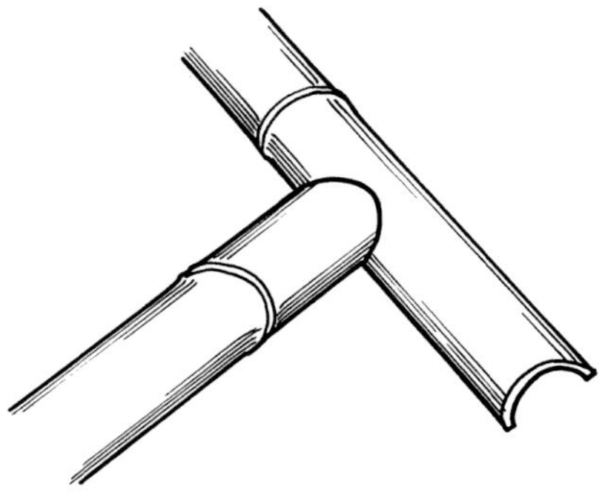

Side view

Cut the end of the round bamboo like this.

Normally, a simply diagonal straight cut is made. But this is not desirable in this case.

The two bamboos match like this. The cut can be made easily with a pointed knife.

Joining two bamboo canes at a corner
(Eg. Kasa-dake)

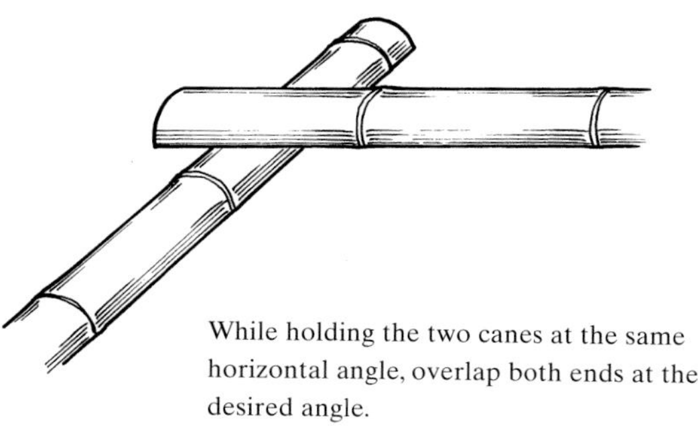

While holding the two canes at the same horizontal angle, overlap both ends at the desired angle.

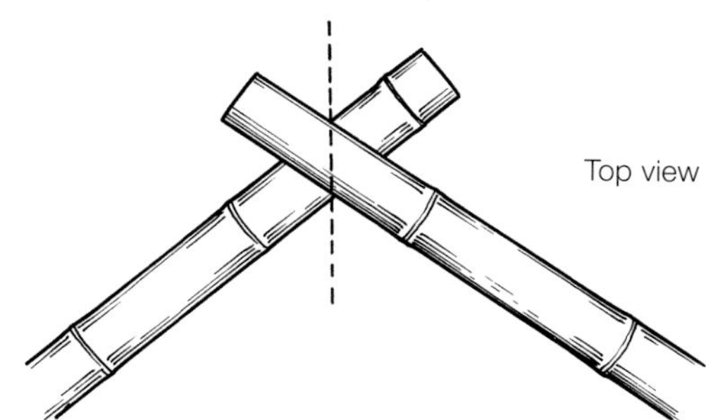

Cut the canes precisely at the center of the intersection using a bamboo saw (takehiki).

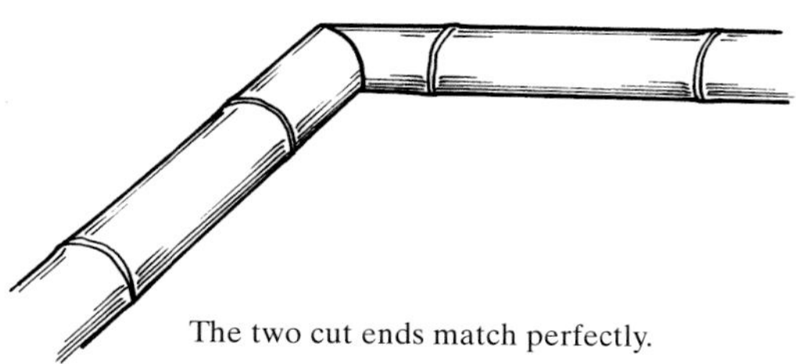

The two cut ends match perfectly.

Tokkuri-musubi ("sake bottle" tie)
(also called unokubi-musubi ["cormorant neck" tie])

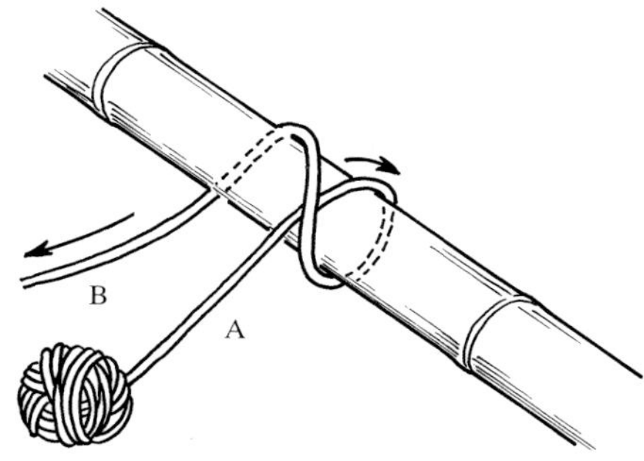

Wind the rope around the pole as shown.

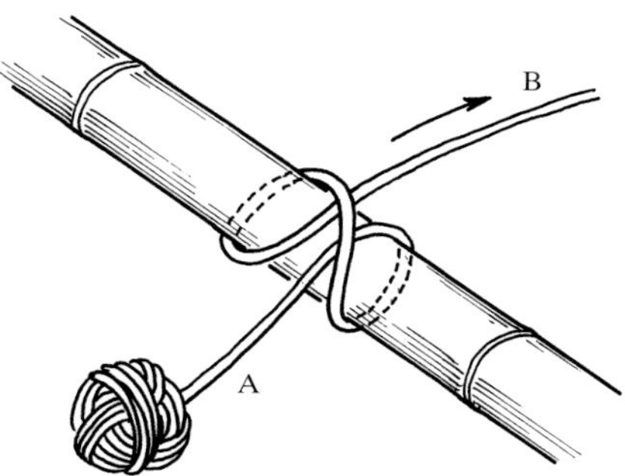

Pass the end of the rope (B) under the rope as shown.

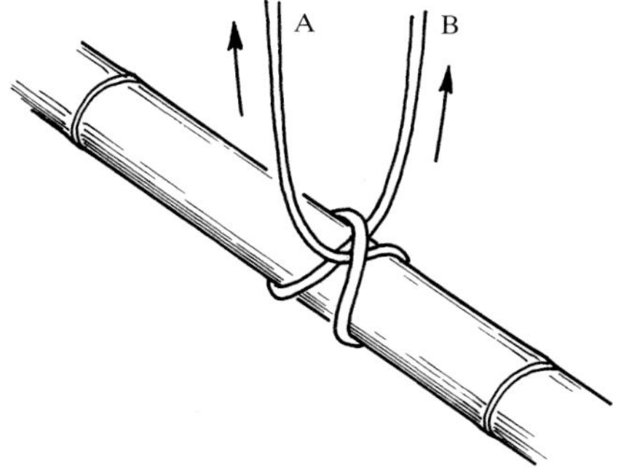

Pull A and B upward and fasten tightly.

Ibo-musubi ("wart" tie)
(also called otoko-musubi ["male" tie])

1

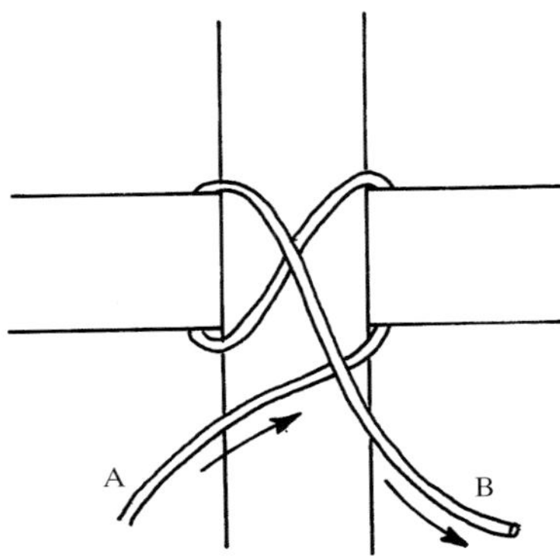

Wind the rope around the horizontal pole so that it crosses itself on the outer surface of the vertical pole.

2

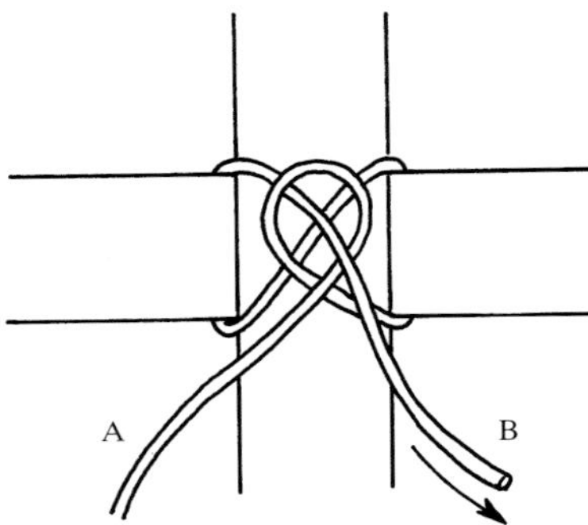

Make a loop around B with the A end, and pull B.

3

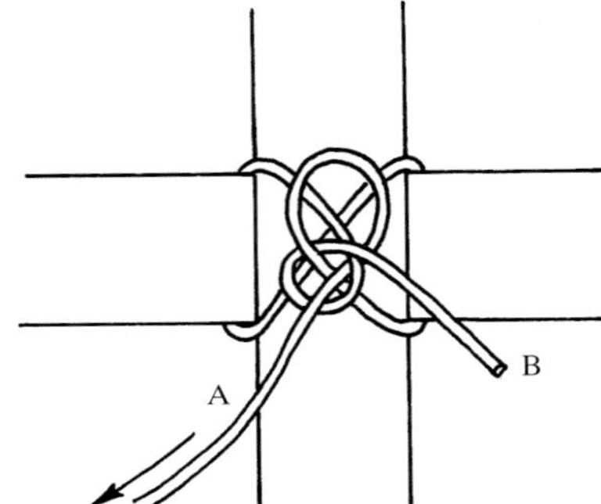

Pass the B end through the loop as shown; then pull the A end until the rope is tightly fastened.

Tying a tamabuchi

1

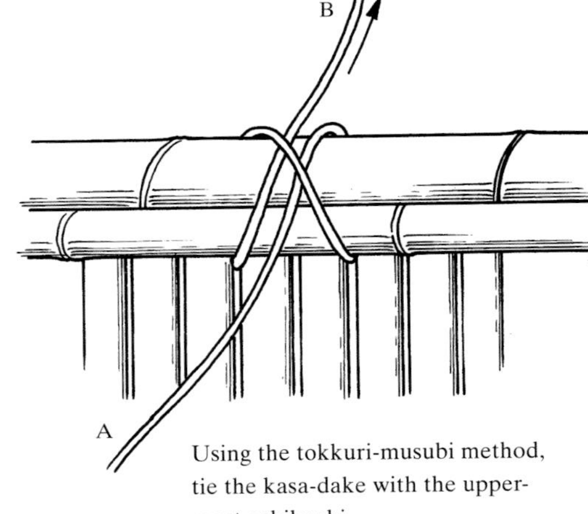

Using the tokkuri-musubi method, tie the kasa-dake with the uppermost oshibuchi.

2

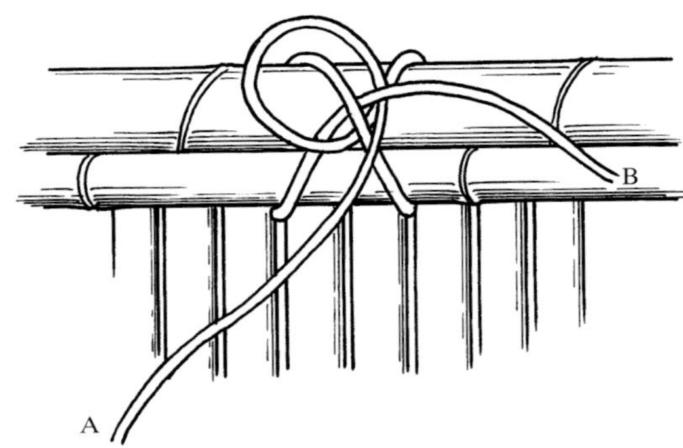

Tie the rope following the same procedure as the ibo-musubi method.

3

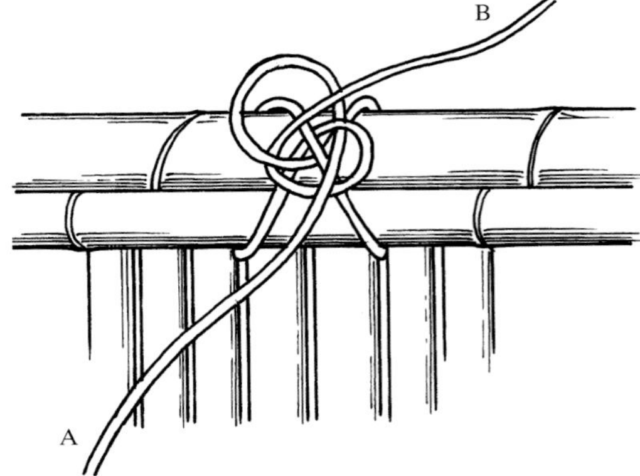

Follow the ibo-musubi method until this step.

4

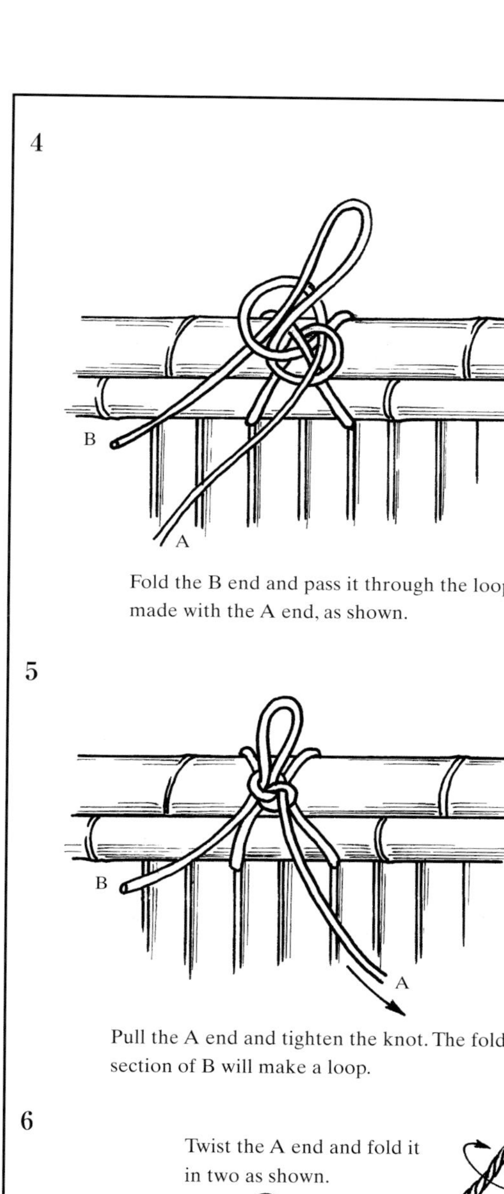

Fold the B end and pass it through the loop made with the A end, as shown.

5

Pull the A end and tighten the knot. The folded section of B will make a loop.

6

Twist the A end and fold it in two as shown.

Approx. 5cm

7

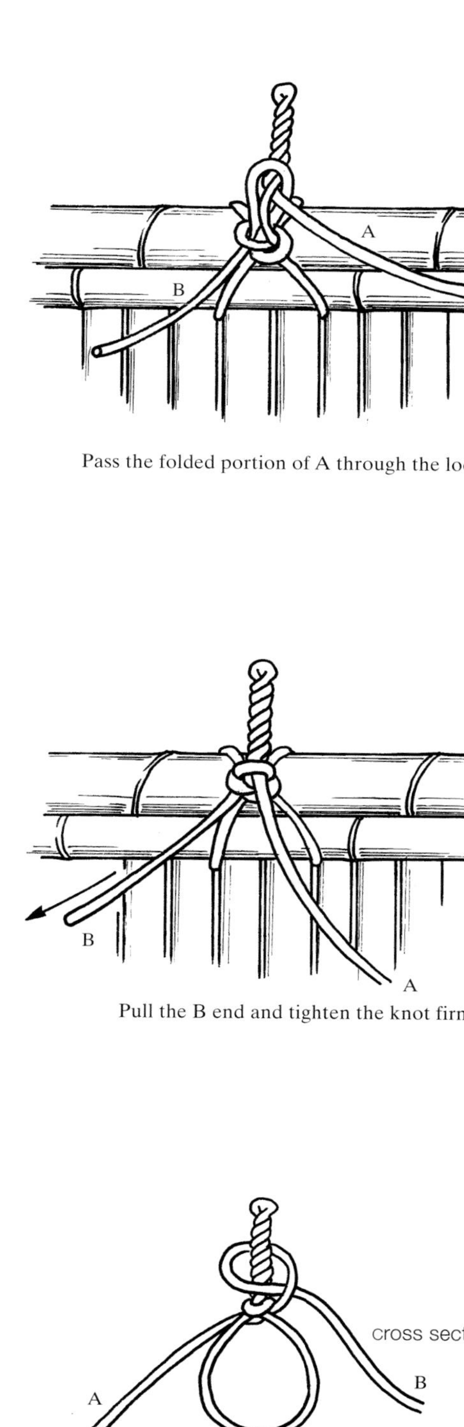

Pass the folded portion of A through the loop.

8

Pull the B end and tighten the knot firmly.

9

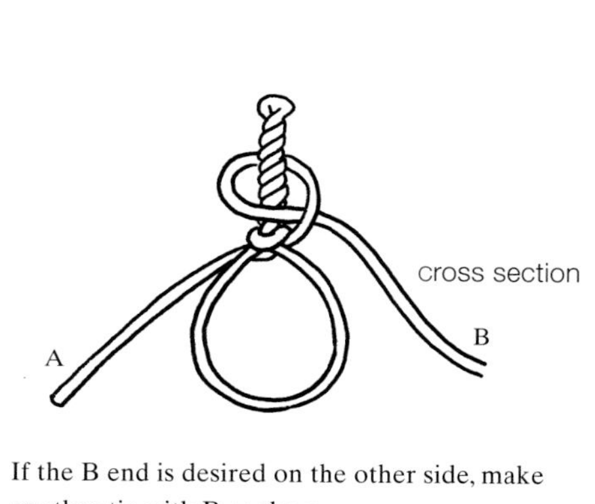

If the B end is desired on the other side, make another tie with B as shown.

Kenninji-gaki (Shin Style)

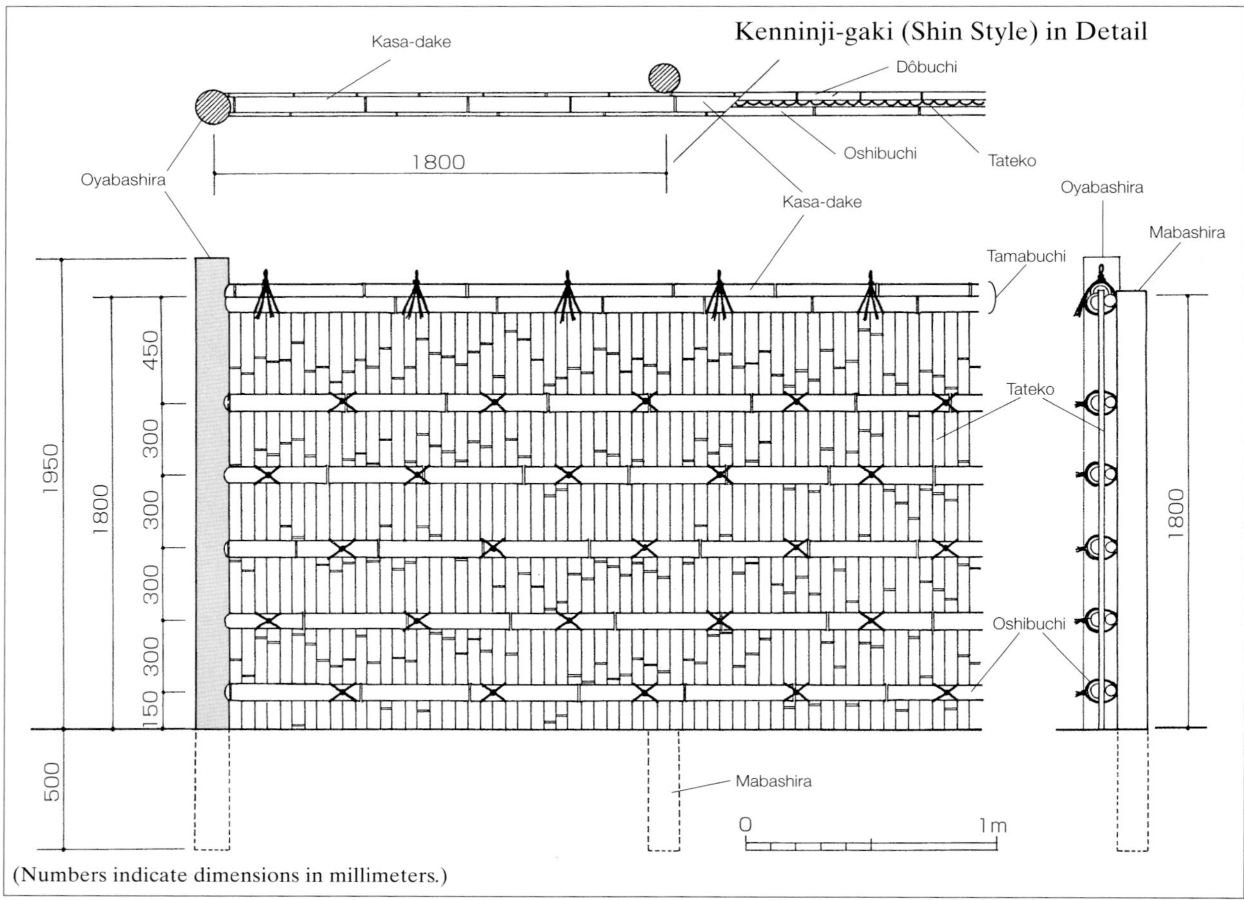

This drawing shows the end result of the fence construction process delineated on the following pages.

The most frequent type of Shahei-gaki seen in Japan, the kenninji-gaki uses many of the basic bamboo fence construction techniques, with tateko held in place by oshibuchi and a molding placed at the top (tamabuchi) to provide balance.

The shin-gyô-sô categorization of calligraphy is used to describe the three styles of kenninji-gaki, the first of which is portrayed in detail here. The shin ("straight," "standard") style has a tamabuchi; the sô ("grass") style has no molding, and the tops of the tateko are varied in height; and the gyô, an intermediate style, also has no molding, but its tateko are leveled off to the same height. (Sô-style kenninji-gaki are seen only rarely, usually as so-called sode-gaki in tea ceremony gardens.)

Construction proceeds by inserting oyabashira into the ground, running dôbuchi, usually of slender Japanese bamboo, between them, and attaching tateko to the rails. There are two basic construction methods: (1) the abbreviated method (shown here), in which the ends of the dôbuchi are cut at an angle and nailed to the posts, and (2) the original method, in which the support rails are inserted into holes in the posts. (The original method results in a sturdier fence; it also allows for support poles of ordinary wood to be used.)

The final appearance of the fence will depend on how many oshibuchi are desired (this will also determine the number of dôbuchi used as well, since the oshibuchi are braced over the tateko at the level of the dôbuchi). The Kansai (Osaka area) style uses relatively stout oshibuchi, so five-level fences are common there. The Kanto (Tokyo area) style uses more-slender oshibuchi, so six-level fences are usually seen; this style is depicted here. Although bamboo canes split in half are ordinarily used for the oshibuchi, an alternative arrangement—several thin bamboo slats bunched together—may be used for the second and fourth oshibuchi from the top.

The tateko may extend to the ground (as shown here), or a row of lining stones (sashi-ishi)or a board may be placed on the ground and the tateko rested on these.

When relatively stout bamboo is used for the oshibuchi, they can be attached with twine to pairs of tateko, as shown above. Ordinarily, however, the twine is tied around single tateko.

Although the kenninji-gaki appears simple, getting one to look nice can be unexpectedly difficult. Take special care when splitting the bamboo for the oshibuchi and tamabuchi. Also, ensure that the joints of the tateko are arranged in a random pattern.

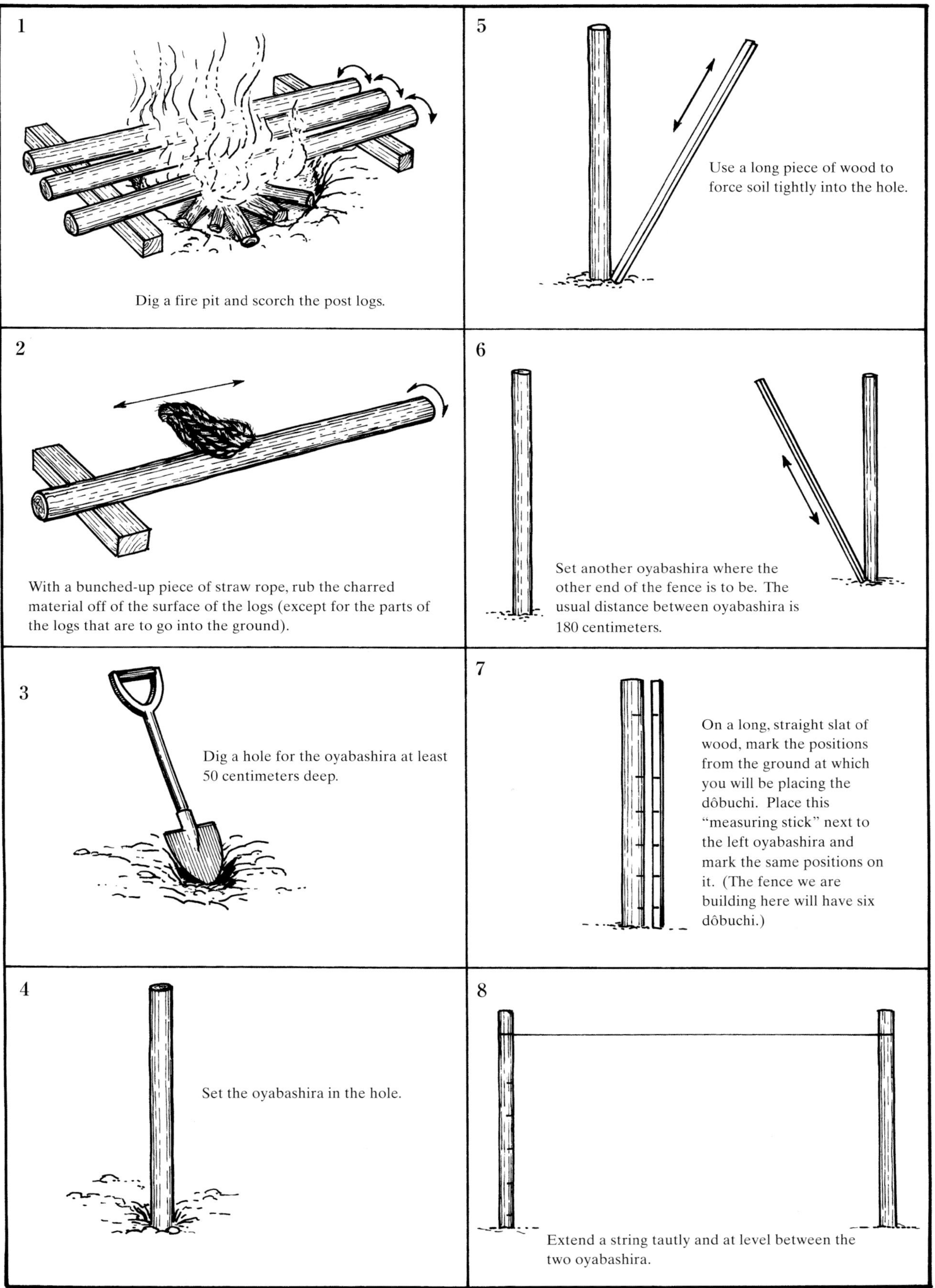
1
Dig a fire pit and scorch the post logs.
2
With a bunched-up piece of straw rope, rub the charred material off of the surface of the logs (except for the parts of the logs that are to go into the ground).
3
Dig a hole for the oyabashira at least 50 centimeters deep.
4
Set the oyabashira in the hole.
5
Use a long piece of wood to force soil tightly into the hole.
6
Set another oyabashira where the other end of the fence is to be. The usual distance between oyabashira is 180 centimeters.
7
On a long, straight slat of wood, mark the positions from the ground at which you will be placing the dôbuchi. Place this "measuring stick" next to the left oyabashira and mark the same positions on it. (The fence we are building here will have six dôbuchi.)
8
Extend a string tautly and at level between the two oyabashira.

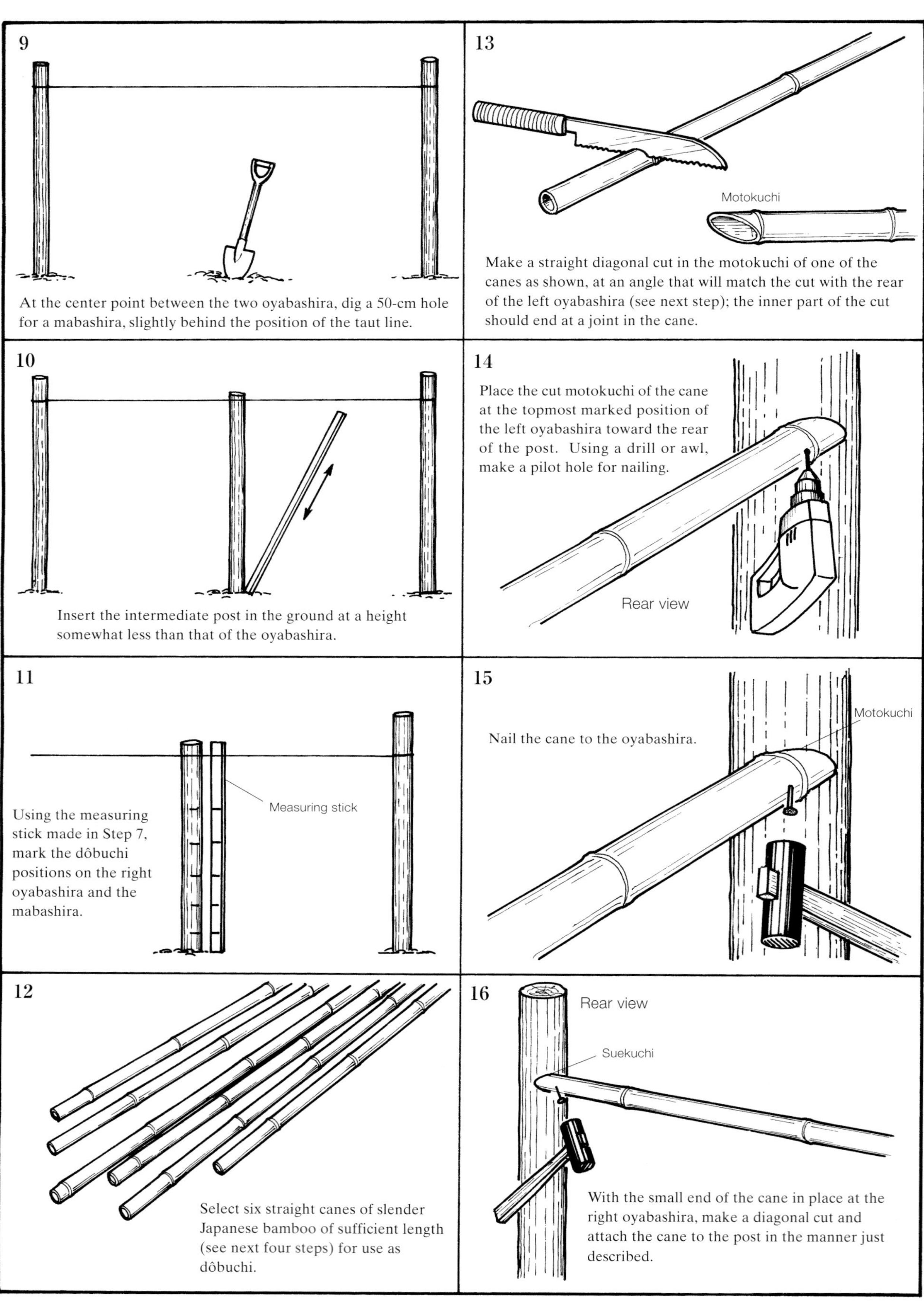
9
At the center point between the two oyabashira, dig a 50-cm hole for a mabashira, slightly behind the position of the taut line.
10
Insert the intermediate post in the ground at a height somewhat less than that of the oyabashira.
11
Measuring stick
Using the measuring stick made in Step 7, mark the dôbuchi positions on the right oyabashira and the mabashira.
12
Select six straight canes of slender Japanese bamboo of sufficient length (see next four steps) for use as dôbuchi.
13
Motokuchi
Make a straight diagonal cut in the motokuchi of one of the canes as shown, at an angle that will match the cut with the rear of the left oyabashira (see next step); the inner part of the cut should end at a joint in the cane.
14
Place the cut motokuchi of the cane at the topmost marked position of the left oyabashira toward the rear of the post. Using a drill or awl, make a pilot hole for nailing.
Rear view
15
Motokuchi
Nail the cane to the oyabashira.
16
Rear view
Suekuchi
With the small end of the cane in place at the right oyabashira, make a diagonal cut and attach the cane to the post in the manner just described.

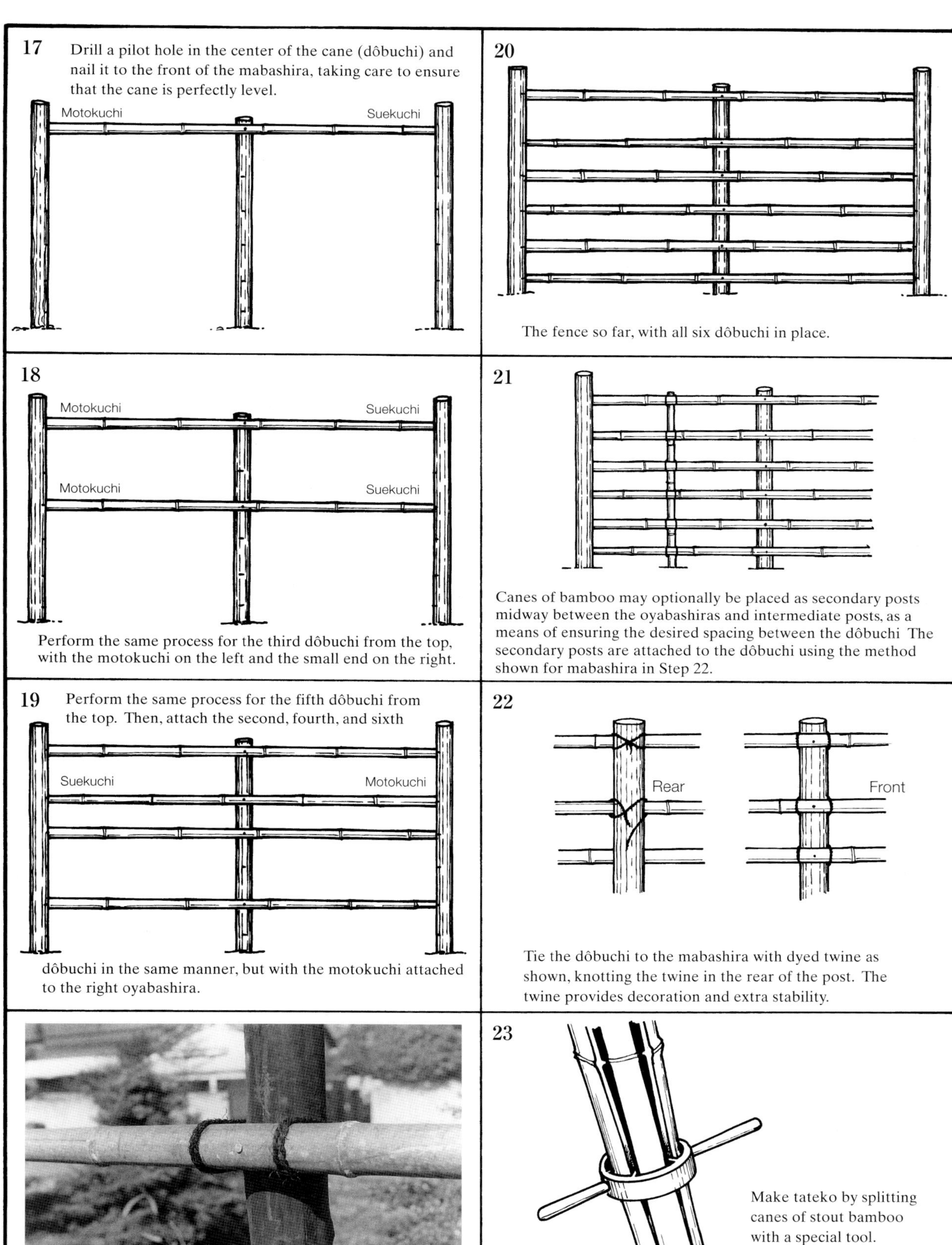

17 Drill a pilot hole in the center of the cane (dôbuchi) and nail it to the front of the mabashira, taking care to ensure that the cane is perfectly level.

18 Perform the same process for the third dôbuchi from the top, with the motokuchi on the left and the small end on the right.

19 Perform the same process for the fifth dôbuchi from the top. Then, attach the second, fourth, and sixth dôbuchi in the same manner, but with the motokuchi attached to the right oyabashira.

Close-up of dôbuchi tied to the mabashira (see Step 22).

20 The fence so far, with all six dôbuchi in place.

21 Canes of bamboo may optionally be placed as secondary posts midway between the oyabashiras and intermediate posts, as a means of ensuring the desired spacing between the dôbuchi The secondary posts are attached to the dôbuchi using the method shown for mabashira in Step 22.

22 Tie the dôbuchi to the mabashira with dyed twine as shown, knotting the twine in the rear of the post. The twine provides decoration and extra stability.

23 Make tateko by splitting canes of stout bamboo with a special tool. Use presplit bamboo if available.

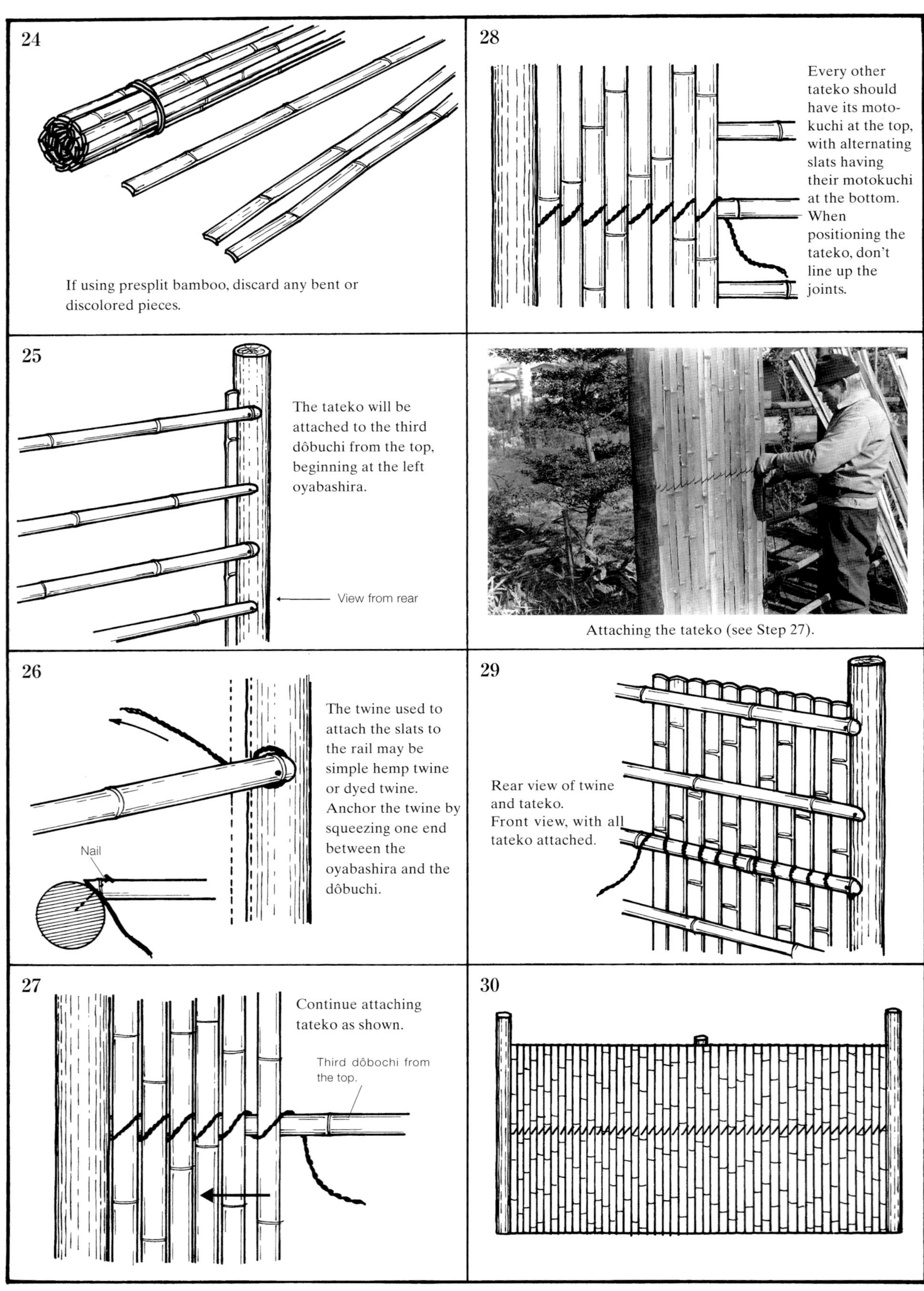

24
If using presplit bamboo, discard any bent or discolored pieces.
25
The tateko will be attached to the third dôbuchi from the top, beginning at the left oyabashira.
View from rear
26
The twine used to attach the slats to the rail may be simple hemp twine or dyed twine. Anchor the twine by squeezing one end between the oyabashira and the dôbuchi.
Nail
27
Continue attaching tateko as shown.
Third dôbochi from the top.
28
Every other tateko should have its motokuchi at the top, with alternating slats having their motokuchi at the bottom. When positioning the tateko, don't line up the joints.
29
Rear view of twine and tateko.
Front view, with all tateko attached.
30

Attaching the tateko (see Step 27).

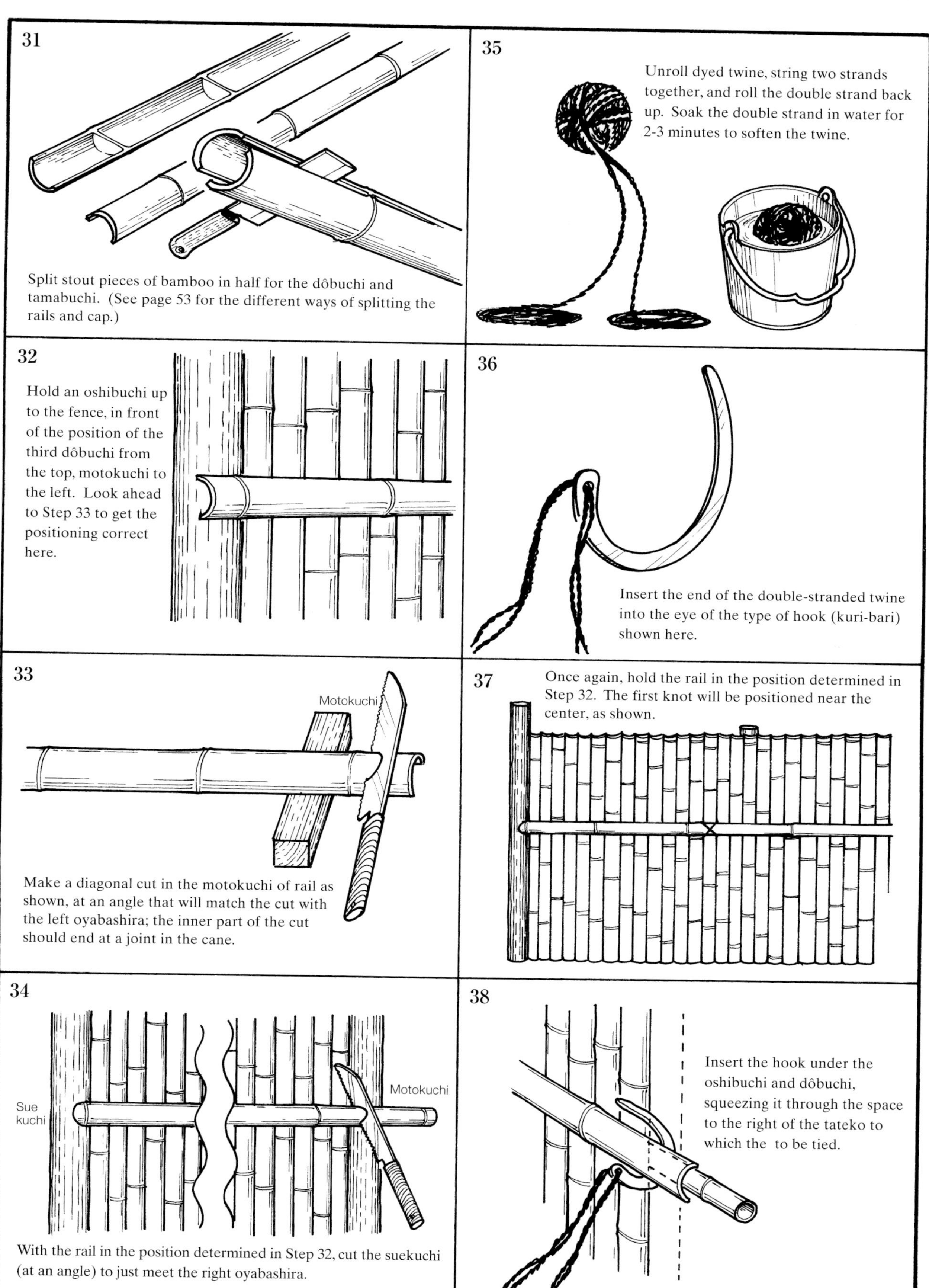
31
Split stout pieces of bamboo in half for the dôbuchi and tamabuchi. (See page 53 for the different ways of splitting the rails and cap.)
32
Hold an oshibuchi up to the fence, in front of the position of the third dôbuchi from the top, motokuchi to the left. Look ahead to Step 33 to get the positioning correct here.
33
Motokuchi
Make a diagonal cut in the motokuchi of rail as shown, at an angle that will match the cut with the left oyabashira; the inner part of the cut should end at a joint in the cane.
34
Sue kuchi
Motokuchi
With the rail in the position determined in Step 32, cut the suekuchi (at an angle) to just meet the right oyabashira.
35
Unroll dyed twine, string two strands together, and roll the double strand back up. Soak the double strand in water for 2-3 minutes to soften the twine.
36
Insert the end of the double-stranded twine into the eye of the type of hook (kuri-bari) shown here.
37
Once again, hold the rail in the position determined in Step 32. The first knot will be positioned near the center, as shown.
38
Insert the hook under the oshibuchi and dôbuchi, squeezing it through the space to the right of the tateko to which the to be tied.

39 Tie as shown.

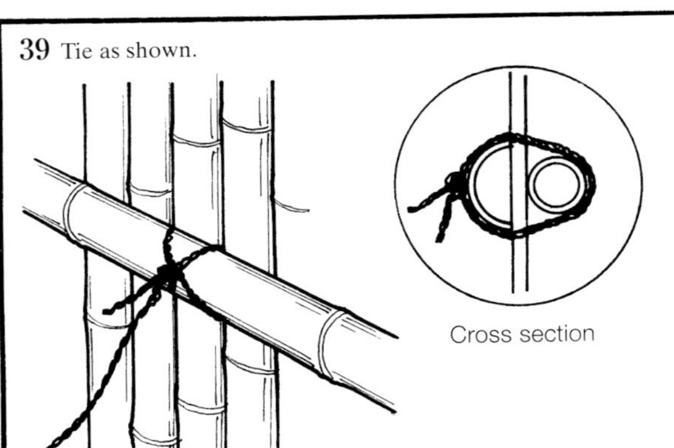

40

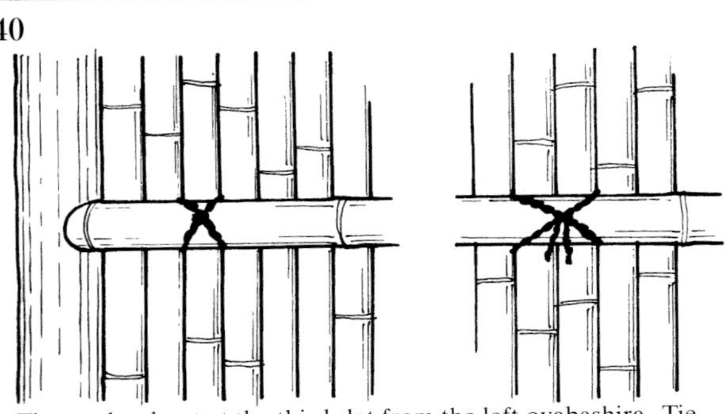

Tie another knot at the third slat from the left oyabashira. Tie additional knots as shown in Step 41. When using stout oshibuchi, you can tie each knot around two tateko, as shown on the right.

41 Attach the second oshibuchi from the top, with the motokuchi of the rail at the right oyabashira. Tie knots in about the positions shown here.

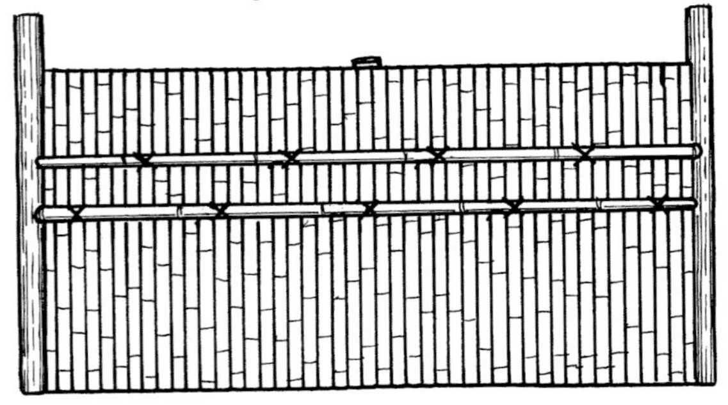

42

Attach the other oshibuchi except the topmost one. Rails 2, 4, and 6 have their motokuchi at the right. Rails 3 and 5 have their motokuchi at the left.

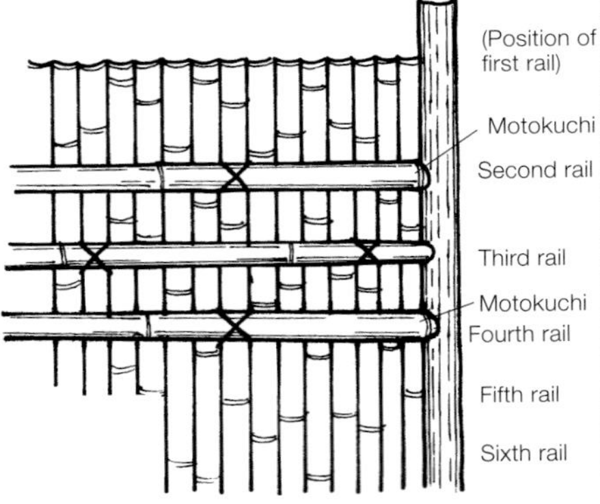

43

The topmost oshibuchi will be attached as shown in the next several steps (with motokuchi at left).

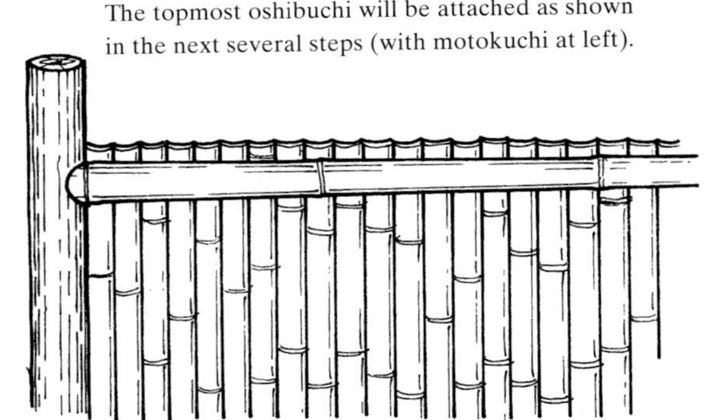

44

Attach the top oshibuchi to its corresponding dôbuchi using a couple of temporary knots.

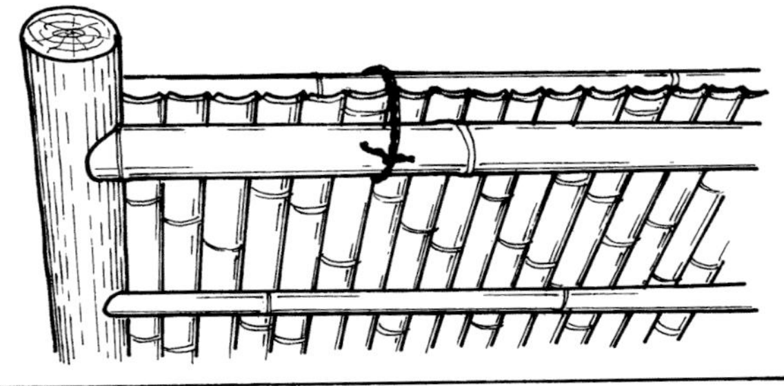

45

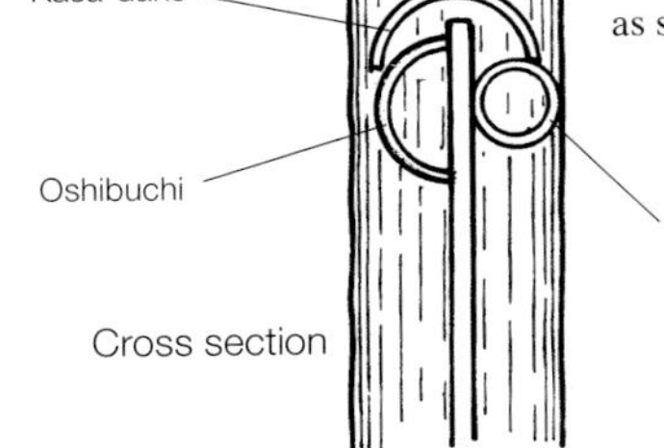

For the kasa-dake, prepare a half-split bamboo cane of sufficient stoutness to cover the oshibuchi and dôbuchi, as shown.

46

Cut the ends of the kasa-dake at an angle and in such a way that they will just slip into place between the oyabashira. Cut the left end first.

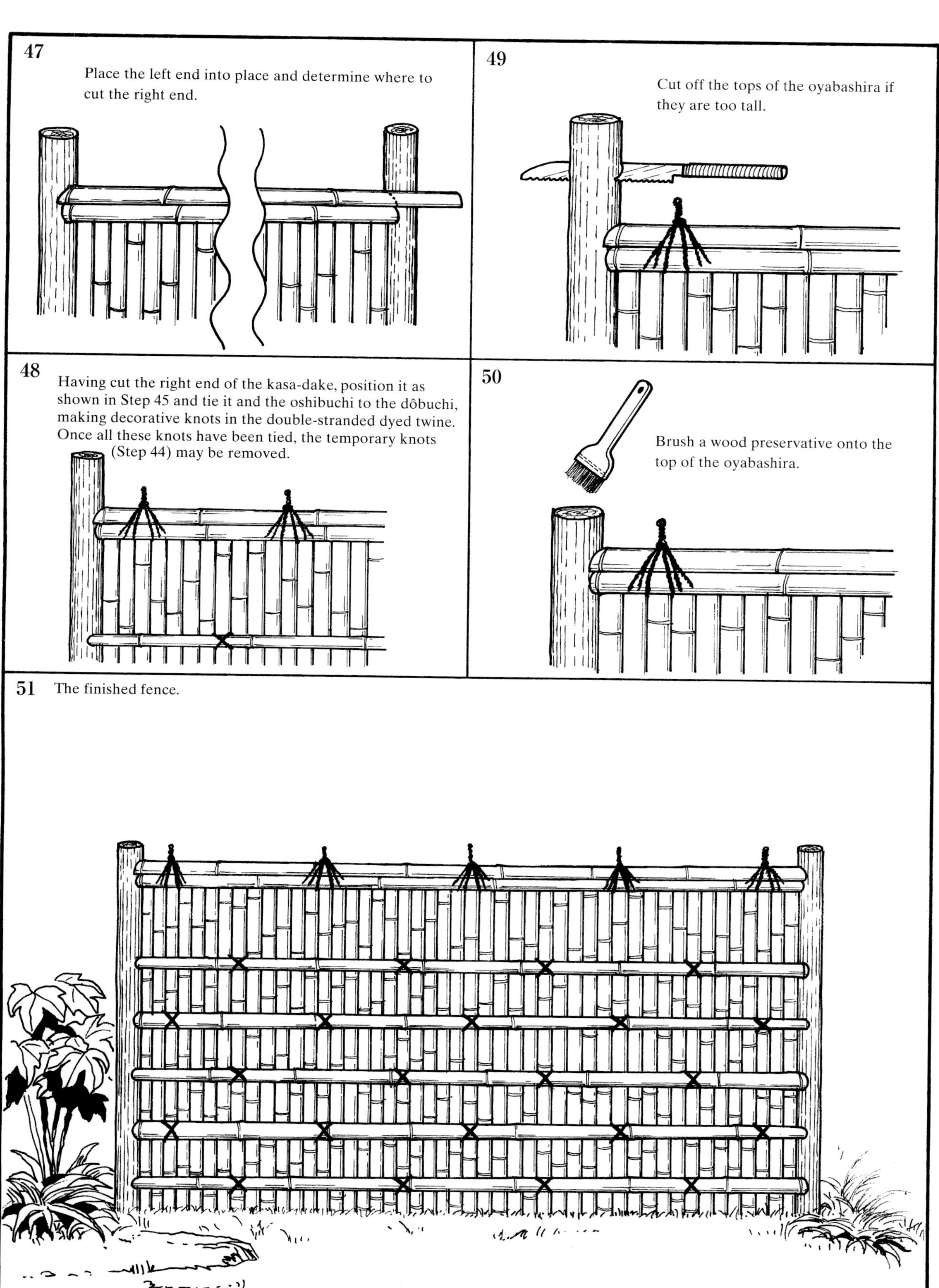

47 Place the left end into place and determine where to cut the right end.

48 Having cut the right end of the kasa-dake, position it as shown in Step 45 and tie it and the oshibuchi to the dôbuchi, making decorative knots in the double-stranded dyed twine. Once all these knots have been tied, the temporary knots (Step 44) may be removed.

49 Cut off the tops of the oyabashira if they are too tall.

50 Brush a wood preservative onto the top of the oyabashira.

51 The finished fence.

Ôtsu-gaki

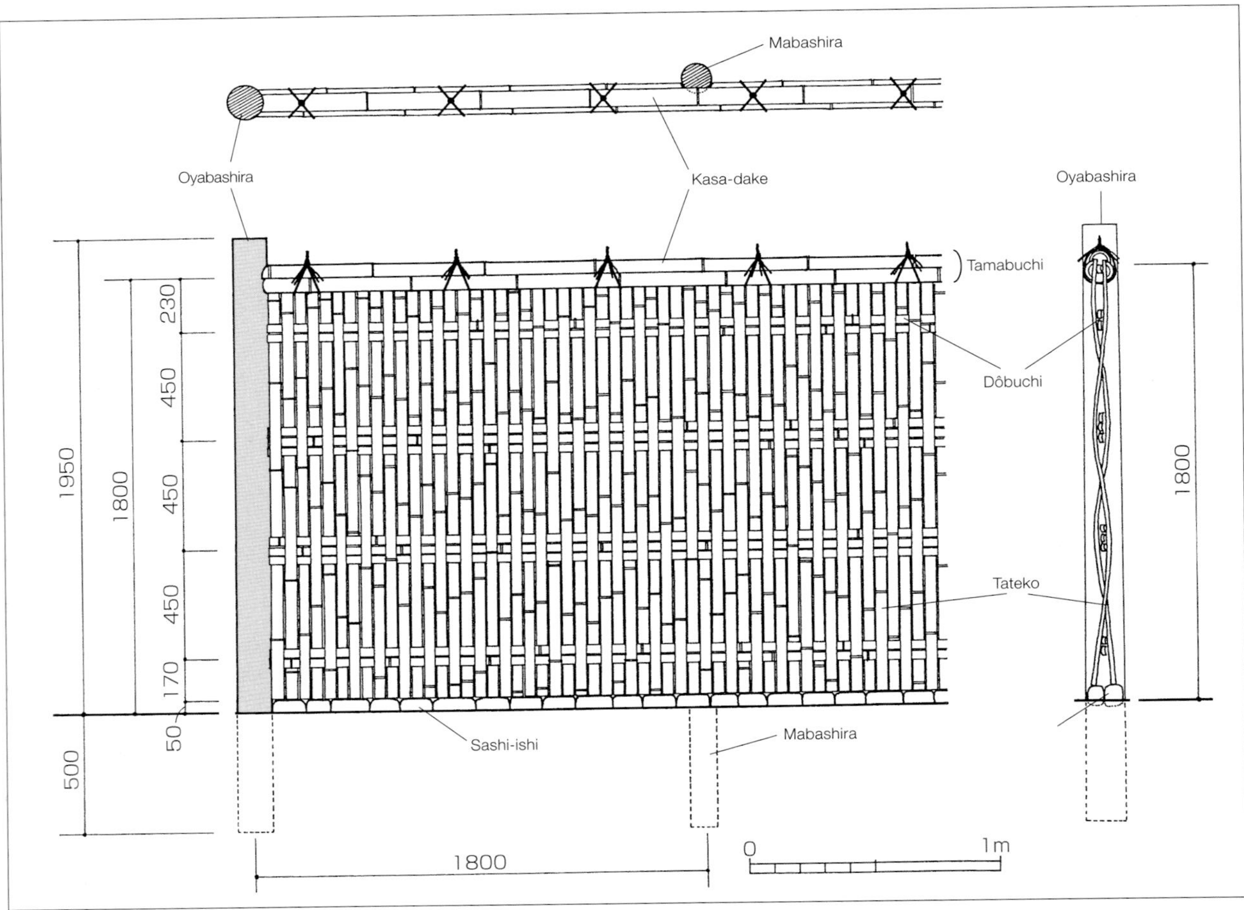

The ôtsu-gaki is a fence with narrow bamboo slats woven vertically and horizontally. Yama wari-dake (split pieces of Japanese bamboo) is normally used for the tateko. Although shino-dake is sometimes used for the tateko, it is not recommended as it is not very desirable. Since long slats are required for dôbuchi, narrow pieces of stout bamboo of the same width are used in most cases.

Make sure the ends of dôbuchi are inserted into the mortises chiseled on the oyabashira, and nailed to them. Using thin slats of bamboo for the dôbuchi will result in a tighter with less gap in the weave.

Dôbuchi in the ôtsu-gaki are used in two ways. In the first way, the dôbuchi is arranged as shown in the illustration above. To add variety and beauty in design, there is a two-piece dôbuchi at the top, two three-piece dôbuchi in the middle, and another two-piece dôbuchi at the bottom. Alternatively, the dôbuchi are made invisible, in which case each dôbuchi is made of one relatively wide piece of bamboo, and covered with oshibuchi. There are varieties of the ôtsu-gaki that combine both styles.

The distance between the uppermost dôbuchi and the tamabuchi, and that between the lowermost dôbuchi and the sashi-ishi must be shorter than the distance between each two sets of dôbuchi, which are positioned at equal intervals. Before placing the tamabuchi at the top, however, be sure to allow a wider distance between the uppermost dôbuchi and the top of the tateko, since the top of the tateko will be covered by the tamabuchi.

Tateko pieces are woven into the dôbuchi, beginning with the one next to the oyabashira. The bottom ends of the tateko are not stuck into the ground; instead, sashi-ishi or a mumeita are used to support them. Each tateko has motokuchi and suekuchi ends. In order to arrange them vertically, be sure to use ones with the motokuchi side up and inverted ones alternately.

Usually, tateko pieces are woven in such a way that every other weave is made on the same side of the dôbuchi as shown in the illustration above. Be sure to finish weaving all tateko before the fence is nailed to the mabashira. Doing so after it has been attached to the mabashira would be very difficult.

Just like in the kenninji-gaki, etc., add a tamabuchi made of the uppermost oshibuchi covered by a kasa-dake. A tamabuchi must be used because the tops of the tateko pieces vary in height.

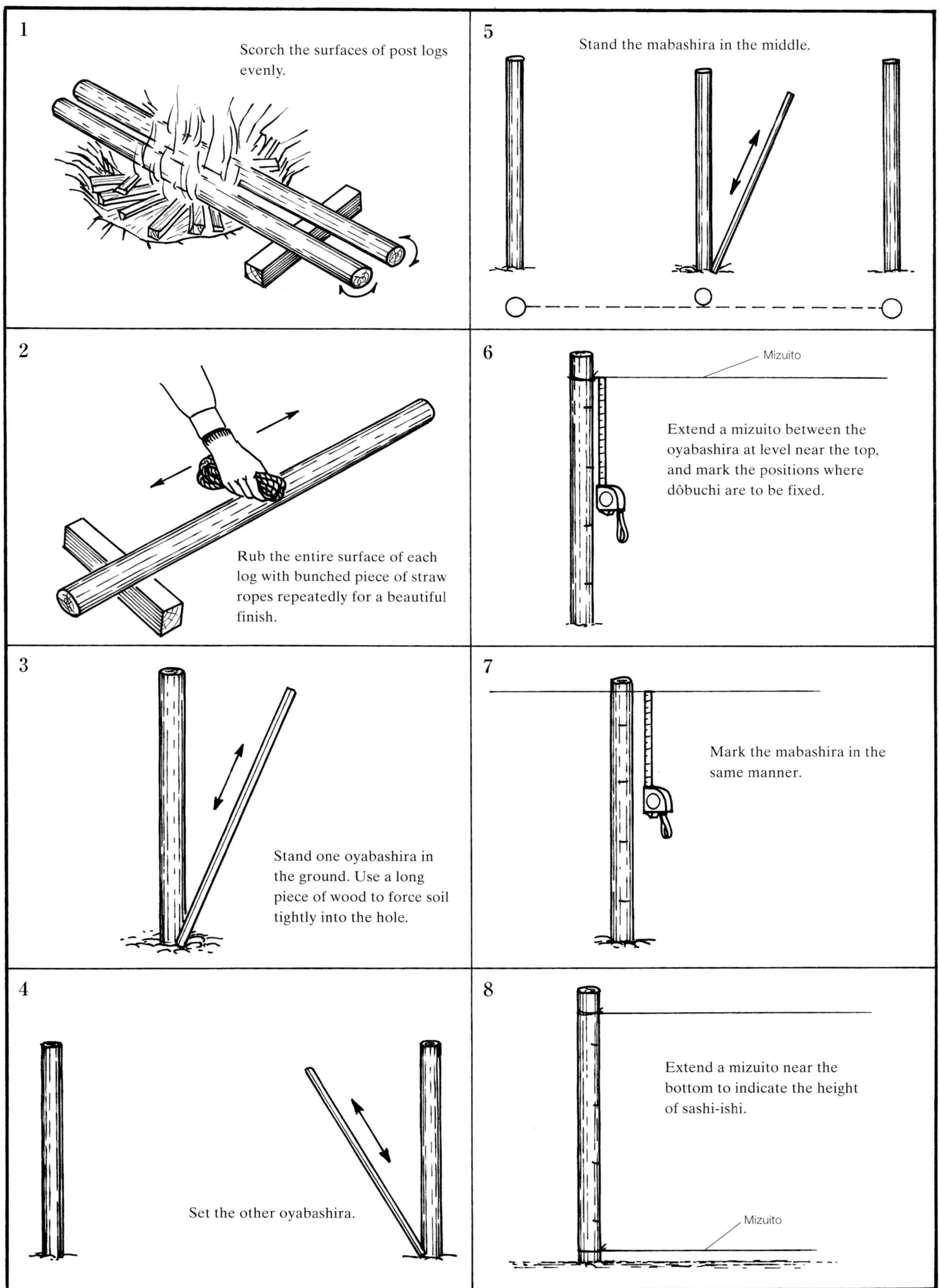
1
Scorch the surfaces of post logs evenly.
2
Rub the entire surface of each log with bunched piece of straw ropes repeatedly for a beautiful finish.
3
Stand one oyabashira in the ground. Use a long piece of wood to force soil tightly into the hole.
4
Set the other oyabashira.
5
Stand the mabashira in the middle.
6
Mizuito
Extend a mizuito between the oyabashira at level near the top, and mark the positions where dôbuchi are to be fixed.
7
Mark the mabashira in the same manner.
8
Extend a mizuito near the bottom to indicate the height of sashi-ishi.
Mizuito

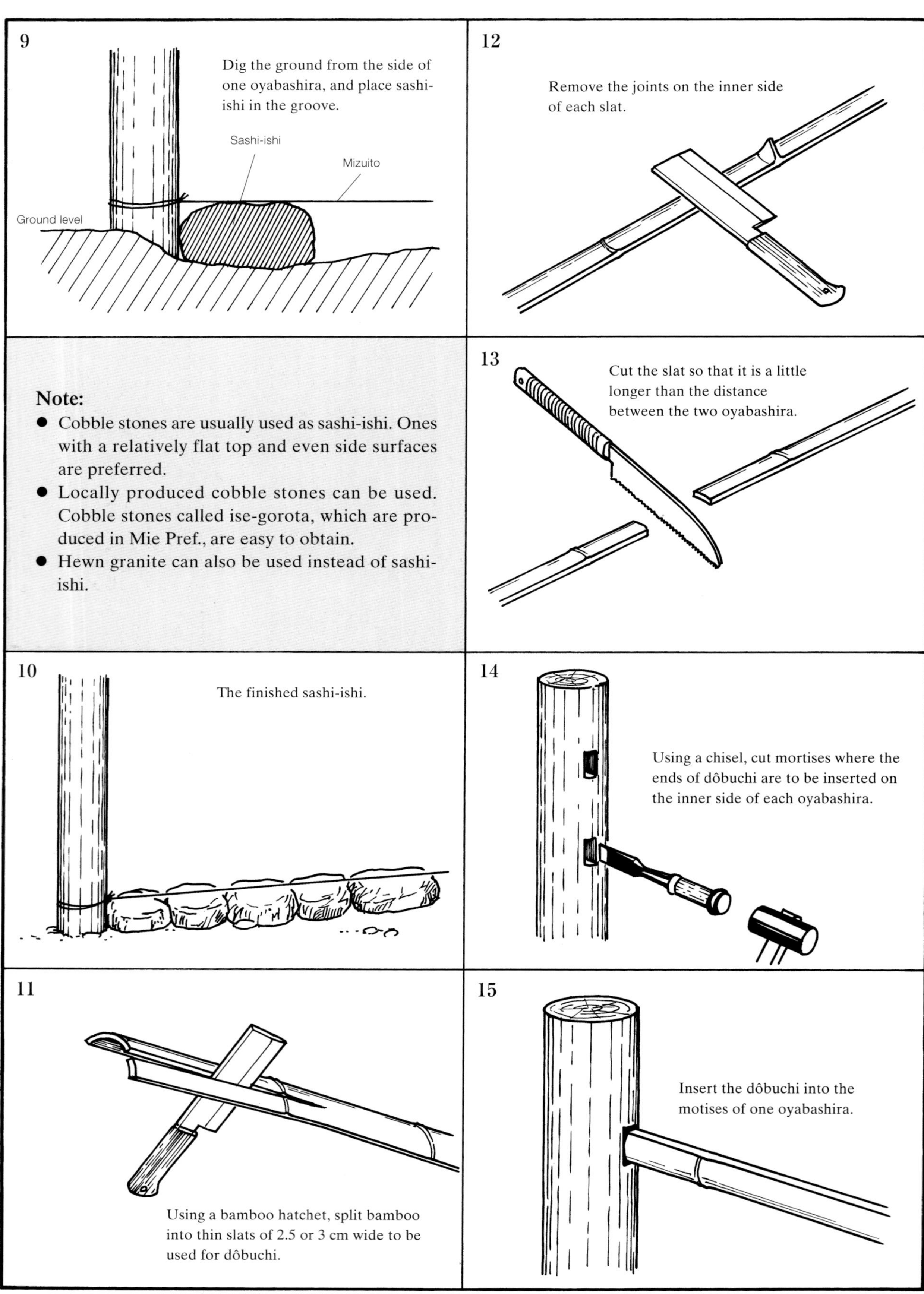

9

Dig the ground from the side of one oyabashira, and place sashi-ishi in the groove.

12

Remove the joints on the inner side of each slat.

Note:

- Cobble stones are usually used as sashi-ishi. Ones with a relatively flat top and even side surfaces are preferred.
- Locally produced cobble stones can be used. Cobble stones called ise-gorota, which are produced in Mie Pref., are easy to obtain.
- Hewn granite can also be used instead of sashi-ishi.

13

Cut the slat so that it is a little longer than the distance between the two oyabashira.

10

The finished sashi-ishi.

14

Using a chisel, cut mortises where the ends of dôbuchi are to be inserted on the inner side of each oyabashira.

11

Using a bamboo hatchet, split bamboo into thin slats of 2.5 or 3 cm wide to be used for dôbuchi.

15

Insert the dôbuchi into the motises of one oyabashira.

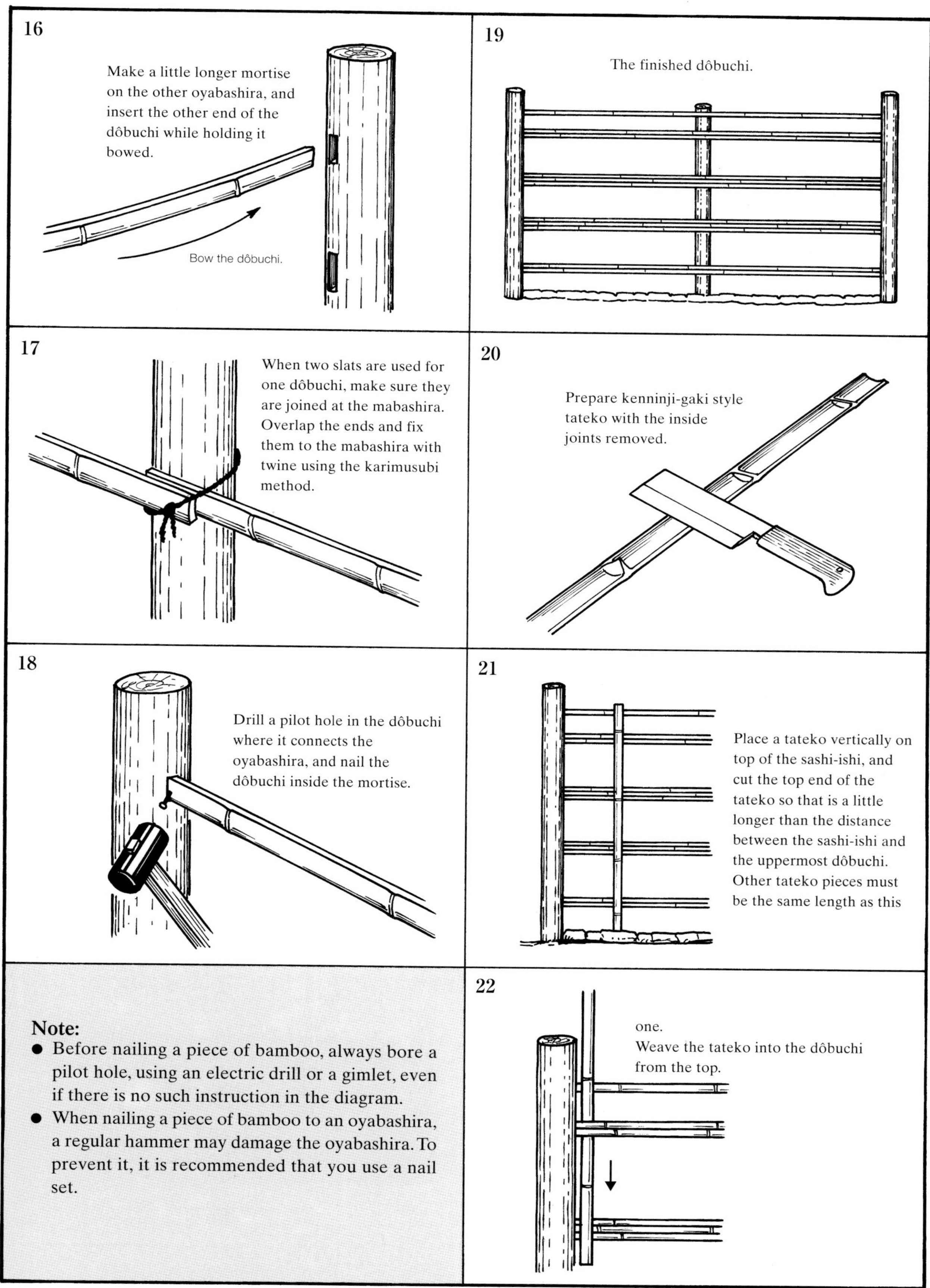
16
Make a little longer mortise on the other oyabashira, and insert the other end of the dôbuchi while holding it bowed.
Bow the dôbuchi.
19
The finished dôbuchi.
17
When two slats are used for one dôbuchi, make sure they are joined at the mabashira. Overlap the ends and fix them to the mabashira with twine using the karimusubi method.
20
Prepare kenninji-gaki style tateko with the inside joints removed.
18
Drill a pilot hole in the dôbuchi where it connects the oyabashira, and nail the dôbuchi inside the mortise.
21
Place a tateko vertically on top of the sashi-ishi, and cut the top end of the tateko so that is a little longer than the distance between the sashi-ishi and the uppermost dôbuchi. Other tateko pieces must be the same length as this
Note:
● Before nailing a piece of bamboo, always bore a pilot hole, using an electric drill or a gimlet, even if there is no such instruction in the diagram.
● When nailing a piece of bamboo to an oyabashira, a regular hammer may damage the oyabashira. To prevent it, it is recommended that you use a nail set.
22
one.
Weave the tateko into the dôbuchi from the top.

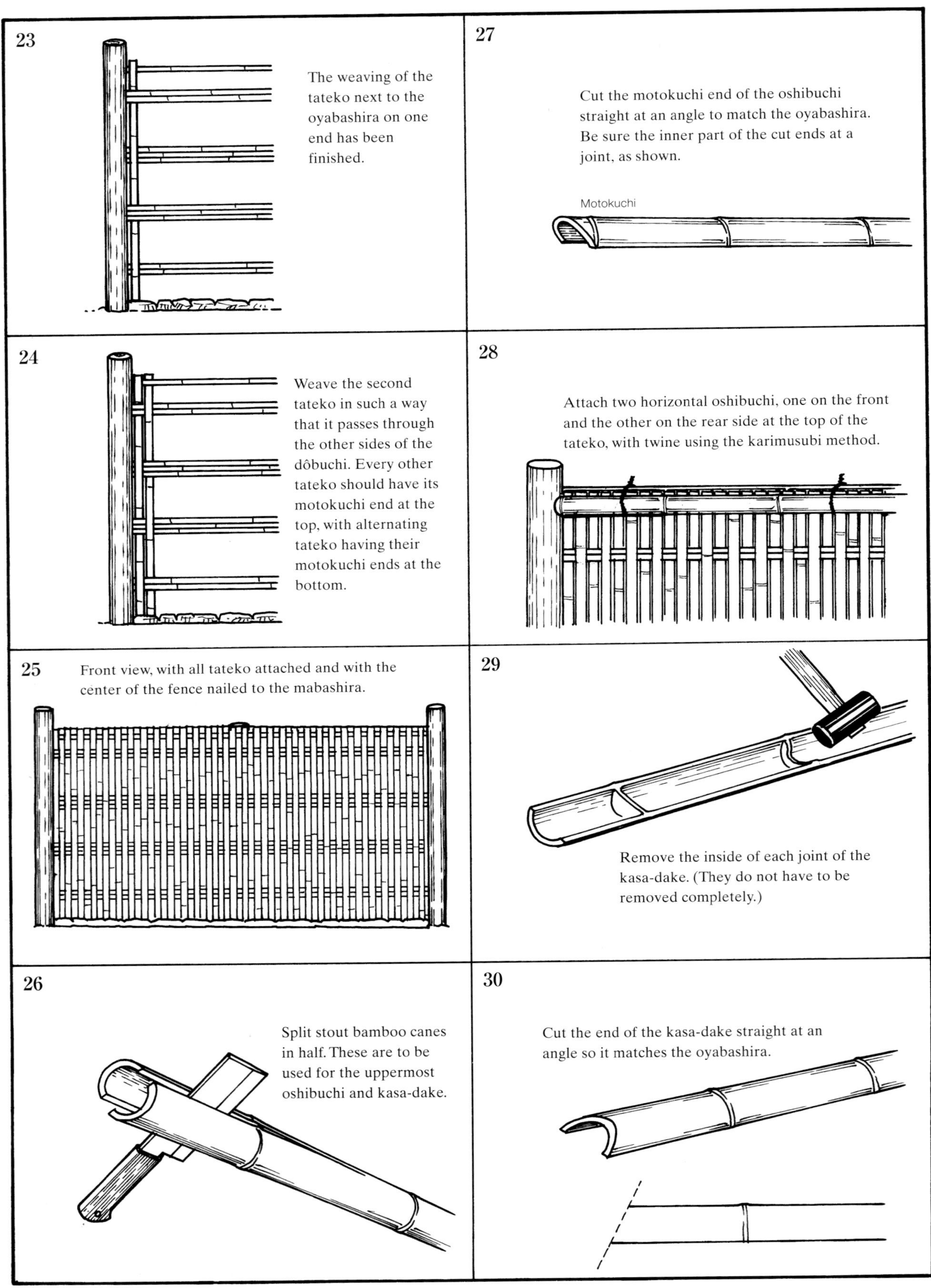
23
The weaving of the tateko next to the oyabashira on one end has been finished.
27
Cut the motokuchi end of the oshibuchi straight at an angle to match the oyabashira. Be sure the inner part of the cut ends at a joint, as shown.
Motokuchi
24
Weave the second tateko in such a way that it passes through the other sides of the dôbuchi. Every other tateko should have its motokuchi end at the top, with alternating tateko having their motokuchi ends at the bottom.
28
Attach two horizontal oshibuchi, one on the front and the other on the rear side at the top of the tateko, with twine using the karimusubi method.
25
Front view, with all tateko attached and with the center of the fence nailed to the mabashira.
29
Remove the inside of each joint of the kasa-dake. (They do not have to be removed completely.)
26
Split stout bamboo canes in half. These are to be used for the uppermost oshibuchi and kasa-dake.
30
Cut the end of the kasa-dake straight at an angle so it matches the oyabashira.

31

Place the kasa-dake at the top and tie the tamabuchi with twine using the karimusubi method.

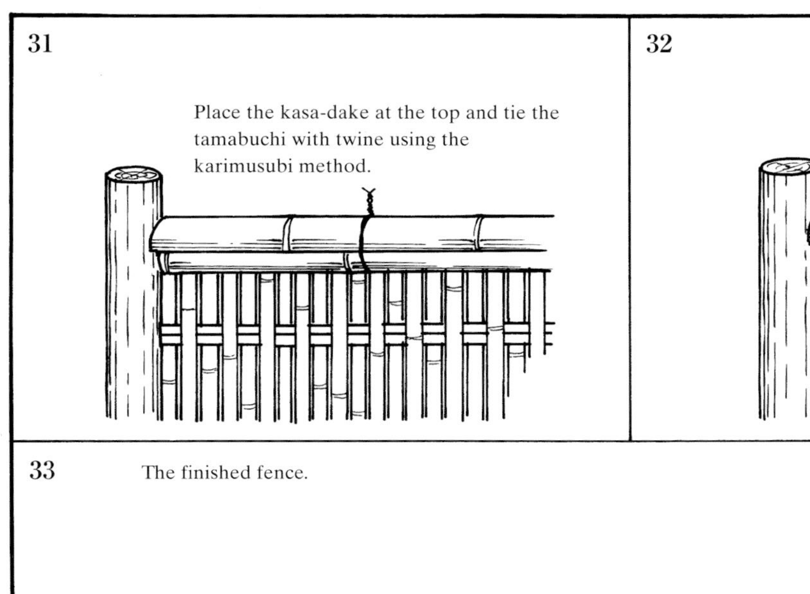

32

Tie kazarimusubi on the tamabuchi.

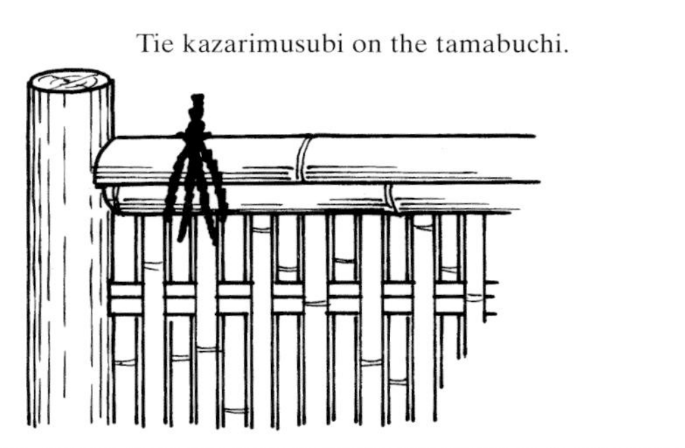

33

The finished fence.

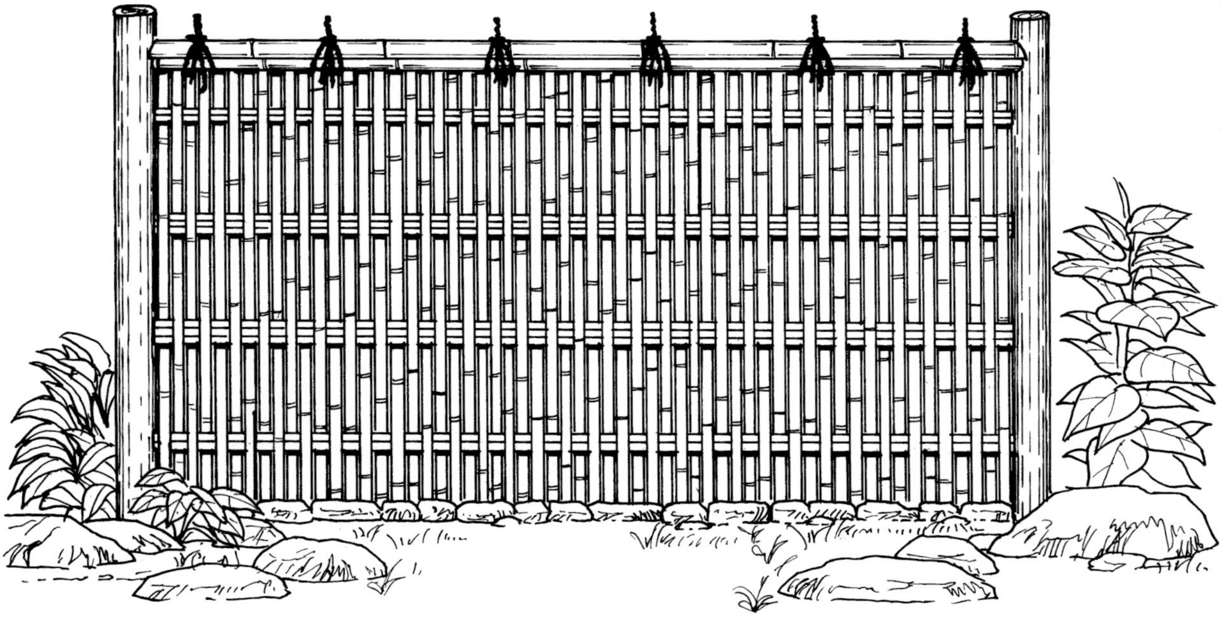

Teppô-gaki (rifle barrel fence)

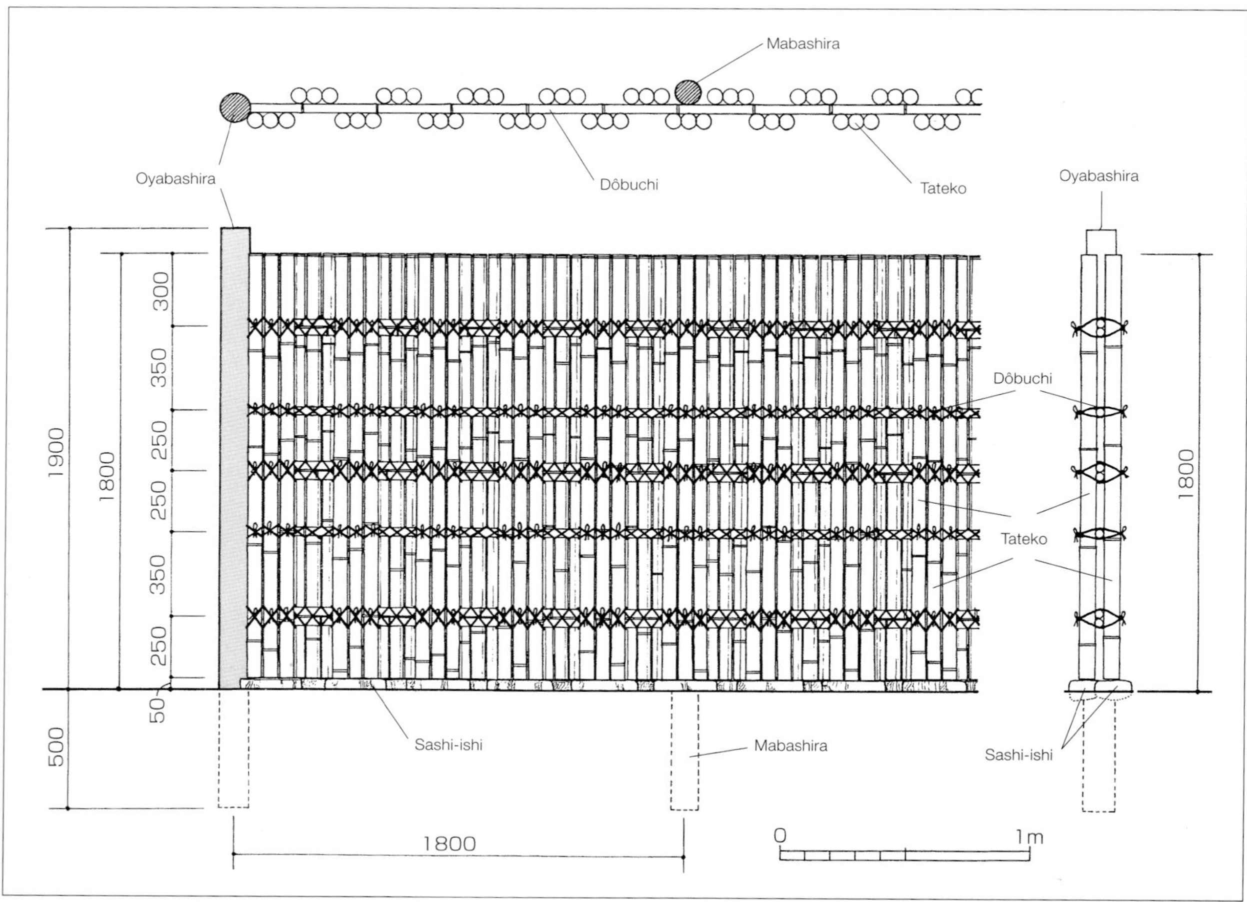

The teppô-gaki has several dôbuchi to which tateko are attached from the front and rear sides at intervals. There are many varieties of teppô-gaki.

While the above illustration shows a teppô-gaki built in the most common style, there is a wide variety using other materials for tateko. Roughly speaking, there are two types of tateko for the teppô-gaki: round bamboo canes, and makitatego. A makitatego is a bundle of bamboo branches, me-dake canes, bush clover (hagi) or spicebush (kuromoji) branches. Bold-looking tateko made of slender logs also exist.

Tateko of round bamboo canes can greatly vary in appearance depending on the thickness of the bamboo used. Teppô-gaki with tateko of especially stout bamboo are called odake-teppô-gaki, an example of which can be seen at the head priest's residence at the Nanzenji Temple in Kyoto.

Usually, gara-dake is used for the dôbuchi, which are inserted tightly into the mortises made on the oyabashira. Every other dôbuchi is made of a pair of garadake instead of one garadake, as shown in the illustration, to add variety.

When round bamboo is used for the tateko, the suekuchi end, which is cut in the fushidome method, must face upward. The number of pieces in one set of tateko can vary as desired. In the case of the fence in the illustration, each set of tateko has three pieces, but there are cases in which five pieces are put together for each set, and cases in which the number of pieces on one side is different from that on the other. The key point here is that no matter how many pieces each set of tateko has, all the pieces must have their suekuchi ends at the top. Although this arrangement makes the bottom wider than the top, all the tateko pieces must be placed in the same direction, and slight gaps between them at the top will not matter. With these gaps, it is easier to tie the tateko pieces using twine.

It is important to place the front and rear tateko at appropriate intervals. They must be positioned in such a way that the mabashira is right behind a set of front tateko, and that each set of front tateko and that of rear tateko slightly overlap by the length of the radius of one tateko piece. This adjustment is made when tateko is tied to the dôbuchi with twine. The most important element in building the teppô-gaki, perhaps, is the twine tying technique.

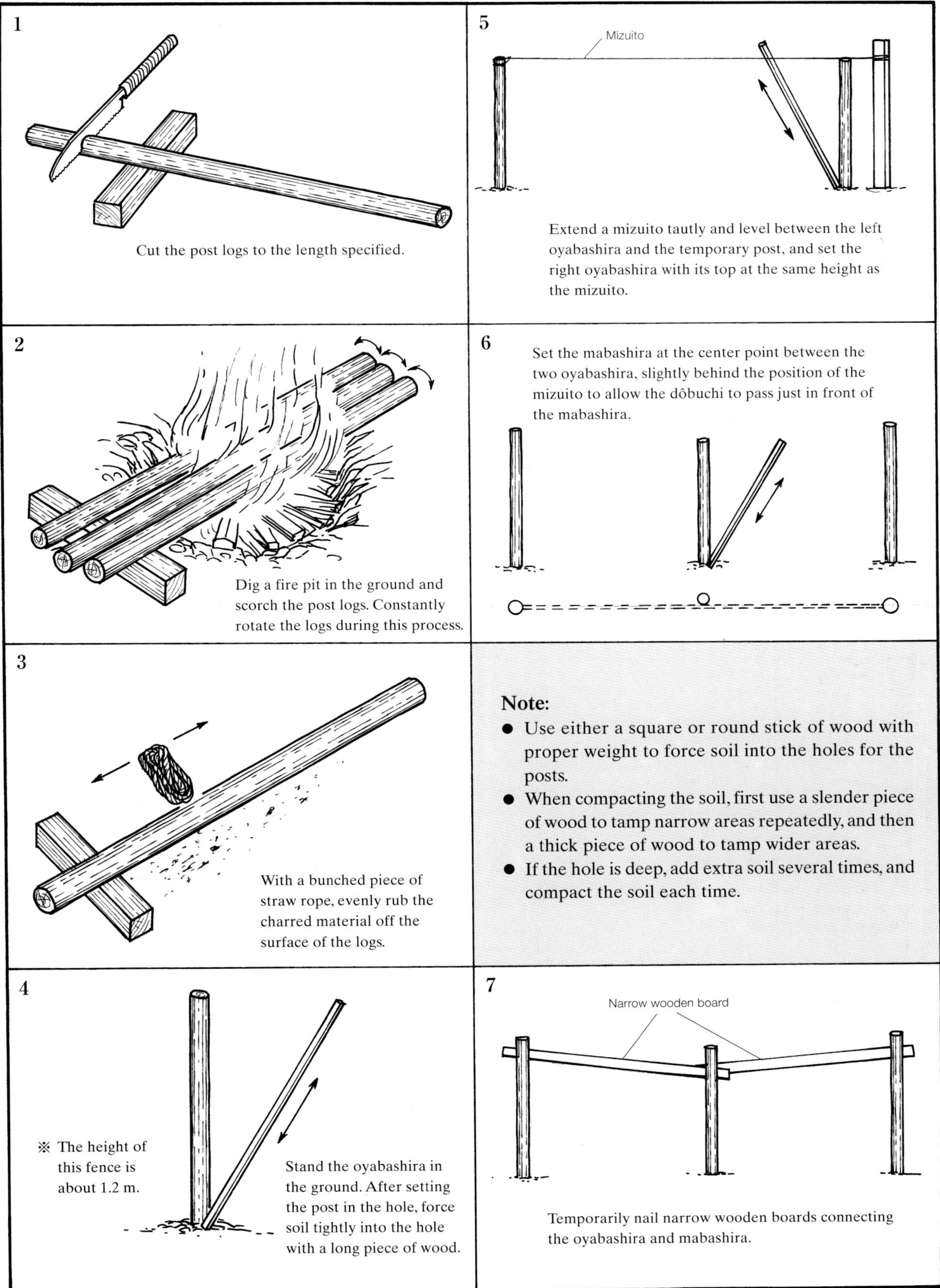

1 Cut the post logs to the length specified.

2 Dig a fire pit in the ground and scorch the post logs. Constantly rotate the logs during this process.

3 With a bunched piece of straw rope, evenly rub the charred material off the surface of the logs.

4 Stand the oyabashira in the ground. After setting the post in the hole, force soil tightly into the hole with a long piece of wood.

※ The height of this fence is about 1.2 m.

5 Extend a mizuito tautly and level between the left oyabashira and the temporary post, and set the right oyabashira with its top at the same height as the mizuito.

6 Set the mabashira at the center point between the two oyabashira, slightly behind the position of the mizuito to allow the dôbuchi to pass just in front of the mabashira.

Note:

- Use either a square or round stick of wood with proper weight to force soil into the holes for the posts.
- When compacting the soil, first use a slender piece of wood to tamp narrow areas repeatedly, and then a thick piece of wood to tamp wider areas.
- If the hole is deep, add extra soil several times, and compact the soil each time.

7 Temporarily nail narrow wooden boards connecting the oyabashira and mabashira.

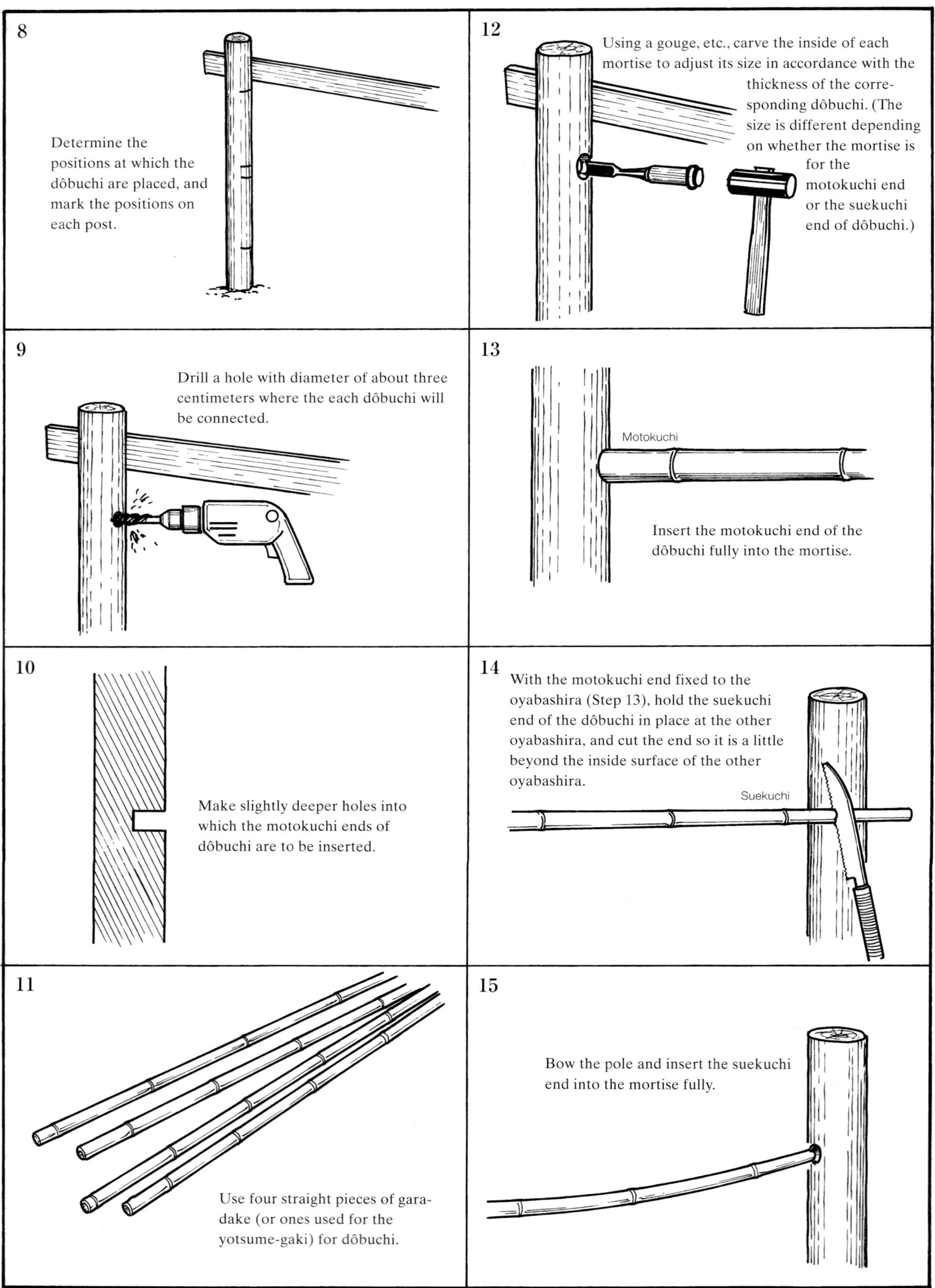
8
Determine the positions at which the dôbuchi are placed, and mark the positions on each post.
9
Drill a hole with diameter of about three centimeters where the each dôbuchi will be connected.
10
Make slightly deeper holes into which the motokuchi ends of dôbuchi are to be inserted.
11
Use four straight pieces of gara-dake (or ones used for the yotsume-gaki) for dôbuchi.
12
Using a gouge, etc., carve the inside of each mortise to adjust its size in accordance with the thickness of the corresponding dôbuchi. (The size is different depending on whether the mortise is for the motokuchi end or the suekuchi end of dôbuchi.)
13
Motokuchi
Insert the motokuchi end of the dôbuchi fully into the mortise.
14
With the motokuchi end fixed to the oyabashira (Step 13), hold the suekuchi end of the dôbuchi in place at the other oyabashira, and cut the end so it is a little beyond the inside surface of the other oyabashira.
Suekuchi
15
Bow the pole and insert the suekuchi end into the mortise fully.

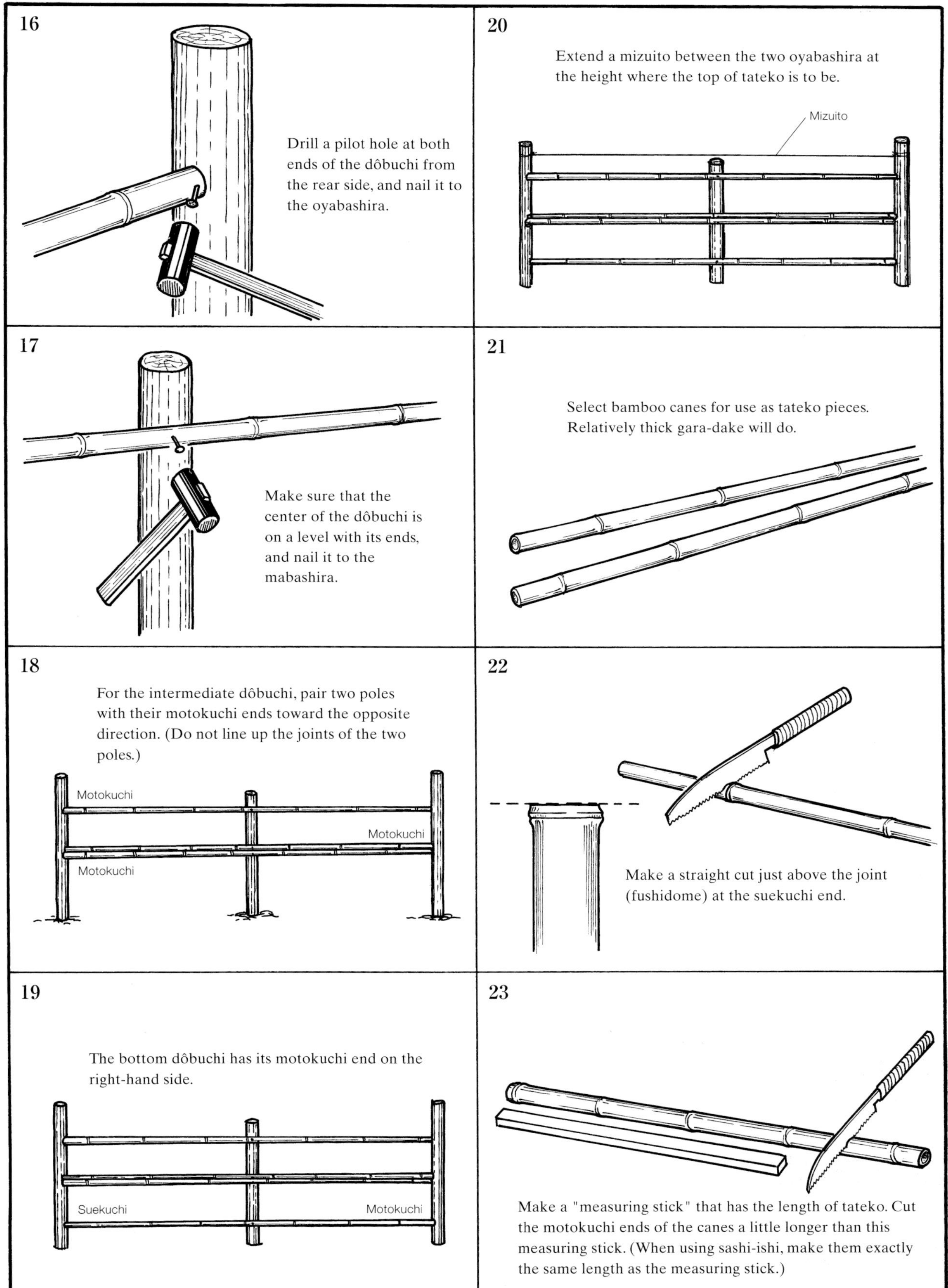
16
Drill a pilot hole at both ends of the dôbuchi from the rear side, and nail it to the oyabashira.
17
Make sure that the center of the dôbuchi is on a level with its ends, and nail it to the mabashira.
18
For the intermediate dôbuchi, pair two poles with their motokuchi ends toward the opposite direction. (Do not line up the joints of the two poles.)
Motokuchi
Motokuchi
Motokuchi
19
The bottom dôbuchi has its motokuchi end on the right-hand side.
Suekuchi
Motokuchi
20
Extend a mizuito between the two oyabashira at the height where the top of tateko is to be.
Mizuito
21
Select bamboo canes for use as tateko pieces. Relatively thick gara-dake will do.
22
Make a straight cut just above the joint (fushidome) at the suekuchi end.
23
Make a "measuring stick" that has the length of tateko. Cut the motokuchi ends of the canes a little longer than this measuring stick. (When using sashi-ishi, make them exactly the same length as the measuring stick.)

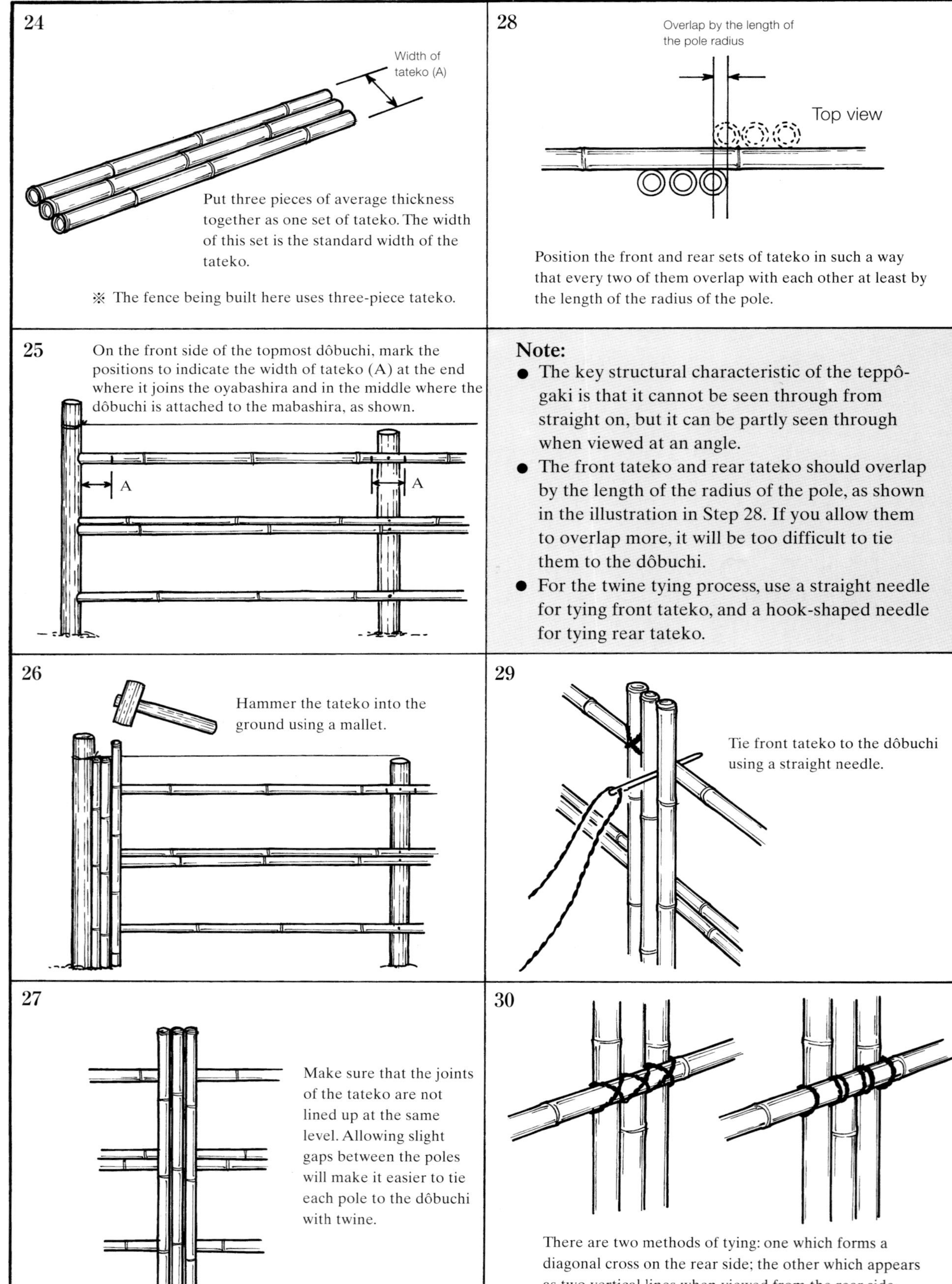

24

Put three pieces of average thickness together as one set of tateko. The width of this set is the standard width of the tateko.

※ The fence being built here uses three-piece tateko.

25

On the front side of the topmost dôbuchi, mark the positions to indicate the width of tateko (A) at the end where it joins the oyabashira and in the middle where the dôbuchi is attached to the mabashira, as shown.

26

Hammer the tateko into the ground using a mallet.

27

Make sure that the joints of the tateko are not lined up at the same level. Allowing slight gaps between the poles will make it easier to tie each pole to the dôbuchi with twine.

28

Position the front and rear sets of tateko in such a way that every two of them overlap with each other at least by the length of the radius of the pole.

Note:

- The key structural characteristic of the teppô-gaki is that it cannot be seen through from straight on, but it can be partly seen through when viewed at an angle.
- The front tateko and rear tateko should overlap by the length of the radius of the pole, as shown in the illustration in Step 28. If you allow them to overlap more, it will be too difficult to tie them to the dôbuchi.
- For the twine tying process, use a straight needle for tying front tateko, and a hook-shaped needle for tying rear tateko.

29

Tie front tateko to the dôbuchi using a straight needle.

30

There are two methods of tying: one which forms a diagonal cross on the rear side; the other which appears as two vertical lines when viewed from the rear side.

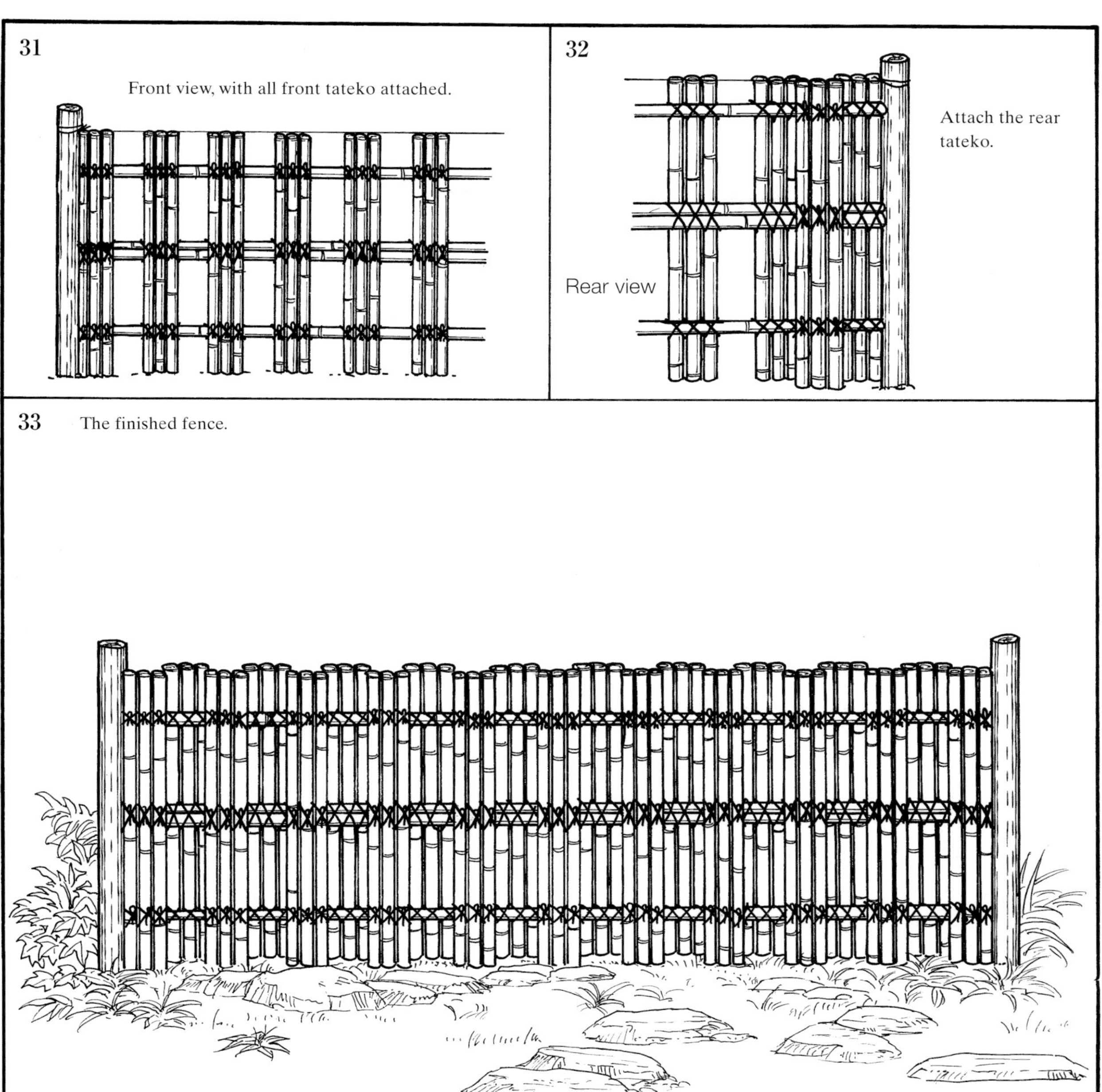
31
Front view, with all front tateko attached.
32
Attach the rear tateko.
Rear view
33
The finished fence.

Tokusa-gaki (Dutch rush fence)

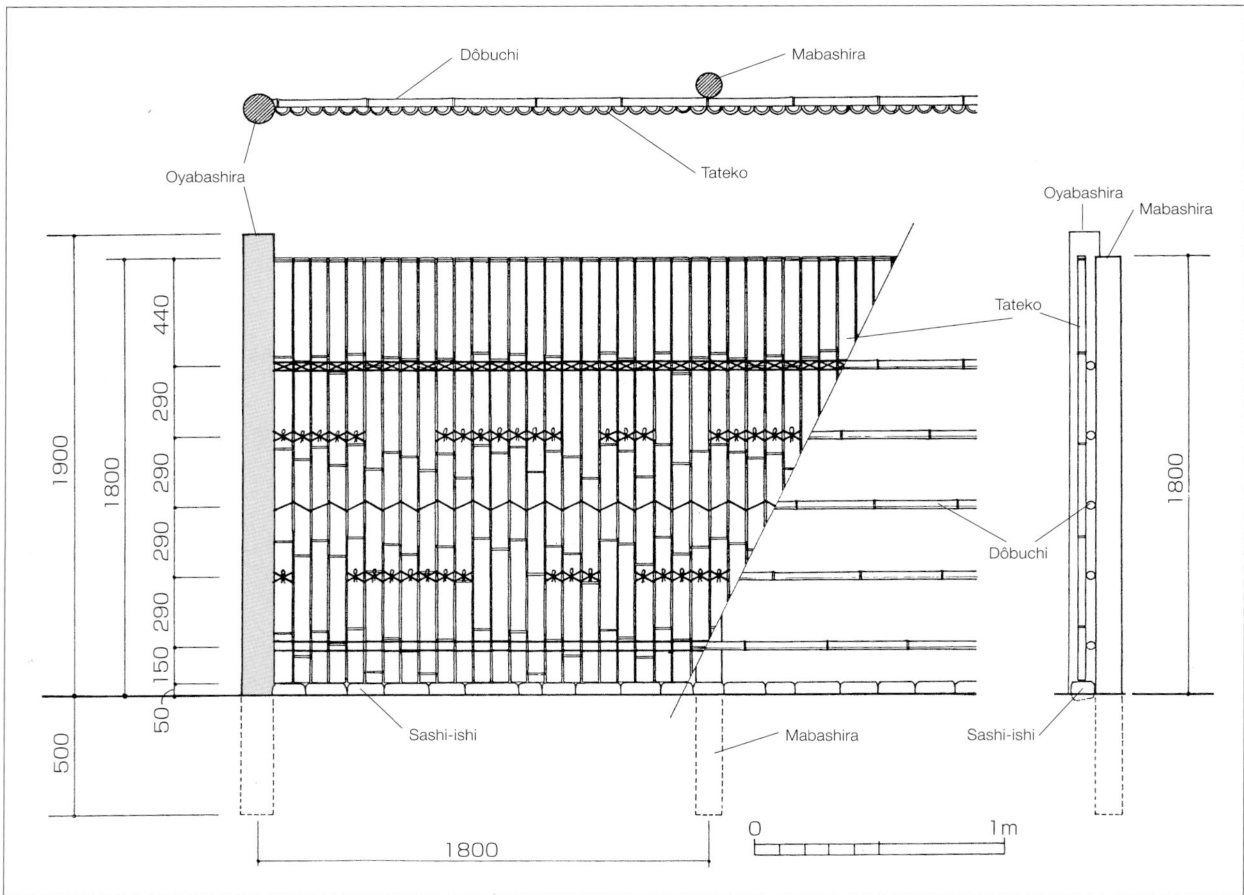

The main characteristic of the tokusa-gaki is that it uses dôbuchi and tateko, but not oshibuchi. There are cases in which gara-dake is used for the dôbuchi, and cases in which long pieces of wood are used. In the former, the tateko pieces are usually tied to the dôbuchi using twine, and in the latter, they are usually nailed to the dôbuchi. Each dôbuchi is made of a piece of round bamboo cane with similar thickness at both ends (motokuchi and suekuchi).

When preparing tateko pieces, split relatively stout round bamboo canes, which are one joint longer than the planned height, in half. Sashi-ishi are used at the bottom to place tateko pieces on them. The tops of the tateko must be cut in the fushidome manner. The tateko should be arranged in such a way that every other piece has its motokuchi end at the top with alternating pieces with their suekuchi ends at the top, so that each piece can be vertically arranged. The reason why they must be prepared longer than the actual height is that each can be used in either direction with a fushidome-cut end at the top. Also, it is important to not line up the joints of the tateko when they are arranged.

In the case of the fence in the illustration above, its beautiful appearance is created by the twine knots on the front. It is especially important to determine the number of tiers of knots (dôbuchi) and how close they are to each other.

The distance between the top of the tateko and the uppermost dôbuchi should be wider than that between lower tiers for good balance. If the tops of the tateko pieces vary in height, another dôbuchi may be used at the top.

Each tateko piece is not tied to the dôbuchi separately. Instead, two long pieces of dyed twine are used to tie the tateko pieces from one end to the other. There are a number of tying methods such as single tying, double tying, cross tying, zigzag tying, etc. (See explanatory illustrations on the following pages for the details of each tying method.)

The topmost tier in the above illustration has a combination of cross tying and double tying. For the middle tier the zigzag tying method is used, and the lowermost tier has the double tying method. The second and fourth tiers from the top has the standard ibo-musubi (also called otoko-musubi) method, but not all the tateko pieces have the knots visible in the front for variety of appearance (chirashi). There is no rule as to where knots are to be shown in the front: however, it is better to use complicated knots for the topmost tier.

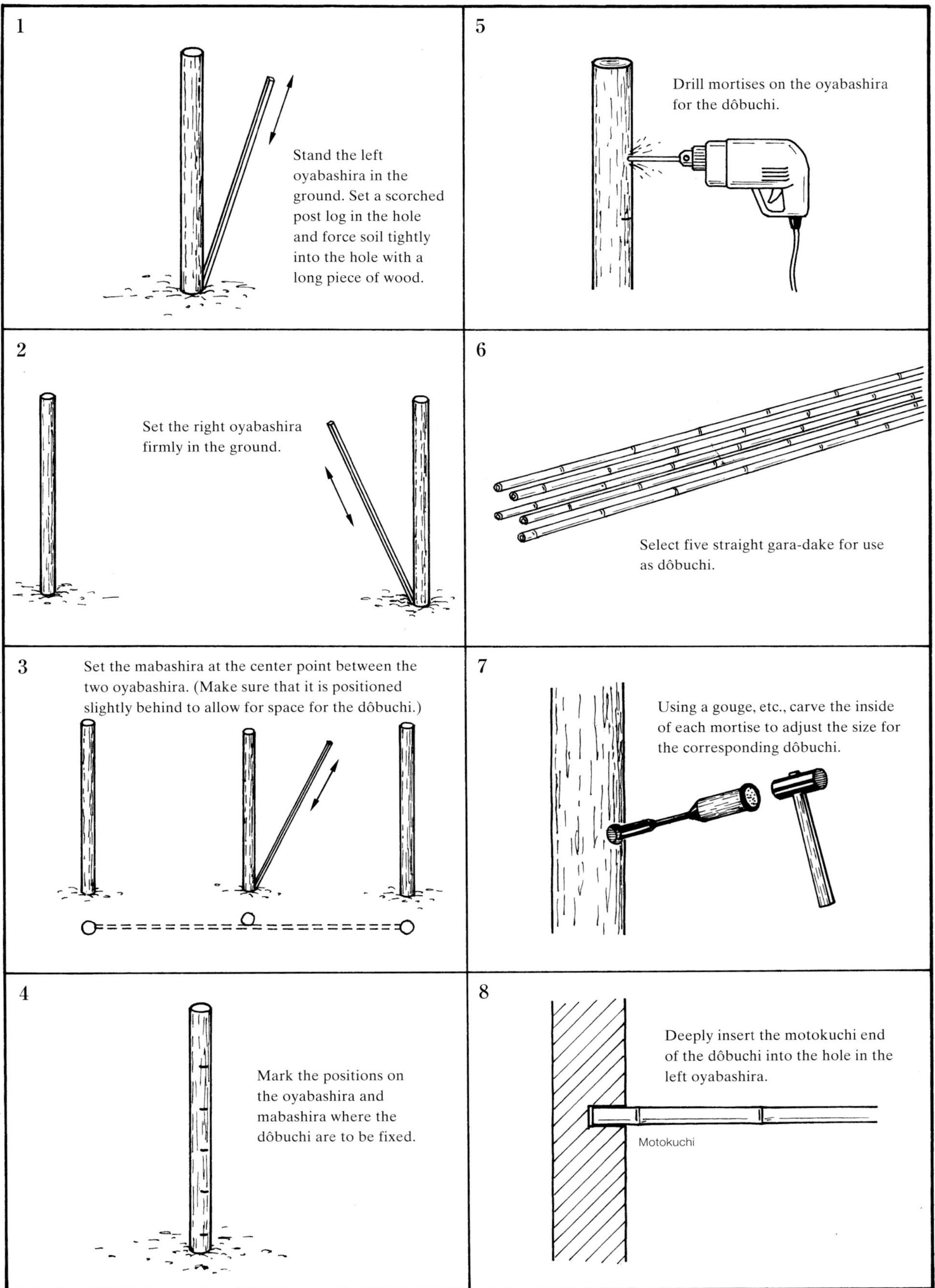
1
Stand the left oyabashira in the ground. Set a scorched post log in the hole and force soil tightly into the hole with a long piece of wood.
2
Set the right oyabashira firmly in the ground.
3
Set the mabashira at the center point between the two oyabashira. (Make sure that it is positioned slightly behind to allow for space for the dôbuchi.)
4
Mark the positions on the oyabashira and mabashira where the dôbuchi are to be fixed.
5
Drill mortises on the oyabashira for the dôbuchi.
6
Select five straight gara-dake for use as dôbuchi.
7
Using a gouge, etc., carve the inside of each mortise to adjust the size for the corresponding dôbuchi.
8
Deeply insert the motokuchi end of the dôbuchi into the hole in the left oyabashira.
Motokuchi

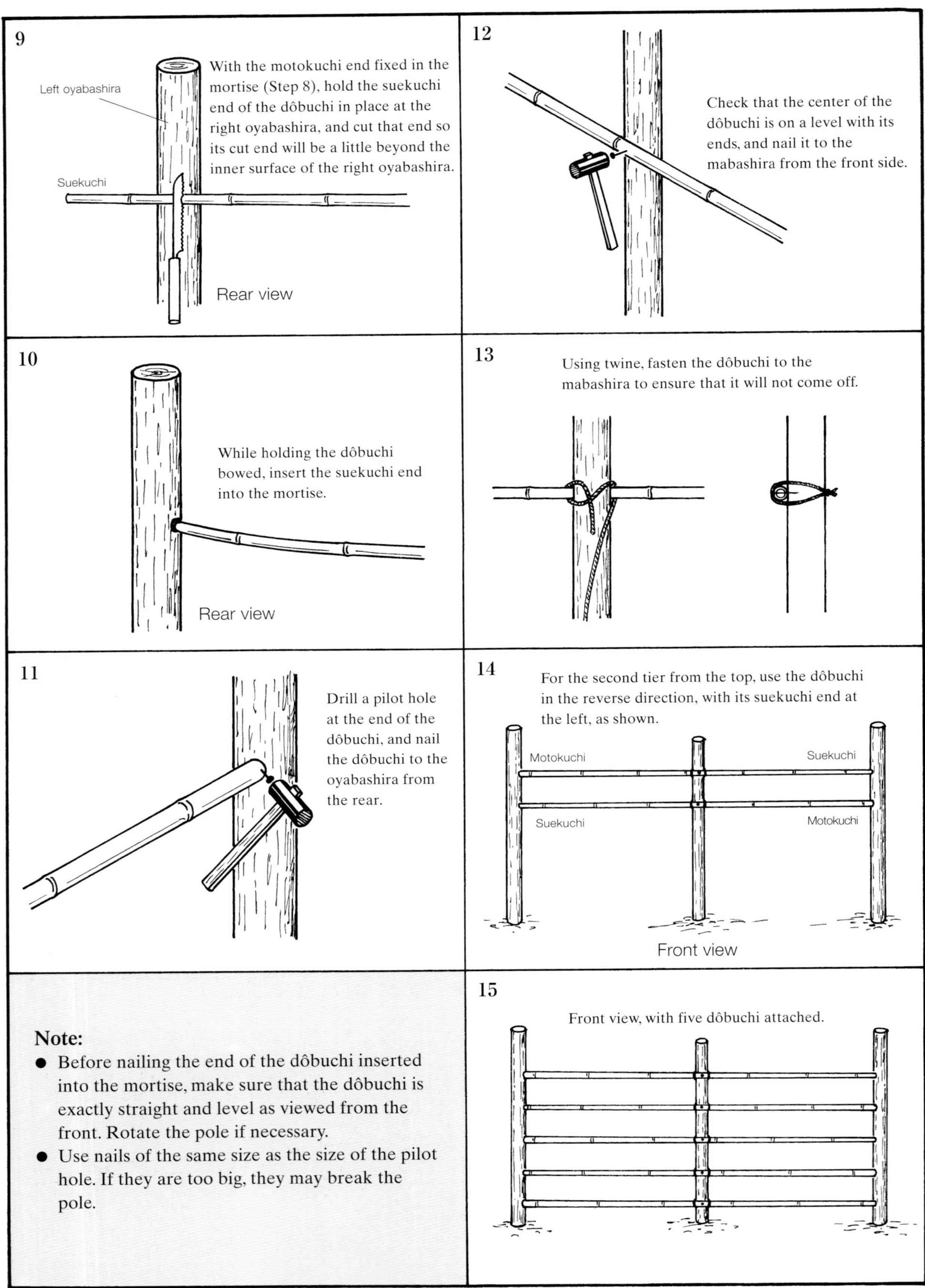
9
Left oyabashira
With the motokuchi end fixed in the mortise (Step 8), hold the suekuchi end of the dôbuchi in place at the right oyabashira, and cut that end so its cut end will be a little beyond the inner surface of the right oyabashira.
Suekuchi
Rear view
10
While holding the dôbuchi bowed, insert the suekuchi end into the mortise.
Rear view
11
Drill a pilot hole at the end of the dôbuchi, and nail the dôbuchi to the oyabashira from the rear.
12
Check that the center of the dôbuchi is on a level with its ends, and nail it to the mabashira from the front side.
13
Using twine, fasten the dôbuchi to the mabashira to ensure that it will not come off.
14
For the second tier from the top, use the dôbuchi in the reverse direction, with its suekuchi end at the left, as shown.
Motokuchi
Suekuchi
Suekuchi
Motokuchi
Front view
15
Front view, with five dôbuchi attached.
Note:
● Before nailing the end of the dôbuchi inserted into the mortise, make sure that the dôbuchi is exactly straight and level as viewed from the front. Rotate the pole if necessary.
● Use nails of the same size as the size of the pilot hole. If they are too big, they may break the pole.

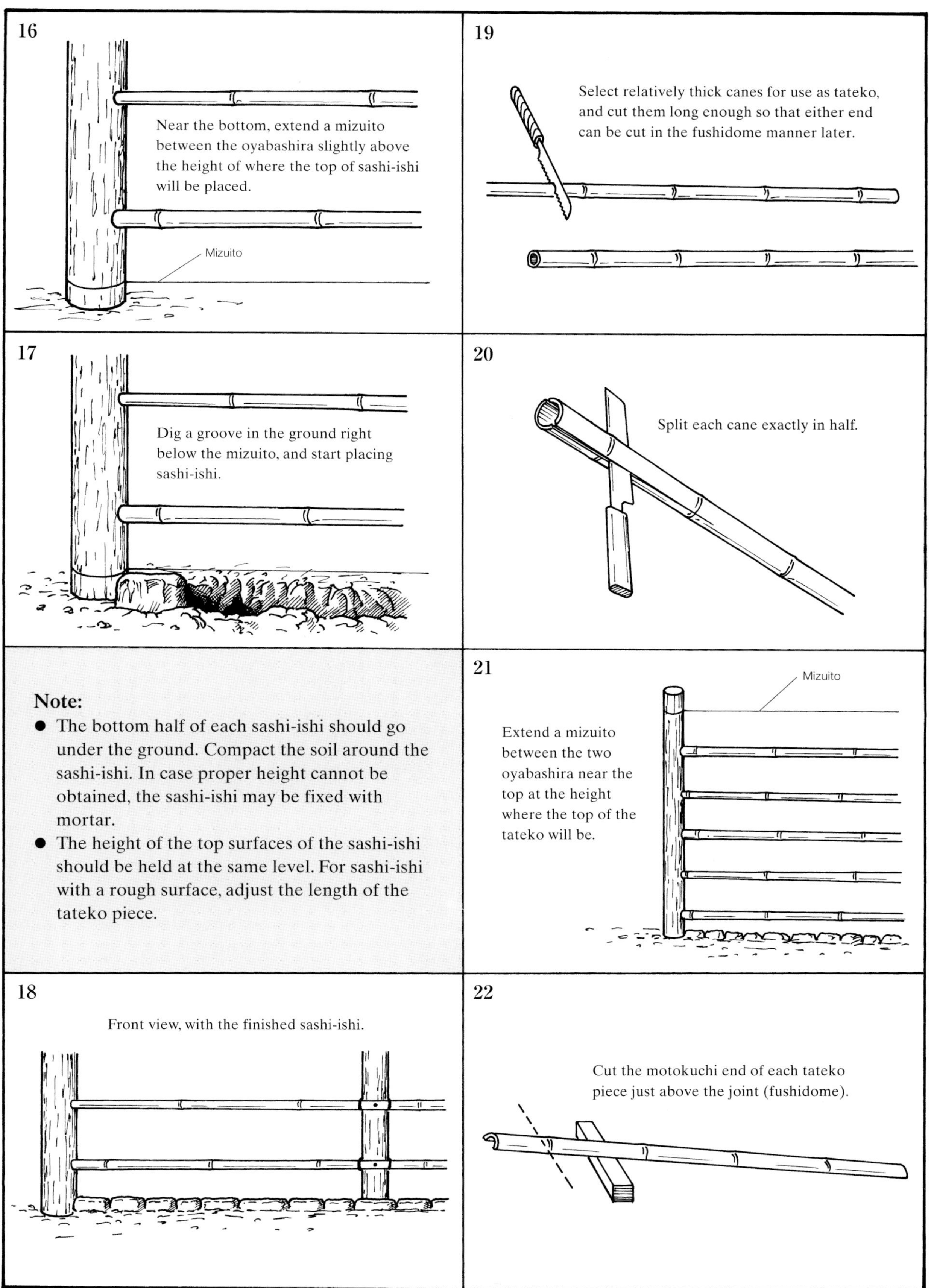

16
Near the bottom, extend a mizuito between the oyabashira slightly above the height of where the top of sashi-ishi will be placed.
Mizuito
17
Dig a groove in the ground right below the mizuito, and start placing sashi-ishi.
18
Front view, with the finished sashi-ishi.
19
Select relatively thick canes for use as tateko, and cut them long enough so that either end can be cut in the fushidome manner later.
20
Split each cane exactly in half.
21
Mizuito
Extend a mizuito between the two oyabashira near the top at the height where the top of the tateko will be.
22
Cut the motokuchi end of each tateko piece just above the joint (fushidome).

Note:

- The bottom half of each sashi-ishi should go under the ground. Compact the soil around the sashi-ishi. In case proper height cannot be obtained, the sashi-ishi may be fixed with mortar.
- The height of the top surfaces of the sashi-ishi should be held at the same level. For sashi-ishi with a rough surface, adjust the length of the tateko piece.

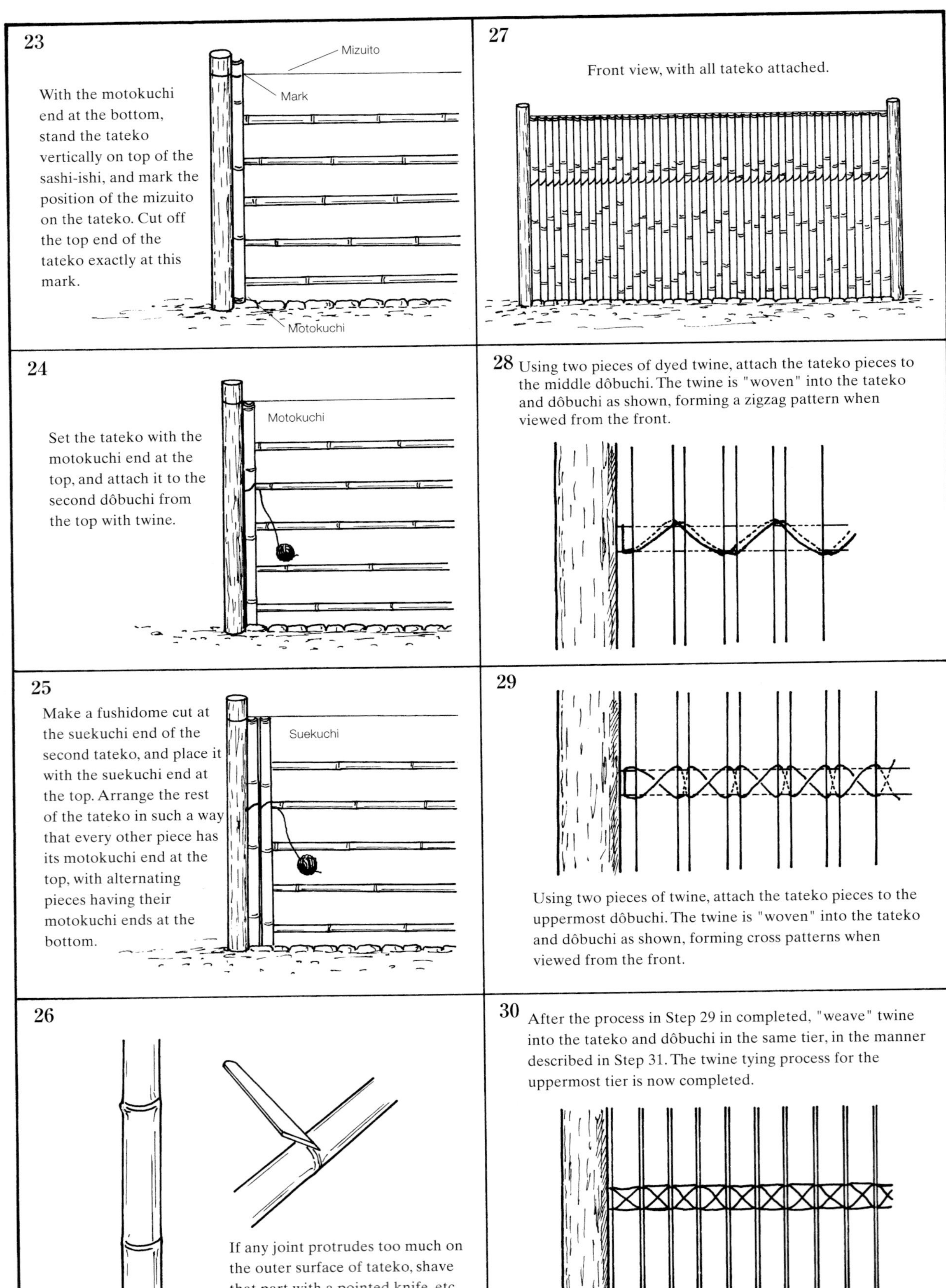

23 With the motokuchi end at the bottom, stand the tateko vertically on top of the sashi-ishi, and mark the position of the mizuito on the tateko. Cut off the top end of the tateko exactly at this mark.

24 Set the tateko with the motokuchi end at the top, and attach it to the second dôbuchi from the top with twine.

25 Make a fushidome cut at the suekuchi end of the second tateko, and place it with the suekuchi end at the top. Arrange the rest of the tateko in such a way that every other piece has its motokuchi end at the top, with alternating pieces having their motokuchi ends at the bottom.

26 If any joint protrudes too much on the outer surface of tateko, shave that part with a pointed knife, etc.

27 Front view, with all tateko attached.

28 Using two pieces of dyed twine, attach the tateko pieces to the middle dôbuchi. The twine is "woven" into the tateko and dôbuchi as shown, forming a zigzag pattern when viewed from the front.

29 Using two pieces of twine, attach the tateko pieces to the uppermost dôbuchi. The twine is "woven" into the tateko and dôbuchi as shown, forming cross patterns when viewed from the front.

30 After the process in Step 29 in completed, "weave" twine into the tateko and dôbuchi in the same tier, in the manner described in Step 31. The twine tying process for the uppermost tier is now completed.

31 Attach the tateko to the lowermost dôbuchi using two pieces of dyed twine. The twine is "woven" into the tateko and dôbuchi as shown, forming the pattern shown when viewed from the front.

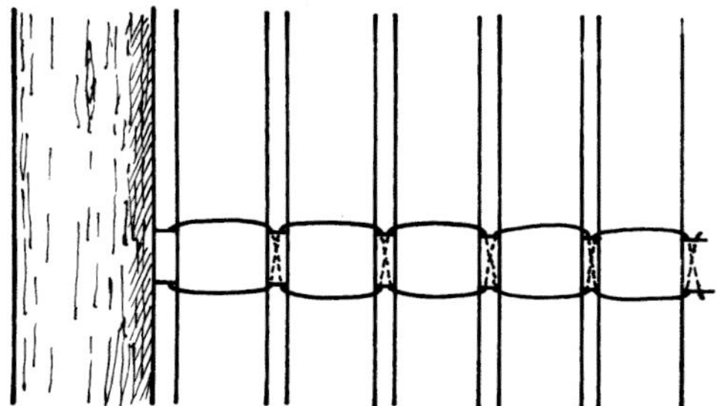

32 Using dyed twine, tie a knot on the front side of selected tateko (chirashi) along the second and fourth dôbuchi from the top.

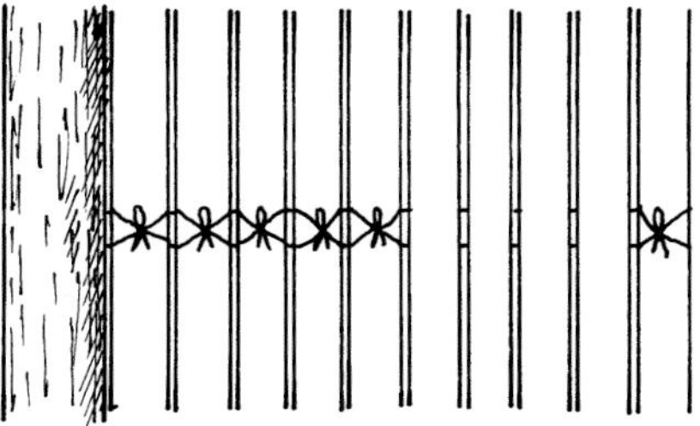

33 The finished fence.

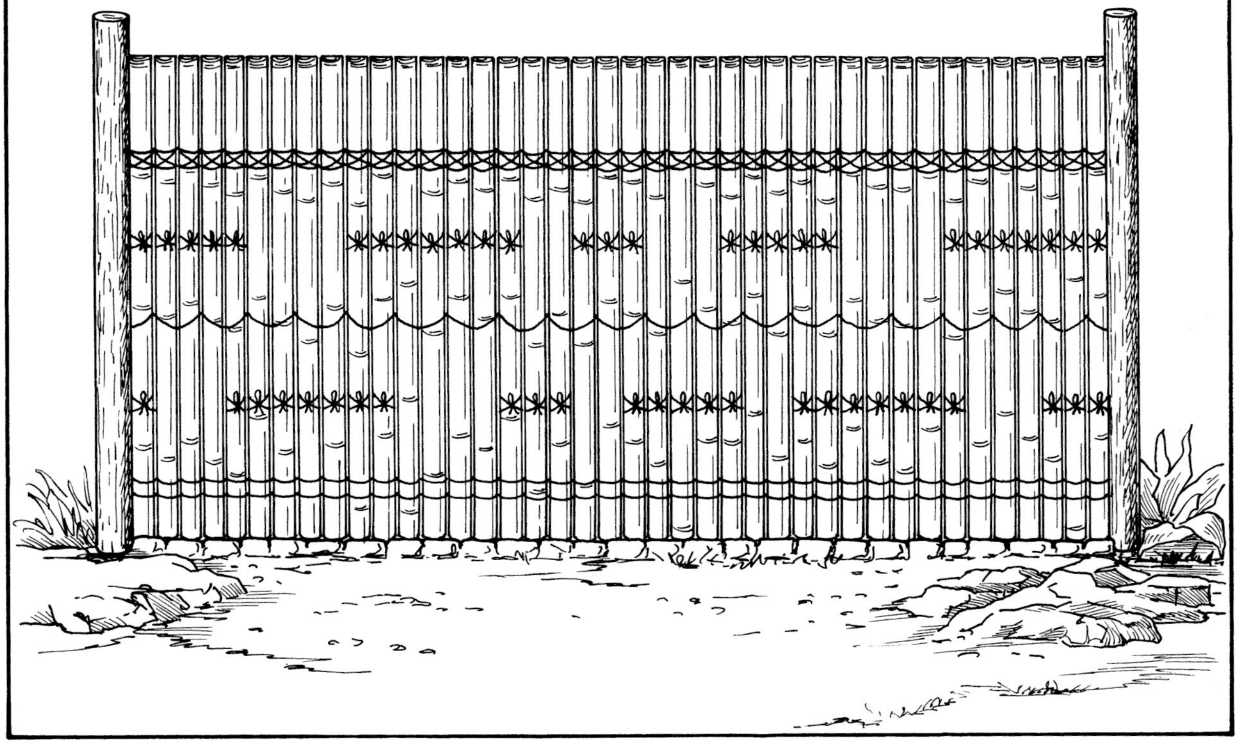

Takeho-gaki (bamboo branch fence)

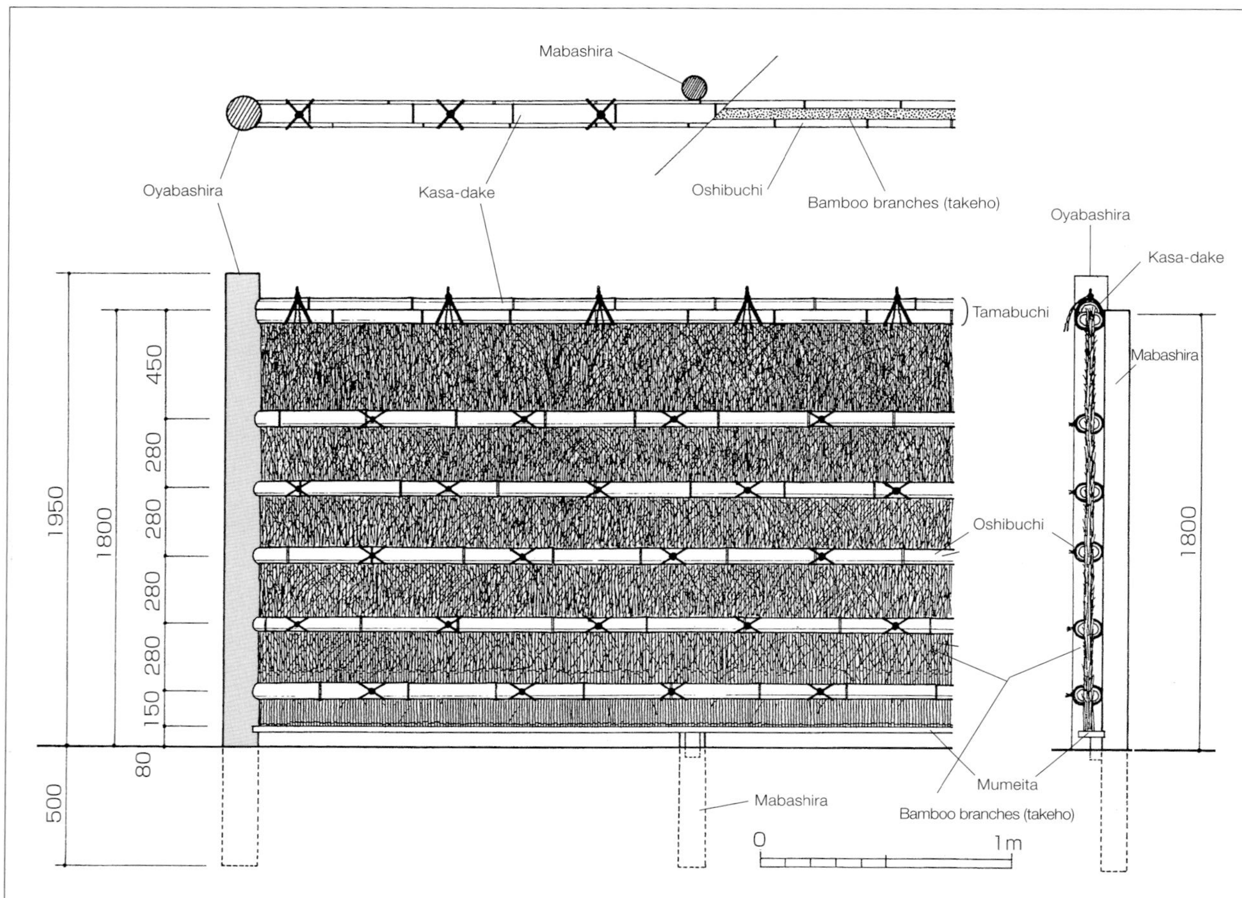

The takeho-gaki is classified into two groups: ones using long "white" branches of môsô-chiku (thick-stemmed bamboo), and those using short "black" branches of kuro-chiku (black bamboo).

While both groups have many varieties, the one described in the illustration above is the most standard type with tiers of vertically arranged "black" branches attached at the bottom.

Structurally speaking, the takeho-gaki is very similar to the kenninji-gaki except that the tateko are made of bamboo branches instead of split bamboo canes, and that the bamboo branches are held in place from front and rear sides with oshibuchi without using any dôbuchi.

When building a takeho-gaki with short "black" branches, there should be more tiers (oshibuchi) than when building one using long "white" branches. For a 180 cm tall fence, for example, there should be six or seven tiers as shown in the illustration above.

Always place sashi-ishi or fix a mumeita at the bottom. The lowermost tier of bamboo branches should never reach the ground.

As explained in the following pages, the tiers of branches are arranged from the rear side and from bottom to top. In the lowermost tier, the joints of the branches must be lined up at the same height for a beautiful appearance when viewed from the front.

Take care to make the rear side of each tier as thin as possible. This will help finish the front side in evenly. Small split bamboo pieces (called shinobi-no-take) are used to hold the branches in place as each tier is arranged. For the details of this process, refer to the explanatory illustrations on the following pages.

The front side should use a few more branches than the rear side, and the arrangement of tiers proceeds from bottom to top. The volume of bamboo branches to be used depends on the thickness of the oyabashira. Take care not to use too many branches as it will make the middle part of the fence too thick.

The illustration above shows a takeho-gaki with a tamabuchi at the top, although there are many cases in which the tops of the branches in the uppermost tier are trimmed evenly and left uncovered.

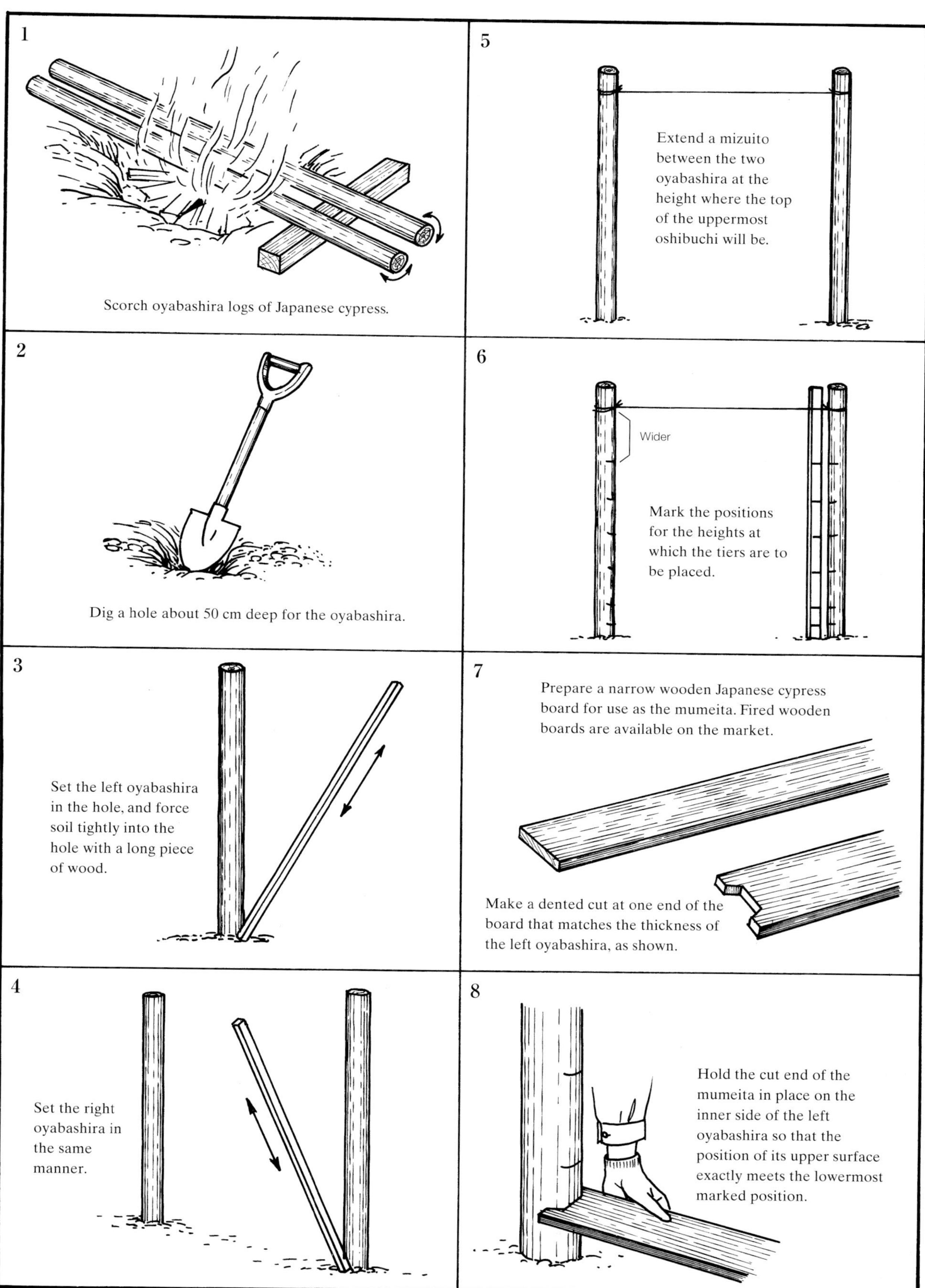
1
Scorch oyabashira logs of Japanese cypress.
2
Dig a hole about 50 cm deep for the oyabashira.
3
Set the left oyabashira in the hole, and force soil tightly into the hole with a long piece of wood.
4
Set the right oyabashira in the same manner.
5
Extend a mizuito between the two oyabashira at the height where the top of the uppermost oshibuchi will be.
6
Wider
Mark the positions for the heights at which the tiers are to be placed.
7
Prepare a narrow wooden Japanese cypress board for use as the mumeita. Fired wooden boards are available on the market.
Make a dented cut at one end of the board that matches the thickness of the left oyabashira, as shown.
8
Hold the cut end of the mumeita in place on the inner side of the left oyabashira so that the position of its upper surface exactly meets the lowermost marked position.

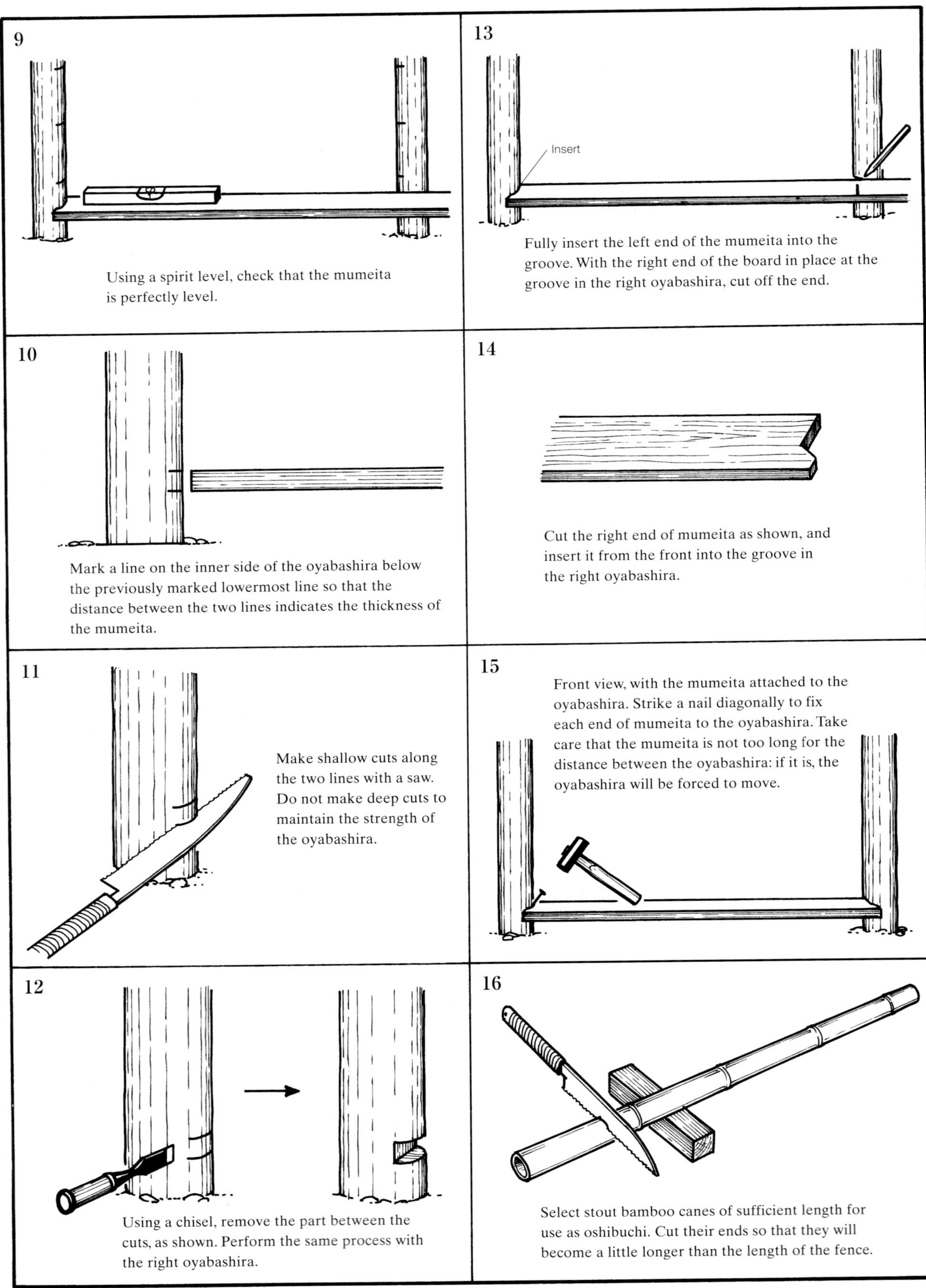

9

Using a spirit level, check that the mumeita is perfectly level.

10

Mark a line on the inner side of the oyabashira below the previously marked lowermost line so that the distance between the two lines indicates the thickness of the mumeita.

11

Make shallow cuts along the two lines with a saw. Do not make deep cuts to maintain the strength of the oyabashira.

12

Using a chisel, remove the part between the cuts, as shown. Perform the same process with the right oyabashira.

13

Fully insert the left end of the mumeita into the groove. With the right end of the board in place at the groove in the right oyabashira, cut off the end.

14

Cut the right end of mumeita as shown, and insert it from the front into the groove in the right oyabashira.

15

Front view, with the mumeita attached to the oyabashira. Strike a nail diagonally to fix each end of mumeita to the oyabashira. Take care that the mumeita is not too long for the distance between the oyabashira: if it is, the oyabashira will be forced to move.

16

Select stout bamboo canes of sufficient length for use as oshibuchi. Cut their ends so that they will become a little longer than the length of the fence.

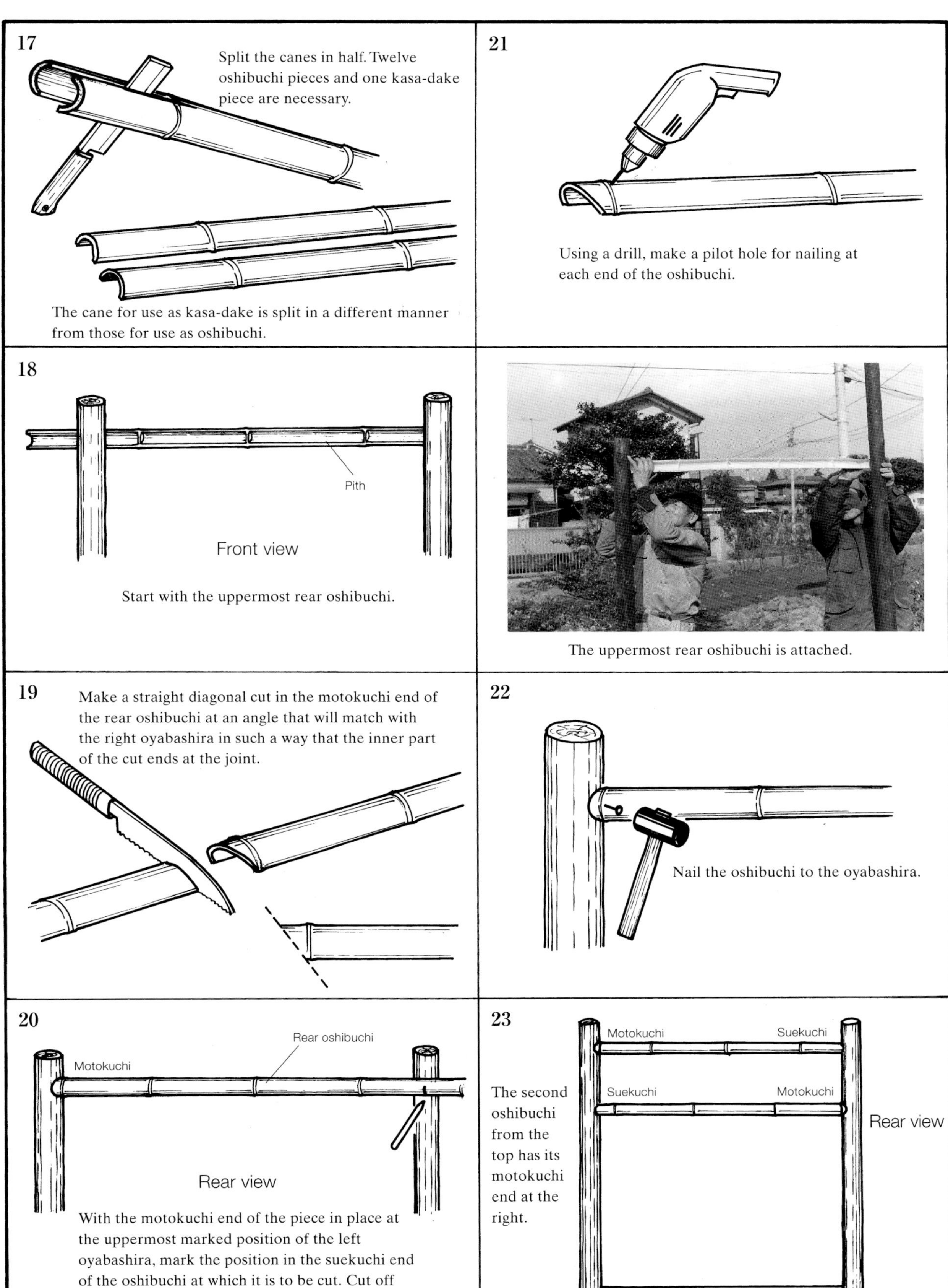
17
Split the canes in half. Twelve oshibuchi pieces and one kasa-dake piece are necessary.
The cane for use as kasa-dake is split in a different manner from those for use as oshibuchi.
21
Using a drill, make a pilot hole for nailing at each end of the oshibuchi.
18
Pith
Front view
Start with the uppermost rear oshibuchi.
The uppermost rear oshibuchi is attached.
19
Make a straight diagonal cut in the motokuchi end of the rear oshibuchi at an angle that will match with the right oyabashira in such a way that the inner part of the cut ends at the joint.
22
Nail the oshibuchi to the oyabashira.
20
Rear oshibuchi
Motokuchi
Rear view
With the motokuchi end of the piece in place at the uppermost marked position of the left oyabashira, mark the position in the suekuchi end of the oshibuchi at which it is to be cut. Cut off the suekuchi end at slightly beyond the mark.
23
Motokuchi
Suekuchi
Suekuchi
Motokuchi
The second oshibuchi from the top has its motokuchi end at the right.
Rear view

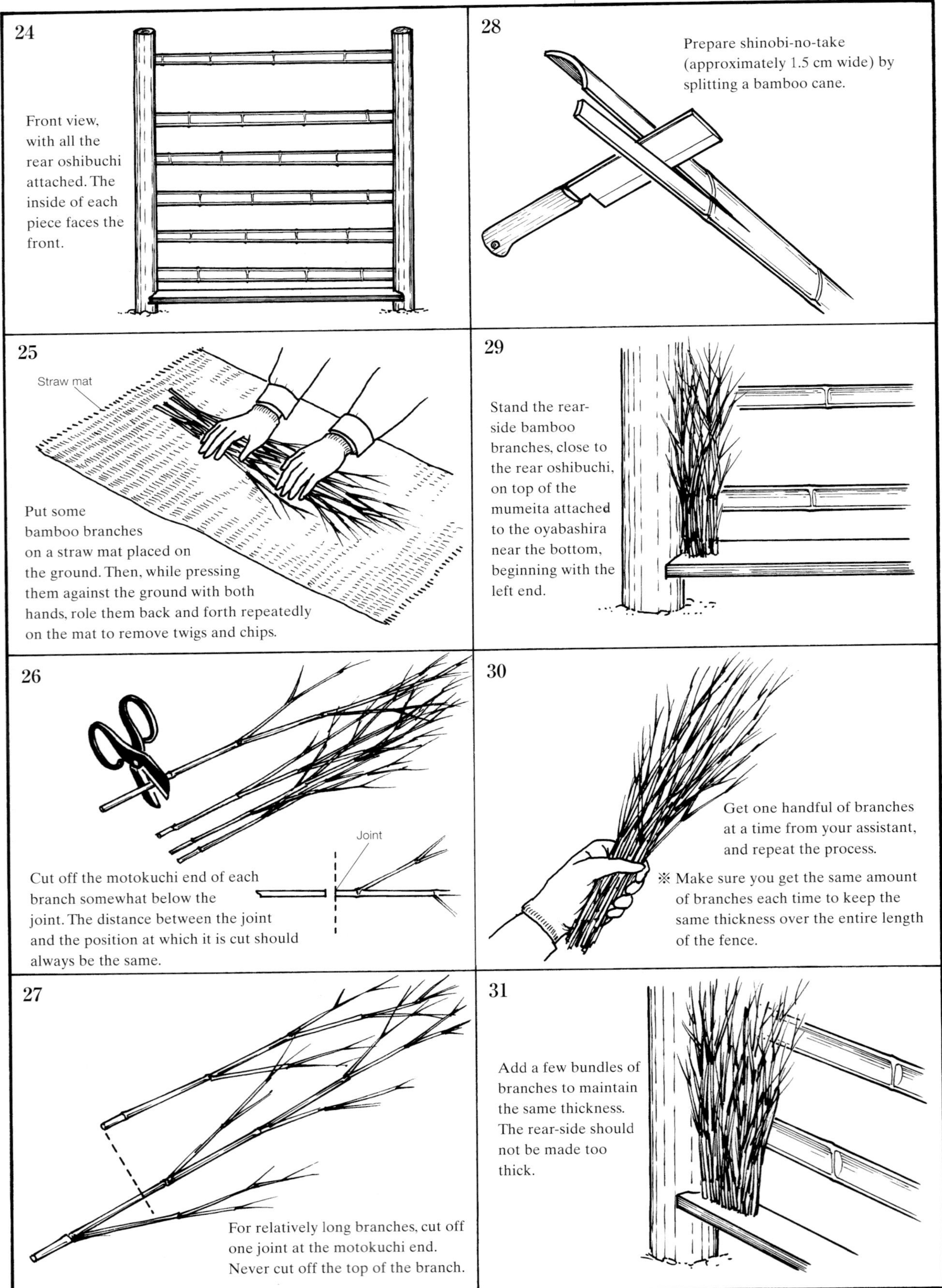
24
Front view, with all the rear oshibuchi attached. The inside of each piece faces the front.
28
Prepare shinobi-no-take (approximately 1.5 cm wide) by splitting a bamboo cane.
25
Straw mat
Put some bamboo branches on a straw mat placed on the ground. Then, while pressing them against the ground with both hands, role them back and forth repeatedly on the mat to remove twigs and chips.
29
Stand the rear-side bamboo branches, close to the rear oshibuchi, on top of the mumeita attached to the oyabashira near the bottom, beginning with the left end.
26
Joint
Cut off the motokuchi end of each branch somewhat below the joint. The distance between the joint and the position at which it is cut should always be the same.
30
Get one handful of branches at a time from your assistant, and repeat the process.
※ Make sure you get the same amount of branches each time to keep the same thickness over the entire length of the fence.
27
For relatively long branches, cut off one joint at the motokuchi end. Never cut off the top of the branch.
31
Add a few bundles of branches to maintain the same thickness. The rear-side should not be made too thick.

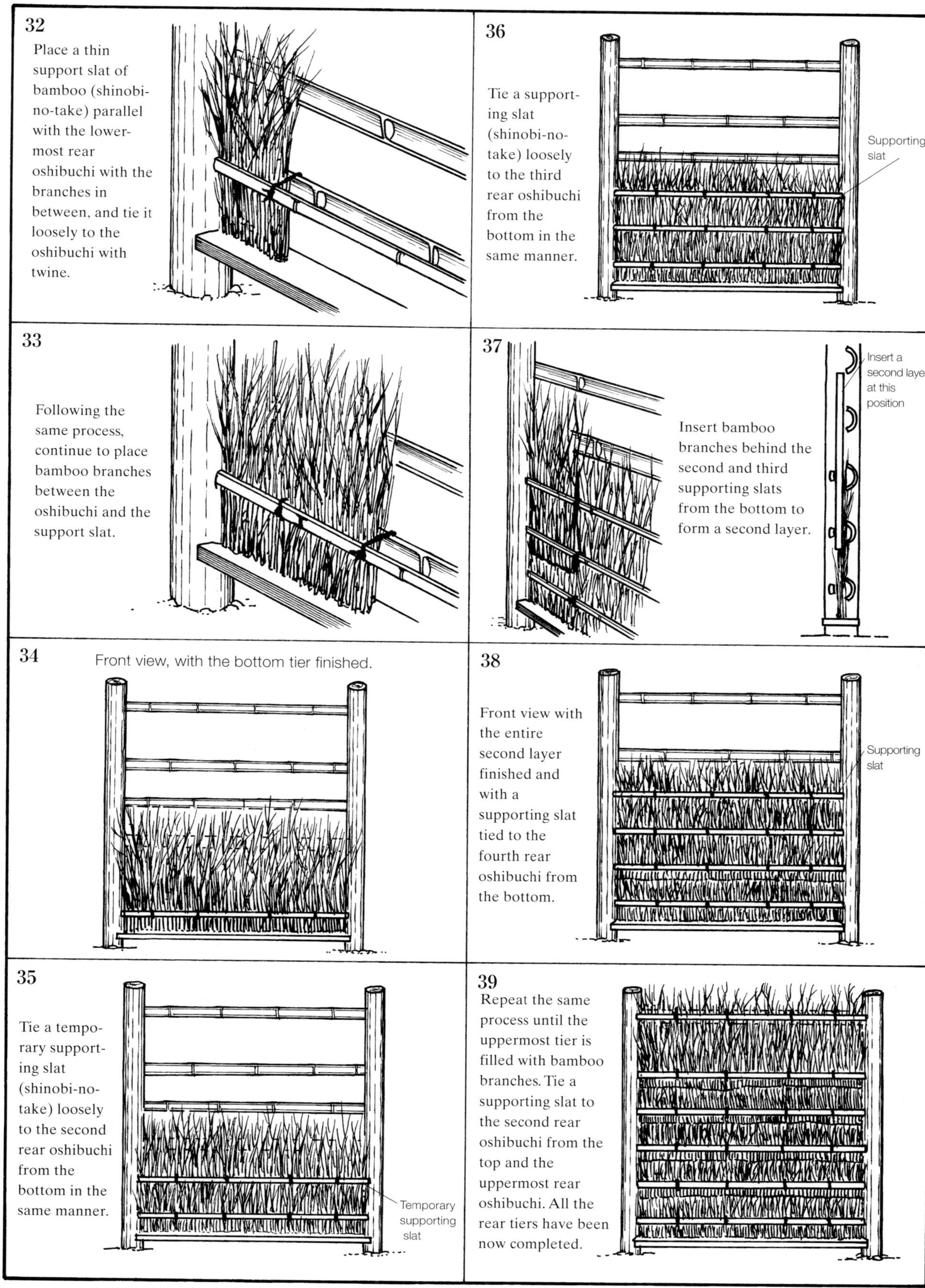
32
Place a thin support slat of bamboo (shinobi-no-take) parallel with the lowermost rear oshibuchi with the branches in between, and tie it loosely to the oshibuchi with twine.
33
Following the same process, continue to place bamboo branches between the oshibuchi and the support slat.
34
Front view, with the bottom tier finished.
35
Tie a temporary supporting slat (shinobi-no-take) loosely to the second rear oshibuchi from the bottom in the same manner.
Temporary supporting slat
36
Tie a supporting slat (shinobi-no-take) loosely to the third rear oshibuchi from the bottom in the same manner.
Supporting slat
37
Insert bamboo branches behind the second and third supporting slats from the bottom to form a second layer.
Insert a second layer at this position
38
Front view with the entire second layer finished and with a supporting slat tied to the fourth rear oshibuchi from the bottom.
Supporting slat
39
Repeat the same process until the uppermost tier is filled with bamboo branches. Tie a supporting slat to the second rear oshibuchi from the top and the uppermost rear oshibuchi. All the rear tiers have been now completed.

40

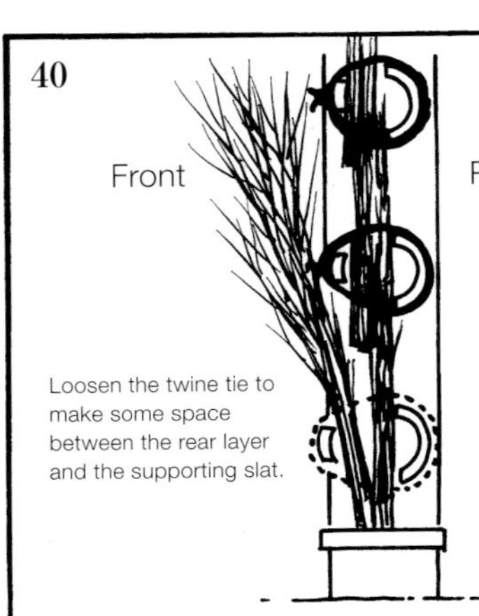

Front
Rear
Loosen the twine tie to make some space between the rear layer and the supporting slat.

Loosen the twine ties in the lowermost tier, and insert bamboo branches to form the front layer.

41

Fill the bottom tier with bamboo branches spread evenly, and attach a supporting slat (shinobi-no-take) to hold them in place.

42

Attach the lowermost front oshibuchi by tying it firmly to the corresponding rear oshibuchi with dyed twine. This process requires two workers with one of them assisting the other on the rear side of the fence. (Use a straight needle to tie the twine.)

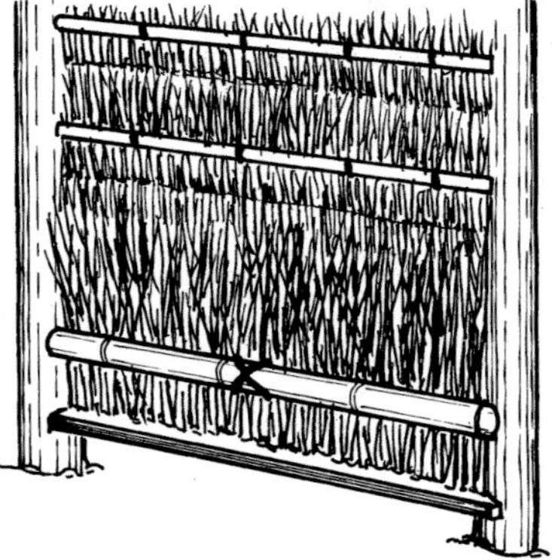

43

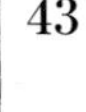

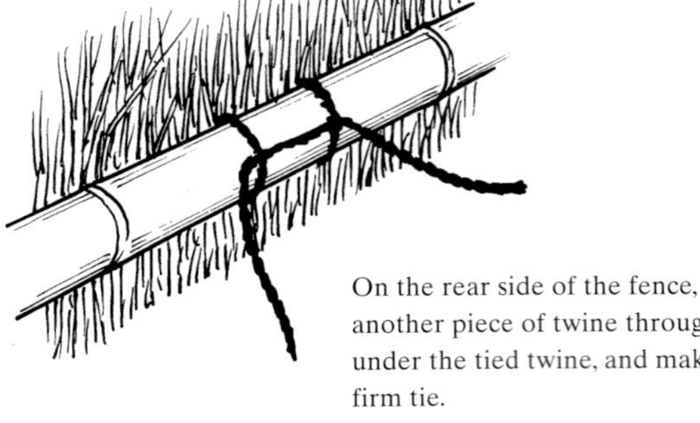

On the rear side of the fence, pass another piece of twine through under the tied twine, and make a firm tie.

44

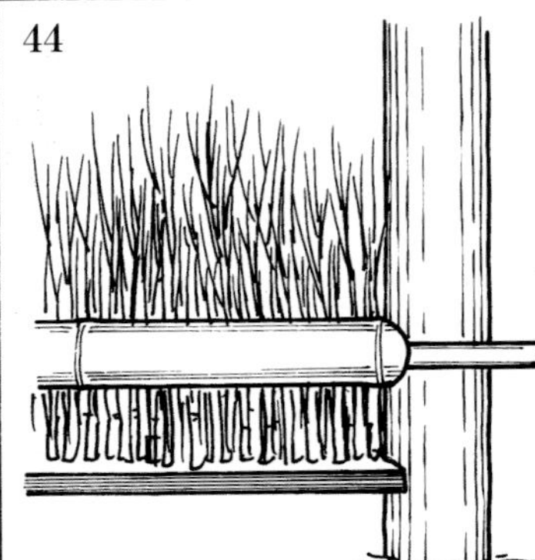

Cut the twine used to tie the supporting slat of bamboo (shinobi-no-take) to the rear oshibuchi, and remove the slat by pulling its end from the oyabashira side.

Then tie the rear and front oshibuchi together with dyed twine.

45

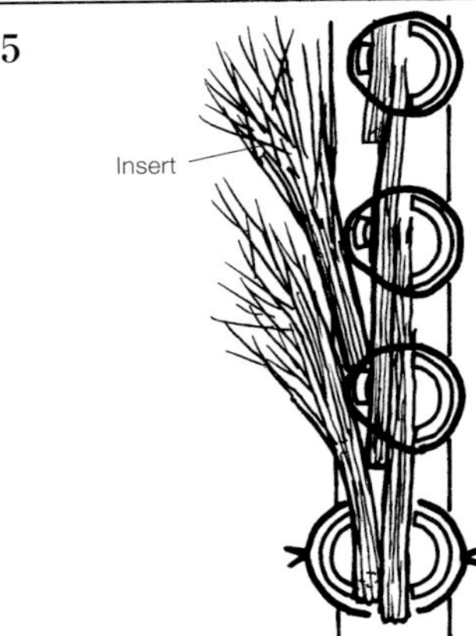

Insert a second layer of bamboo branches inside the first layer.

Insert bamboo branches and arrange them evenly.

46

Fill the second tier from the bottom with bamboo branches, and attach the corresponding oshibuchi. (Remove the supporting slat in the same manner. Do the same with the rest of the tiers.)

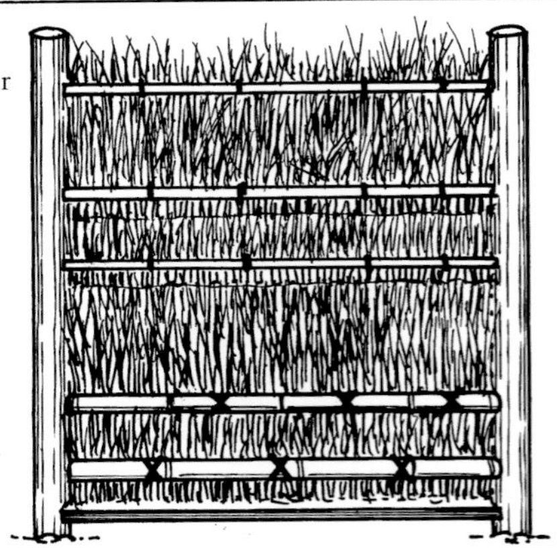

47

In the same manner, fill the other tiers with bamboo branches, and hold them in place with oshibuchi. The uppermost oshibuchi should be temporarily attached.

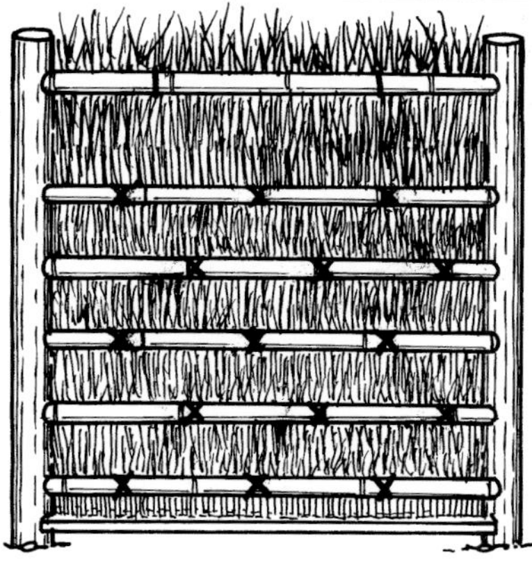

48 Cut the tops of the branches to an even height— about one centimeter above the uppermost oshibuchi.

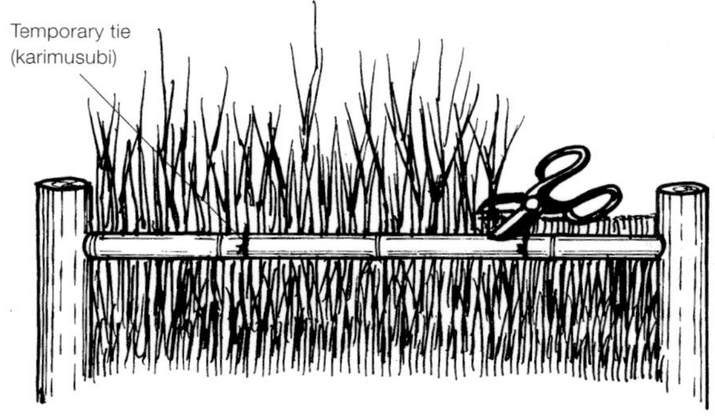

49

Add extra branches, with their motokuchi ends cut off, at the top so that the top part cannot be seen through.

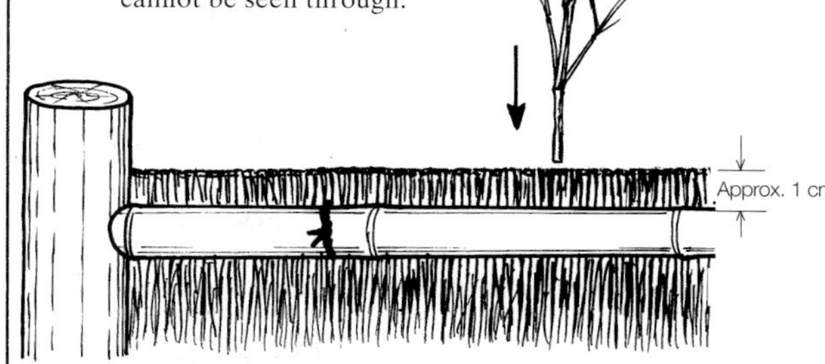

50

Cover the top of the fence with a kasa-dake, forming a tamabuchi with three decorative knots (kazari-musubi).

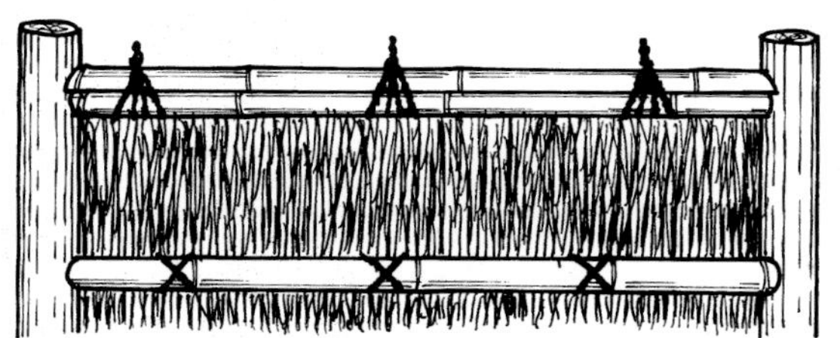

51 The finished fence.

Mino-gaki (raincoat fence)

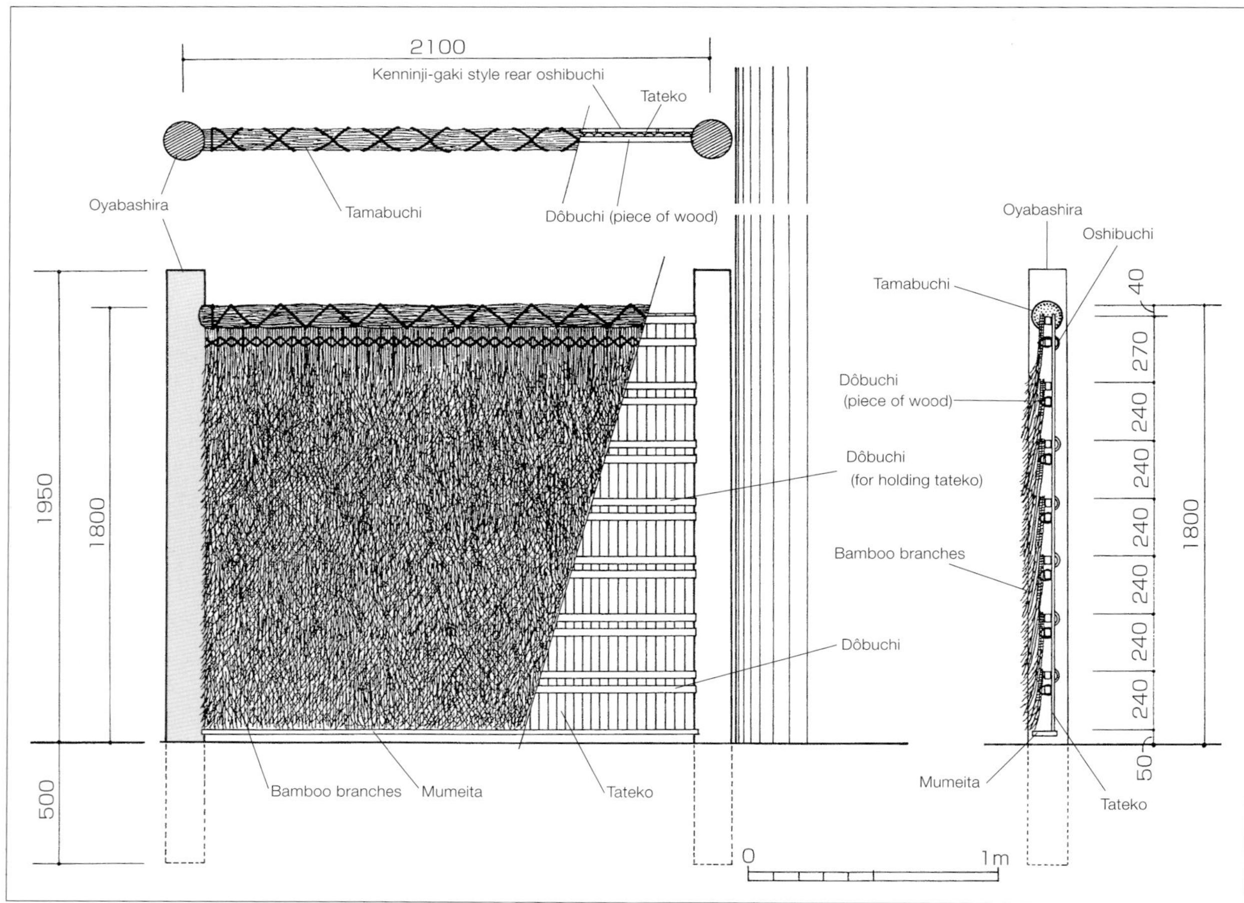

Although mino-gaki (raincoat fences) are regarded as a kind of bamboo fence today, they are, in fact, not all bamboo fences because some of them use bush clover or miscellaneous tree branches for their front surfaces. These days, however, ones using bamboo branches are seen most often. In the Kantô area, especially, branches of black bamboo (kuroho) are most commonly used. Therefore, the mino-gaki we are going to build here is one using black bamboo branches.

The major characteristic of this fence is that it has bamboo branches upside down, and this creates the rural wabi aesthetic that has been popular over the ages.

In some cases, bamboo branches are attached to both sides of the fence, but in most cases, they are attached to the front side only, with the rear side constructed in the kenninji-gaki style.

Such a fence is shown in the illustration above, which, in part, shows the structure of the inner dôbuchi.

As indicated in this diagram, each dôbuchi consists of paired long pieces of wood which are positioned with their centers approximately 4-5 cm apart. The lower piece has the original function of dôbuchi, and the upper is used to hold the tateko in place (furedome). The function of this furedome is different in nature from the regular furedome that is attached at the top of a bamboo fence.

Many bundles of bamboo branches of even thickness and length should be prepared beforehand. They are to be attached to the front surface of the fence, beginning with the lowermost tier, with two pieces of twine, using the cross-tying method. In order to fix them securely to the dôbuchi, place the top of each bundle slightly above the upper piece.

Using bundles of rather thin bamboo branches will make the fence look more delicate and elegant, although this requires time and labor. Repeat the process described in the previous paragraph and continue to attach bamboo branches from bottom up. The uppermost dôbuchi, should be tied neatly with relatively thick twine for a better appearance since the twine can be seen from the front. Usually, a tamabuchi of bundled bamboo branches or rolled-up small bamboo branches is placed at the top, tied to the uppermost dôbuchi with neatly arranged twine.

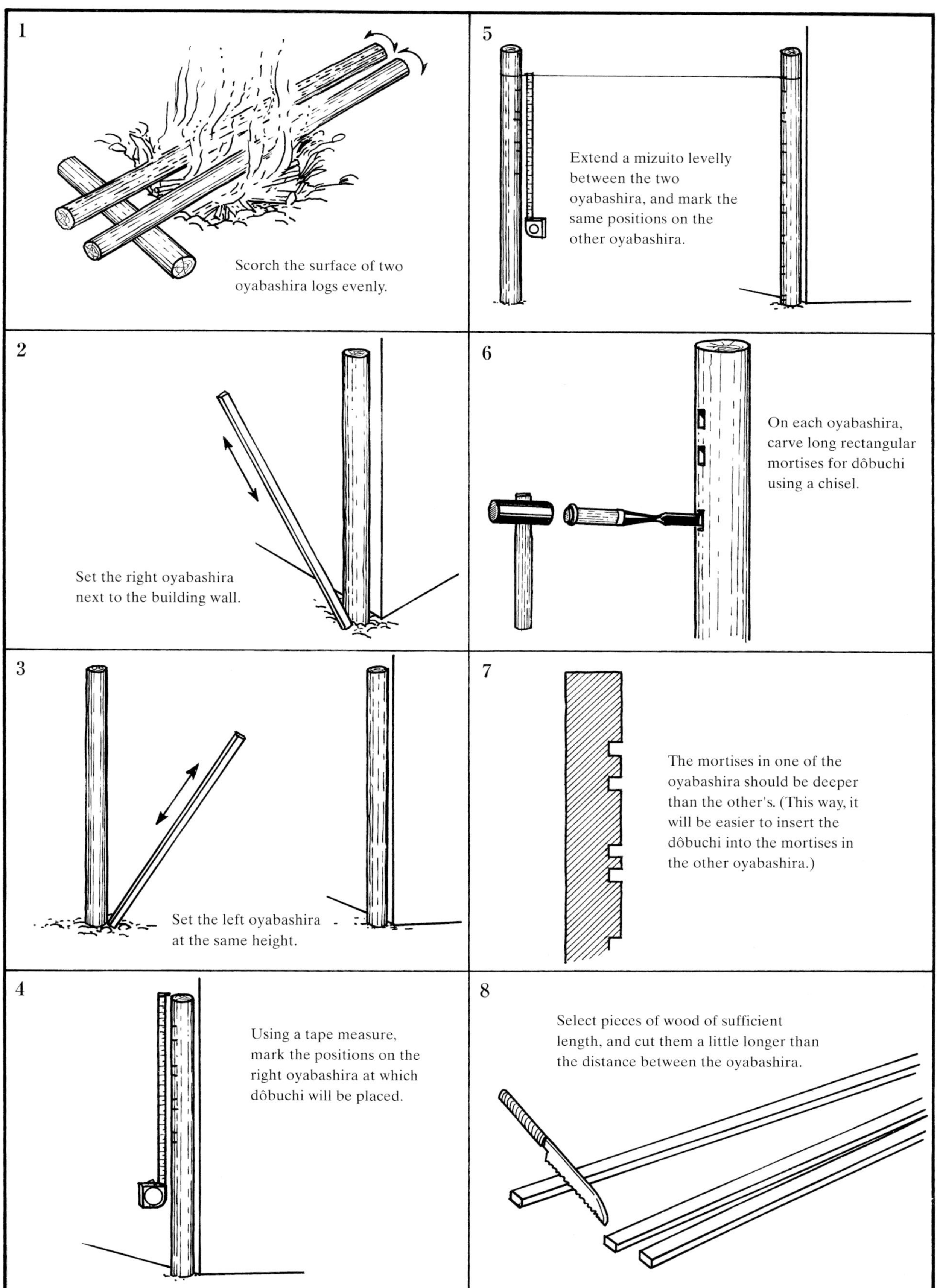
1
Scorch the surface of two oyabashira logs evenly.
2
Set the right oyabashira next to the building wall.
3
Set the left oyabashira at the same height.
4
Using a tape measure, mark the positions on the right oyabashira at which dôbuchi will be placed.
5
Extend a mizuito levelly between the two oyabashira, and mark the same positions on the other oyabashira.
6
On each oyabashira, carve long rectangular mortises for dôbuchi using a chisel.
7
The mortises in one of the oyabashira should be deeper than the other's. (This way, it will be easier to insert the dôbuchi into the mortises in the other oyabashira.)
8
Select pieces of wood of sufficient length, and cut them a little longer than the distance between the oyabashira.

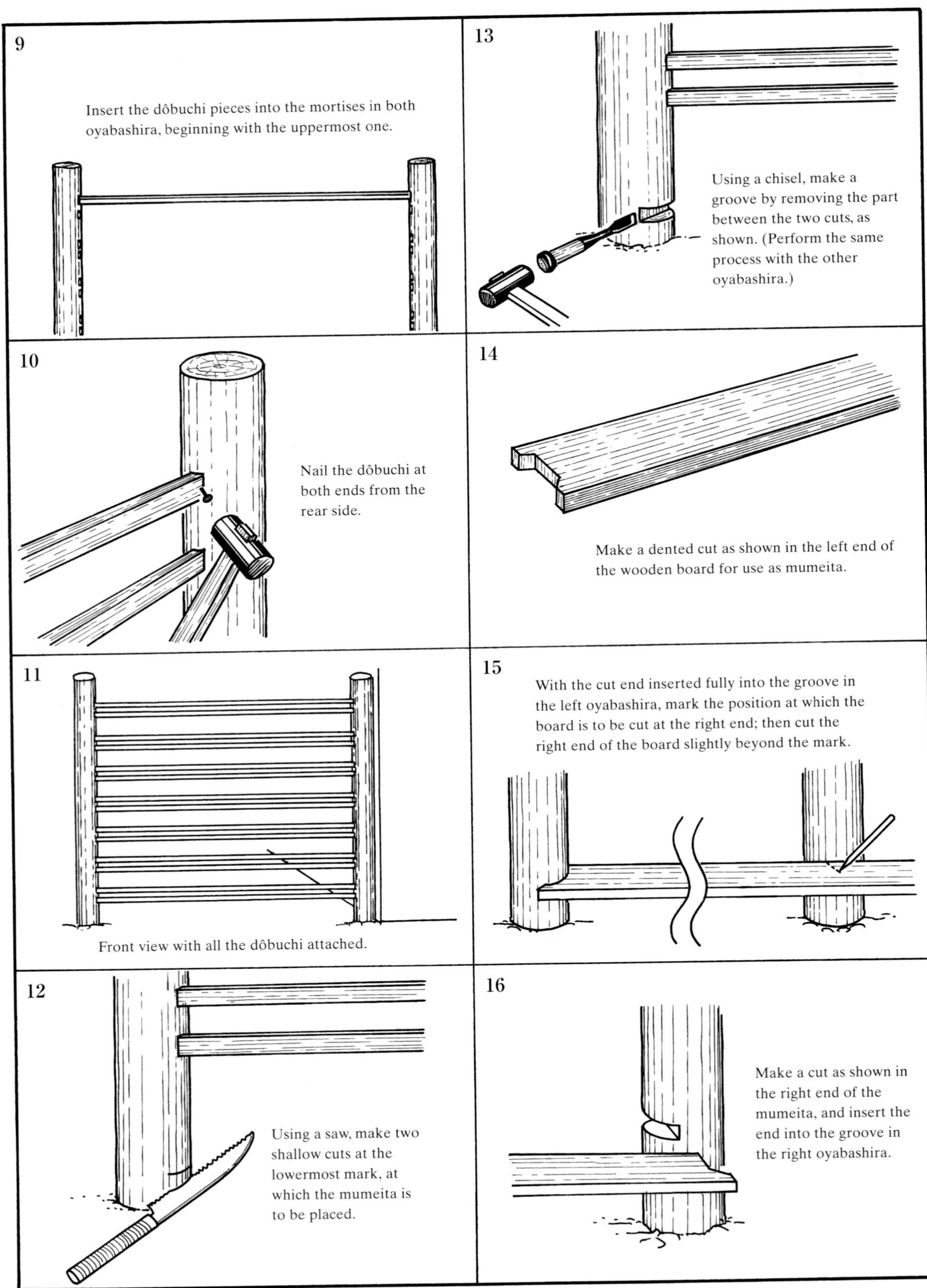
9
Insert the dôbuchi pieces into the mortises in both oyabashira, beginning with the uppermost one.
10
Nail the dôbuchi at both ends from the rear side.
11
Front view with all the dôbuchi attached.
12
Using a saw, make two shallow cuts at the lowermost mark, at which the mumeita is to be placed.
13
Using a chisel, make a groove by removing the part between the two cuts, as shown. (Perform the same process with the other oyabashira.)
14
Make a dented cut as shown in the left end of the wooden board for use as mumeita.
15
With the cut end inserted fully into the groove in the left oyabashira, mark the position at which the board is to be cut at the right end; then cut the right end of the board slightly beyond the mark.
16
Make a cut as shown in the right end of the mumeita, and insert the end into the groove in the right oyabashira.

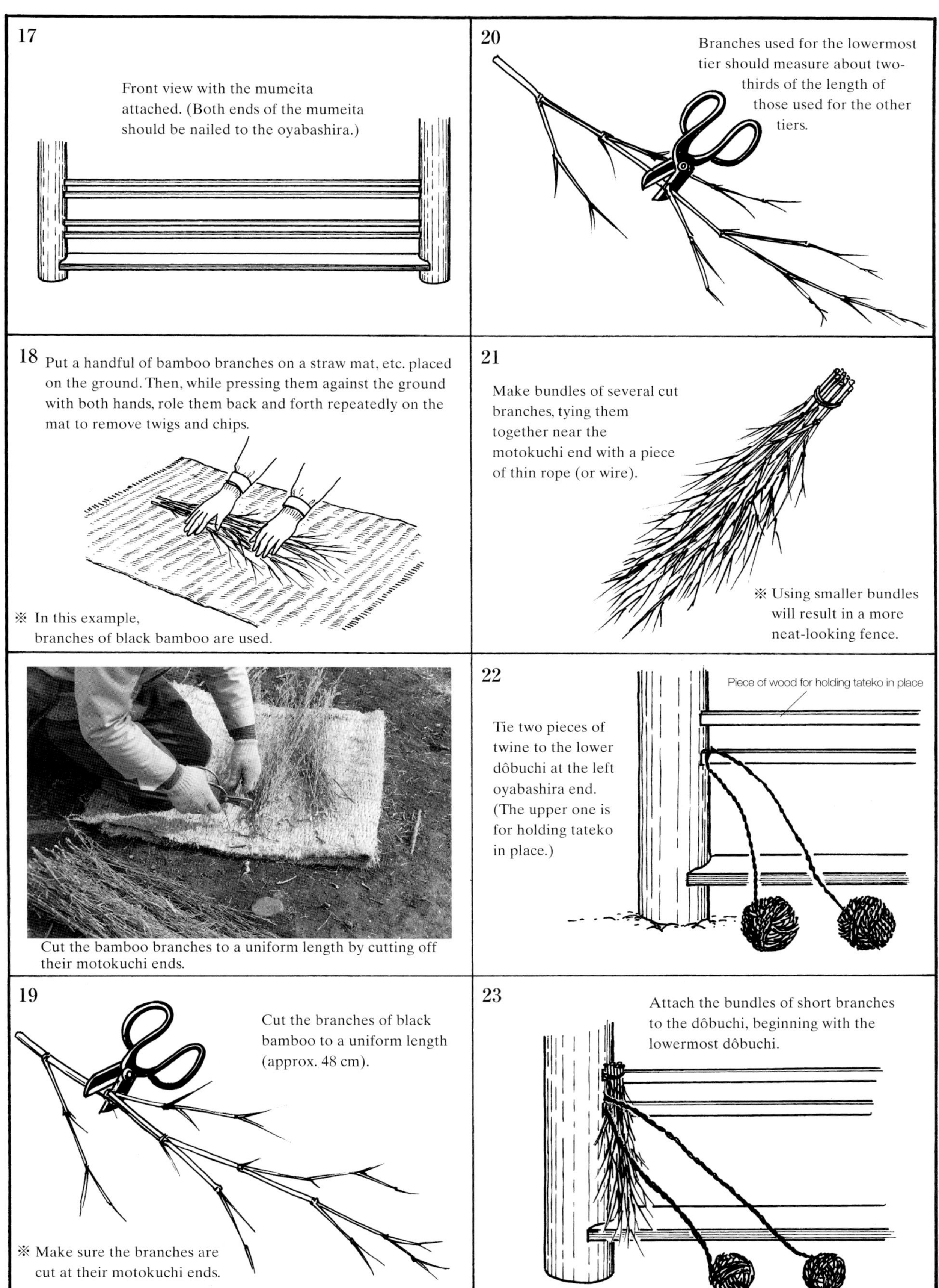
17
Front view with the mumeita attached. (Both ends of the mumeita should be nailed to the oyabashira.)
18
Put a handful of bamboo branches on a straw mat, etc. placed on the ground. Then, while pressing them against the ground with both hands, role them back and forth repeatedly on the mat to remove twigs and chips.
※ In this example, branches of black bamboo are used.
Cut the bamboo branches to a uniform length by cutting off their motokuchi ends.
19
Cut the branches of black bamboo to a uniform length (approx. 48 cm).
※ Make sure the branches are cut at their motokuchi ends.
20
Branches used for the lowermost tier should measure about two-thirds of the length of those used for the other tiers.
21
Make bundles of several cut branches, tying them together near the motokuchi end with a piece of thin rope (or wire).
※ Using smaller bundles will result in a more neat-looking fence.
22
Tie two pieces of twine to the lower dôbuchi at the left oyabashira end. (The upper one is for holding tateko in place.)
Piece of wood for holding tateko in place
23
Attach the bundles of short branches to the dôbuchi, beginning with the lowermost dôbuchi.

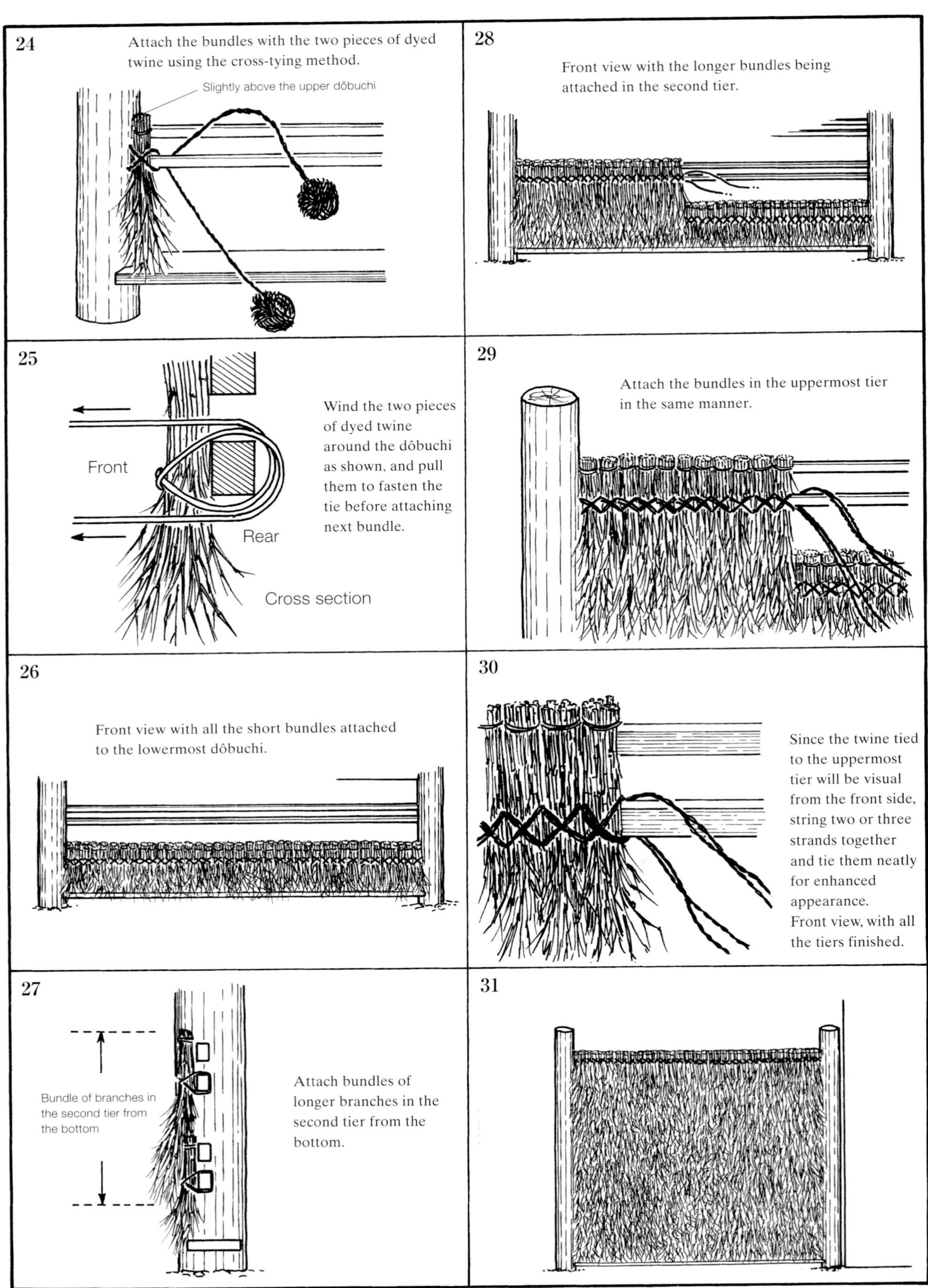

24
Attach the bundles with the two pieces of dyed twine using the cross-tying method.
Slightly above the upper dôbuchi
28
Front view with the longer bundles being attached in the second tier.
25
Front
Rear
Cross section
Wind the two pieces of dyed twine around the dôbuchi as shown, and pull them to fasten the tie before attaching next bundle.
29
Attach the bundles in the uppermost tier in the same manner.
26
Front view with all the short bundles attached to the lowermost dôbuchi.
30
Since the twine tied to the uppermost tier will be visual from the front side, string two or three strands together and tie them neatly for enhanced appearance.
Front view, with all the tiers finished.
27
Bundle of branches in the second tier from the bottom
Attach bundles of longer branches in the second tier from the bottom.
31

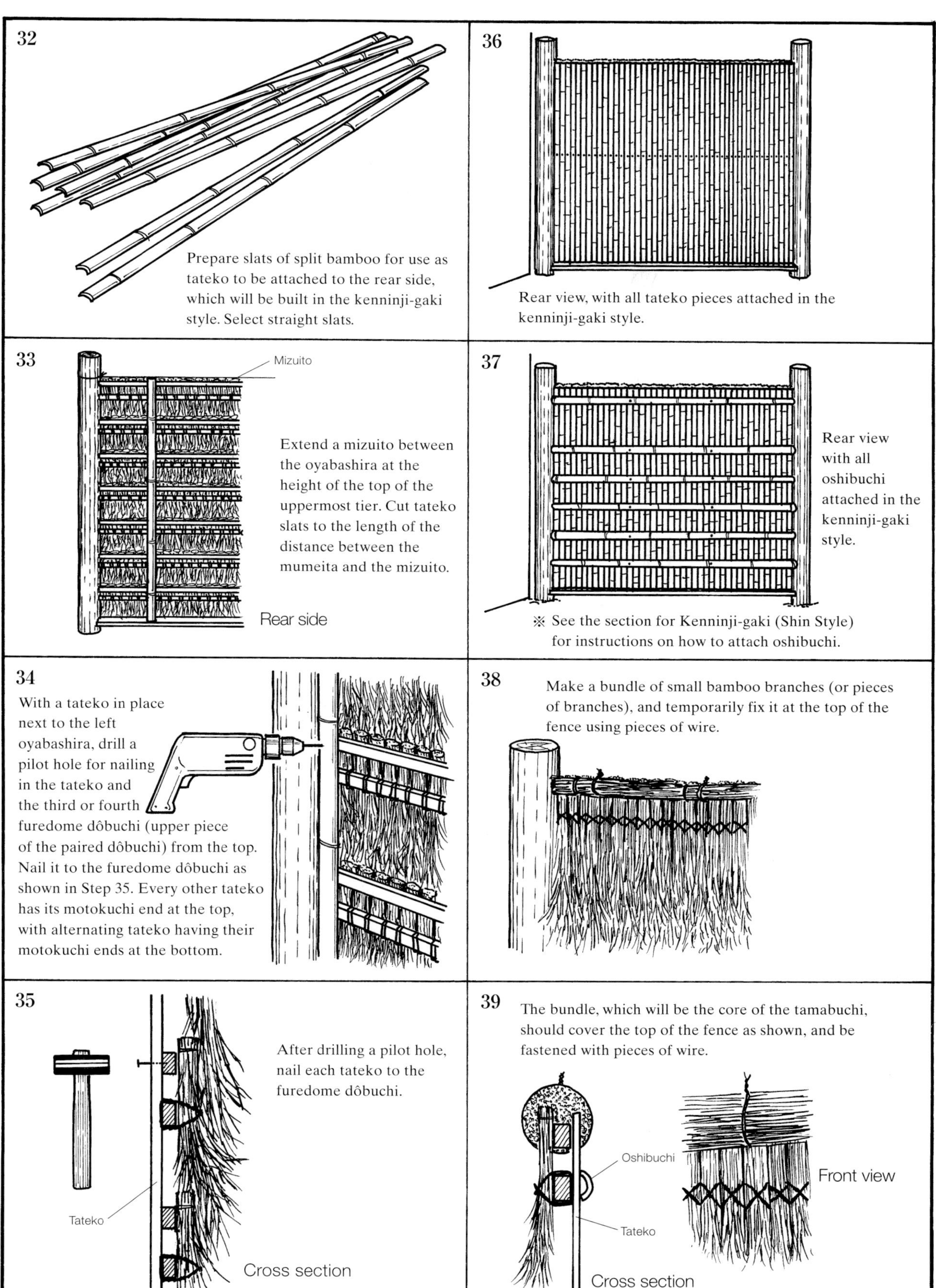

32

Prepare slats of split bamboo for use as tateko to be attached to the rear side, which will be built in the kenninji-gaki style. Select straight slats.

33

Extend a mizuito between the oyabashira at the height of the top of the uppermost tier. Cut tateko slats to the length of the distance between the mumeita and the mizuito.

34

With a tateko in place next to the left oyabashira, drill a pilot hole for nailing in the tateko and the third or fourth furedome dôbuchi (upper piece of the paired dôbuchi) from the top. Nail it to the furedome dôbuchi as shown in Step 35. Every other tateko has its motokuchi end at the top, with alternating tateko having their motokuchi ends at the bottom.

35

After drilling a pilot hole, nail each tateko to the furedome dôbuchi.

36

Rear view, with all tateko pieces attached in the kenninji-gaki style.

37

Rear view with all oshibuchi attached in the kenninji-gaki style.

※ See the section for Kenninji-gaki (Shin Style) for instructions on how to attach oshibuchi.

38

Make a bundle of small bamboo branches (or pieces of branches), and temporarily fix it at the top of the fence using pieces of wire.

39

The bundle, which will be the core of the tamabuchi, should cover the top of the fence as shown, and be fastened with pieces of wire.

40

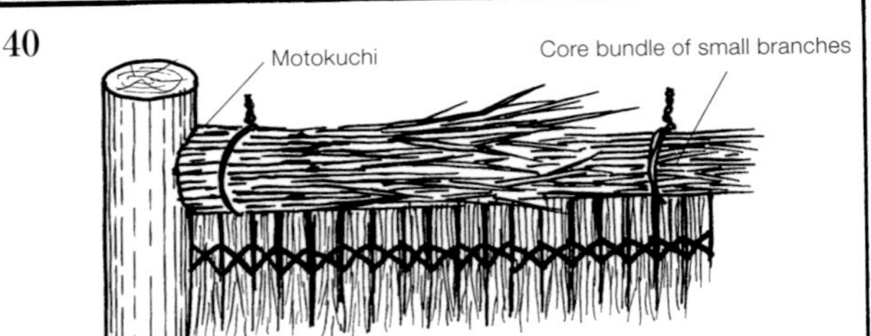

Wrap the core bundle with bamboo branches with their motokuchi ends toward the oyabashira side, and temporarily fasten them together with wire. (The bamboo branches used for the right half of the tamabuchi should have their motokuchi ends toward the right oyabashira.)

41

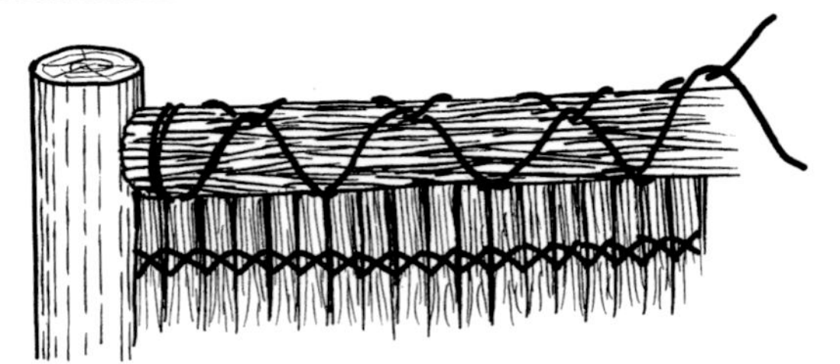

Use two strands of dyed twine to fasten the outer layer of the tamabuchi. (The twine also serves as decoration. Use any tying method of your choice.)

42 The finished fence.

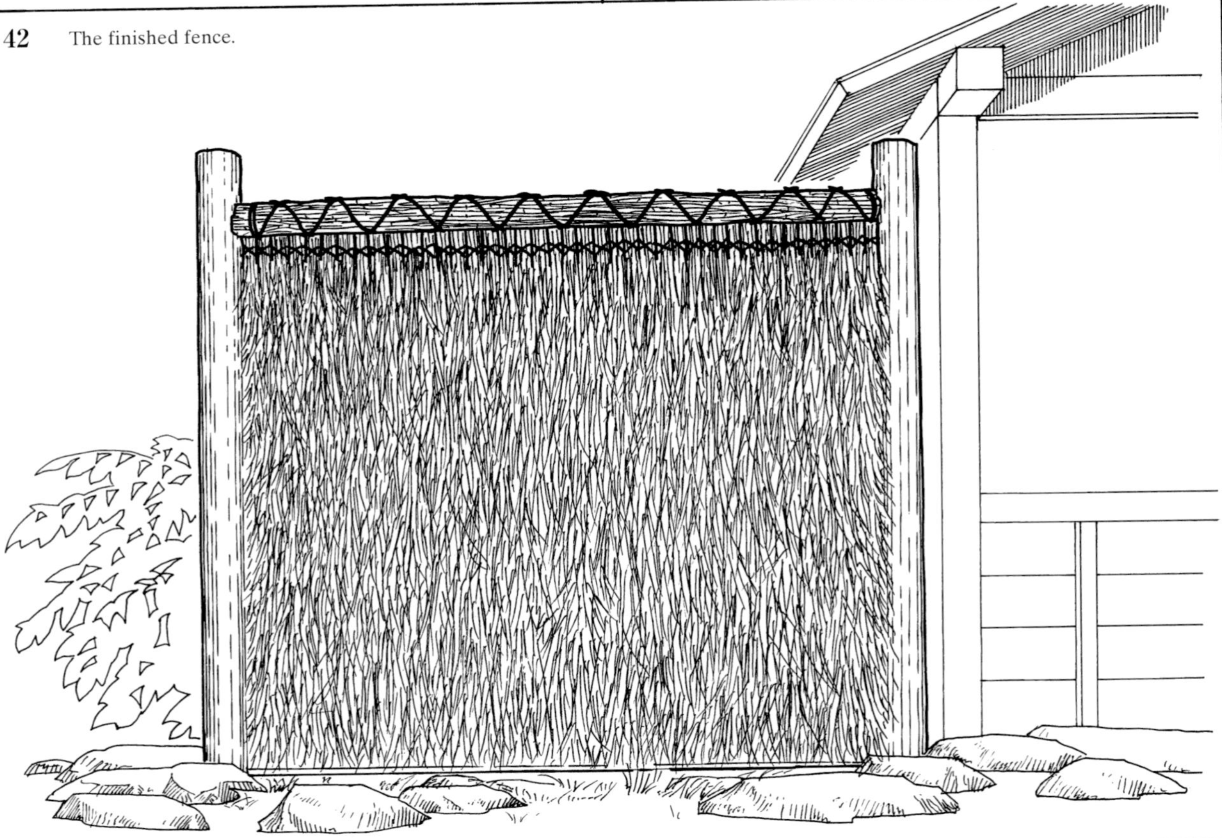

Yotsume-gaki (four-eyed fence)

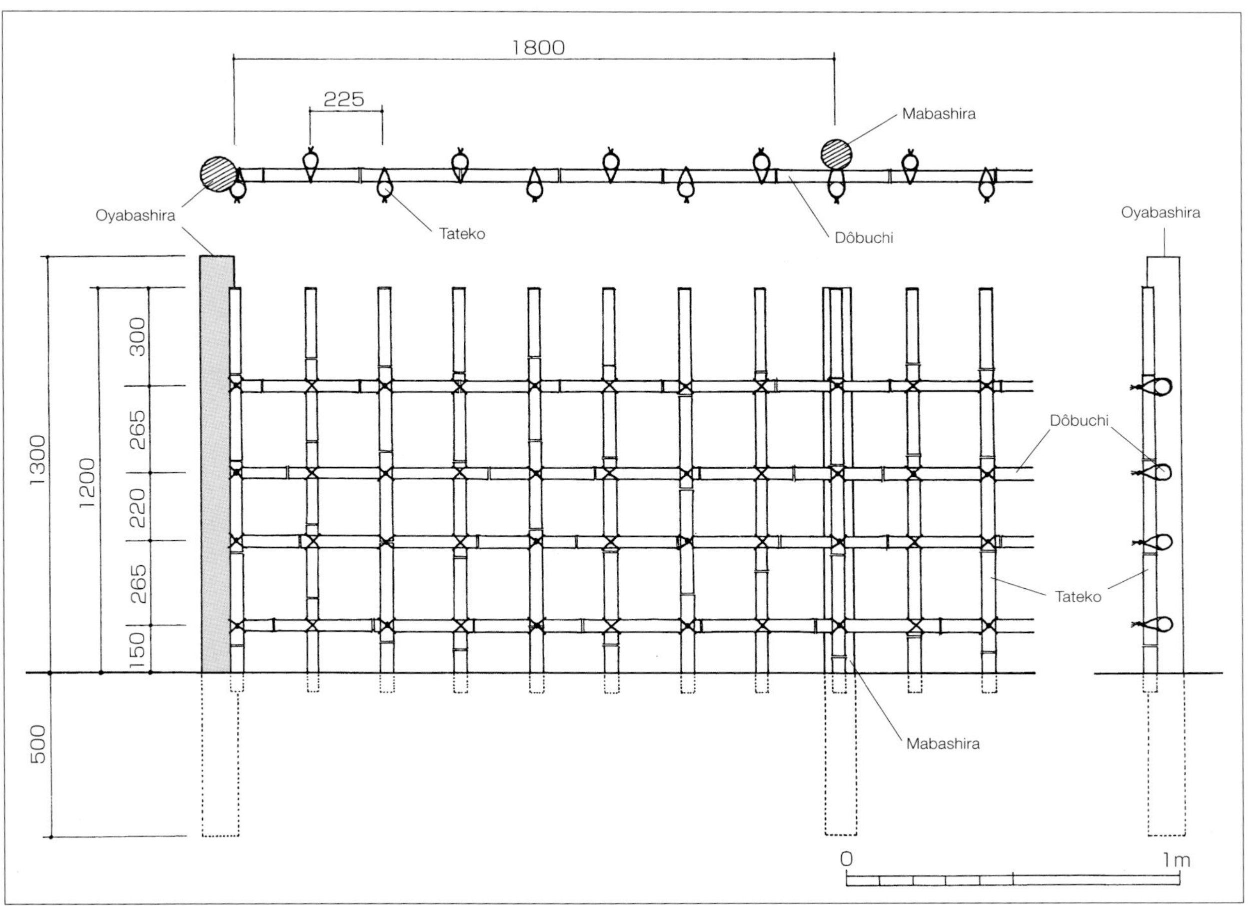

The yotsume-gaki (four-eyed fence) is the most typical see-through fence (sukashi-gaki) and probably the most widely constructed bamboo fence in Japan. The structure is quite simple with only dôbuchi placed horizontally and tateko attached on them. However, because of its simple construction, the arrangement of dôbuchi and tateko requires fine judgement and it is unexpectedly difficult to make an attractive fence. Especially as the yotsume-gaki is an essential component for a tea ceremony garden it must have not only an austere elegance but also well-ordered features.

Using gara-dake for everything except the oyabashira and the mabashira is the characteristic of yotsume-gaki, but the number of levels of dôbuchi will also affect the features greatly. These days, yotsume-gaki with three levels seem to be common but they are limited to low fences. It can be said that the traditional yotsume-gaki is with four levels as shown in the above diagram.

The spacing of the dôbuchi can be determined by your preference, but arranging the second and the third dôbuchi from the top a little closer and making a square space with tateko gives a good balance.

In the traditional yotsume-gaki, tateko poles are inserted into the ground and this is the basic rule for the fence built in a tea ceremony garden. The minimalist sense of the beauty of simplicity is reflected here. Making the length of tateko above the first dôbuchi from the top longer than the others below will give a well-balanced appearance; if the length is short, the whole fence looks tasteless.

Using gara-dake, which has a slight bend, building a yotsume-gaki is ideal for learning the basic skills of how to use bamboo like this for building a fence.

Four pieces of gara-dake with the least bend are used for the dôbuchi. When building a long yotsume-gaki, dôbuchi are extended by connecting with others on the mabashira. In the traditional method, the dôbuchi are put into the holes made on oyabashira, but recently few people employ this method.

Every tateko must be cut just above a joint at the end (fushidome), placed and then tied with a rope by ensuring that they have the least bend when viewed from the front. A special joining method using ropes called "karage shuhô" is often used here. This will be introduced later.

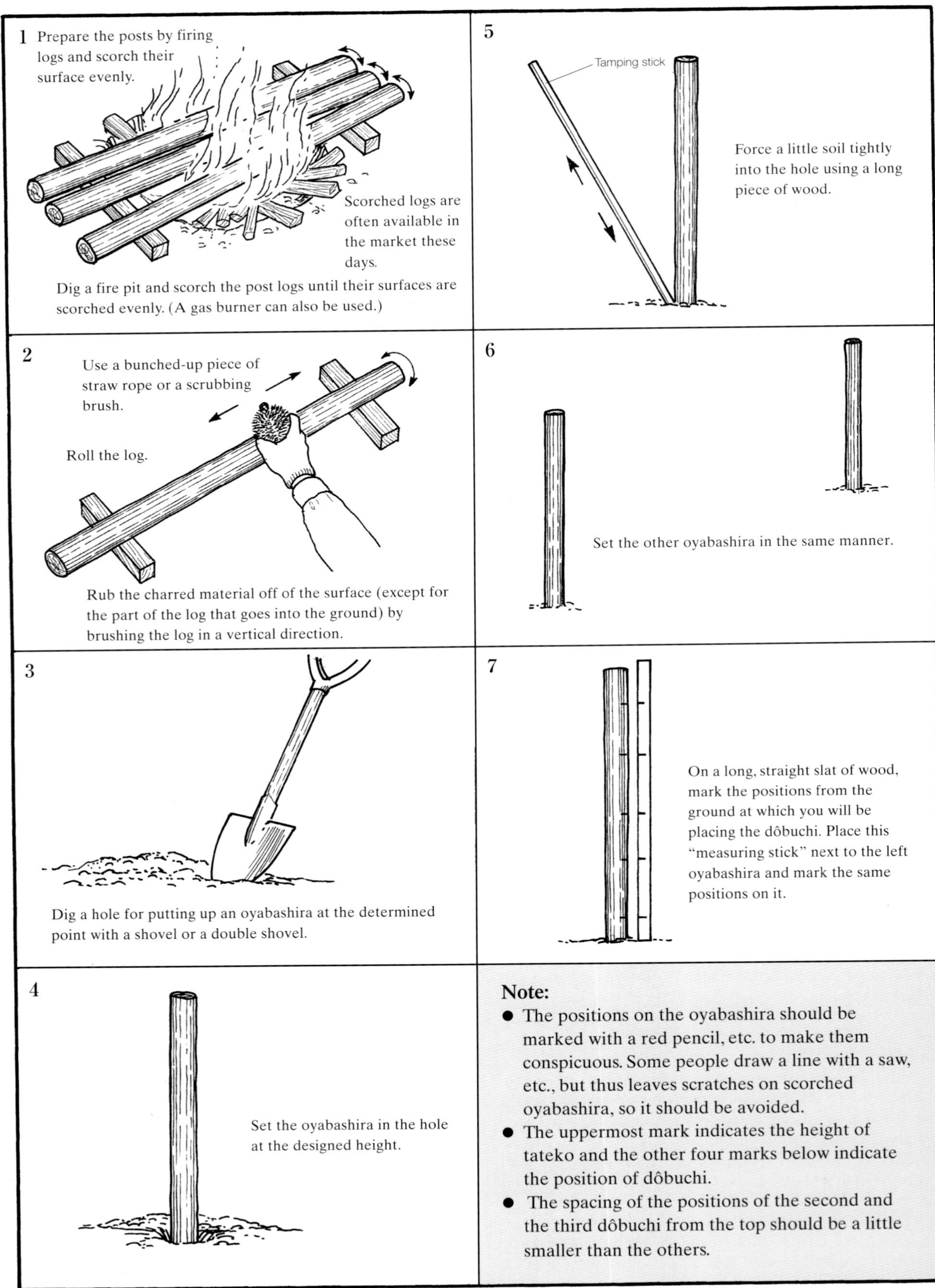
1 Prepare the posts by firing logs and scorch their surface evenly.
Scorched logs are often available in the market these days.
Dig a fire pit and scorch the post logs until their surfaces are scorched evenly. (A gas burner can also be used.)
2 Use a bunched-up piece of straw rope or a scrubbing brush.
Roll the log.
Rub the charred material off of the surface (except for the part of the log that goes into the ground) by brushing the log in a vertical direction.
3
Dig a hole for putting up an oyabashira at the determined point with a shovel or a double shovel.
4
Set the oyabashira in the hole at the designed height.
5
Tamping stick
Force a little soil tightly into the hole using a long piece of wood.
6
Set the other oyabashira in the same manner.
7
On a long, straight slat of wood, mark the positions from the ground at which you will be placing the dôbuchi. Place this "measuring stick" next to the left oyabashira and mark the same positions on it.
Note:
● The positions on the oyabashira should be marked with a red pencil, etc. to make them conspicuous. Some people draw a line with a saw, etc., but thus leaves scratches on scorched oyabashira, so it should be avoided.
● The uppermost mark indicates the height of tateko and the other four marks below indicate the position of dôbuchi.
● The spacing of the positions of the second and the third dôbuchi from the top should be a little smaller than the others.

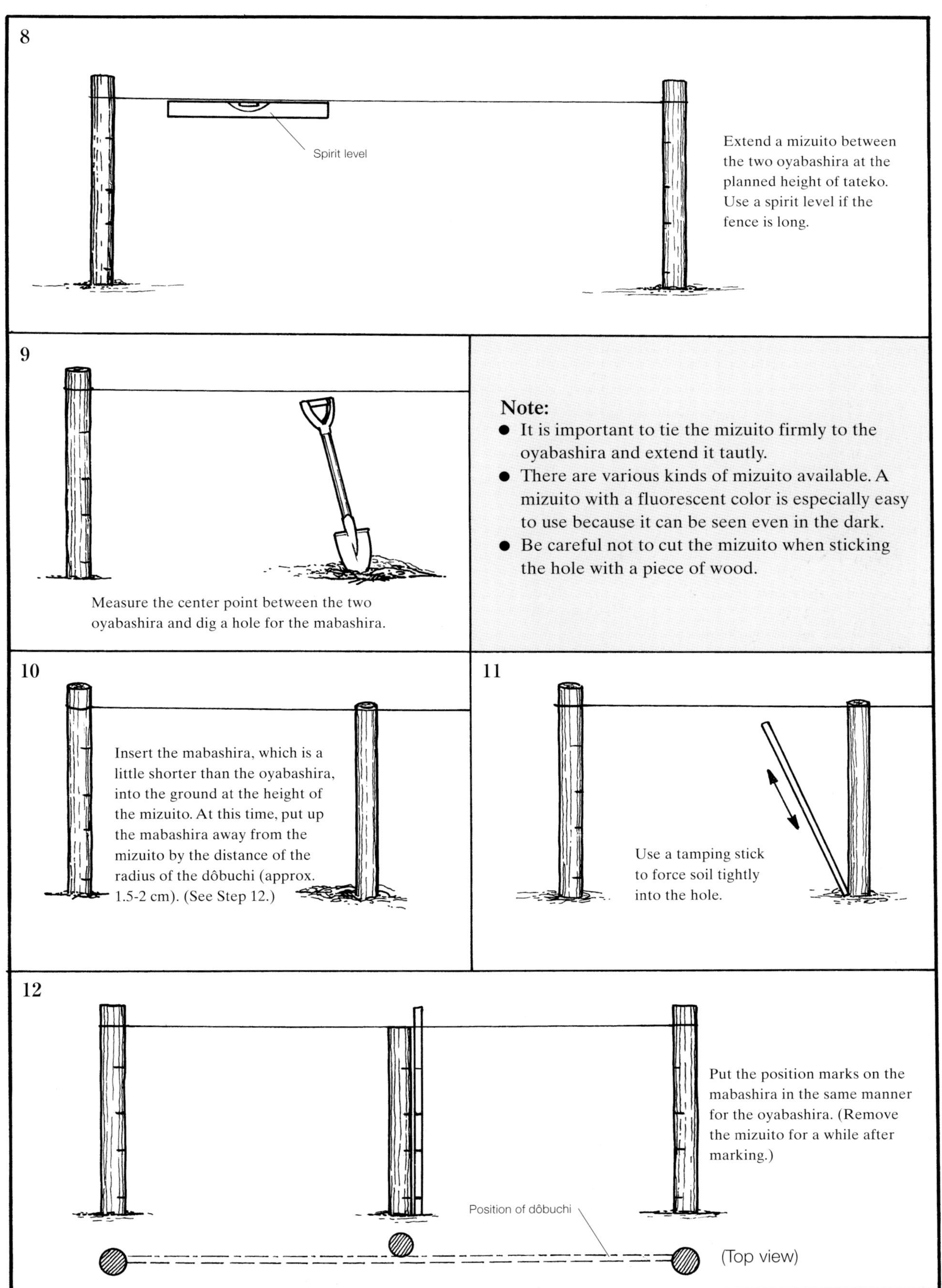

8

Extend a mizuito between the two oyabashira at the planned height of tateko. Use a spirit level if the fence is long.

9

Measure the center point between the two oyabashira and dig a hole for the mabashira.

Note:

- It is important to tie the mizuito firmly to the oyabashira and extend it tautly.
- There are various kinds of mizuito available. A mizuito with a fluorescent color is especially easy to use because it can be seen even in the dark.
- Be careful not to cut the mizuito when sticking the hole with a piece of wood.

10

Insert the mabashira, which is a little shorter than the oyabashira, into the ground at the height of the mizuito. At this time, put up the mabashira away from the mizuito by the distance of the radius of the dôbuchi (approx. 1.5-2 cm). (See Step 12.)

11

Use a tamping stick to force soil tightly into the hole.

12

Put the position marks on the mabashira in the same manner for the oyabashira. (Remove the mizuito for a while after marking.)

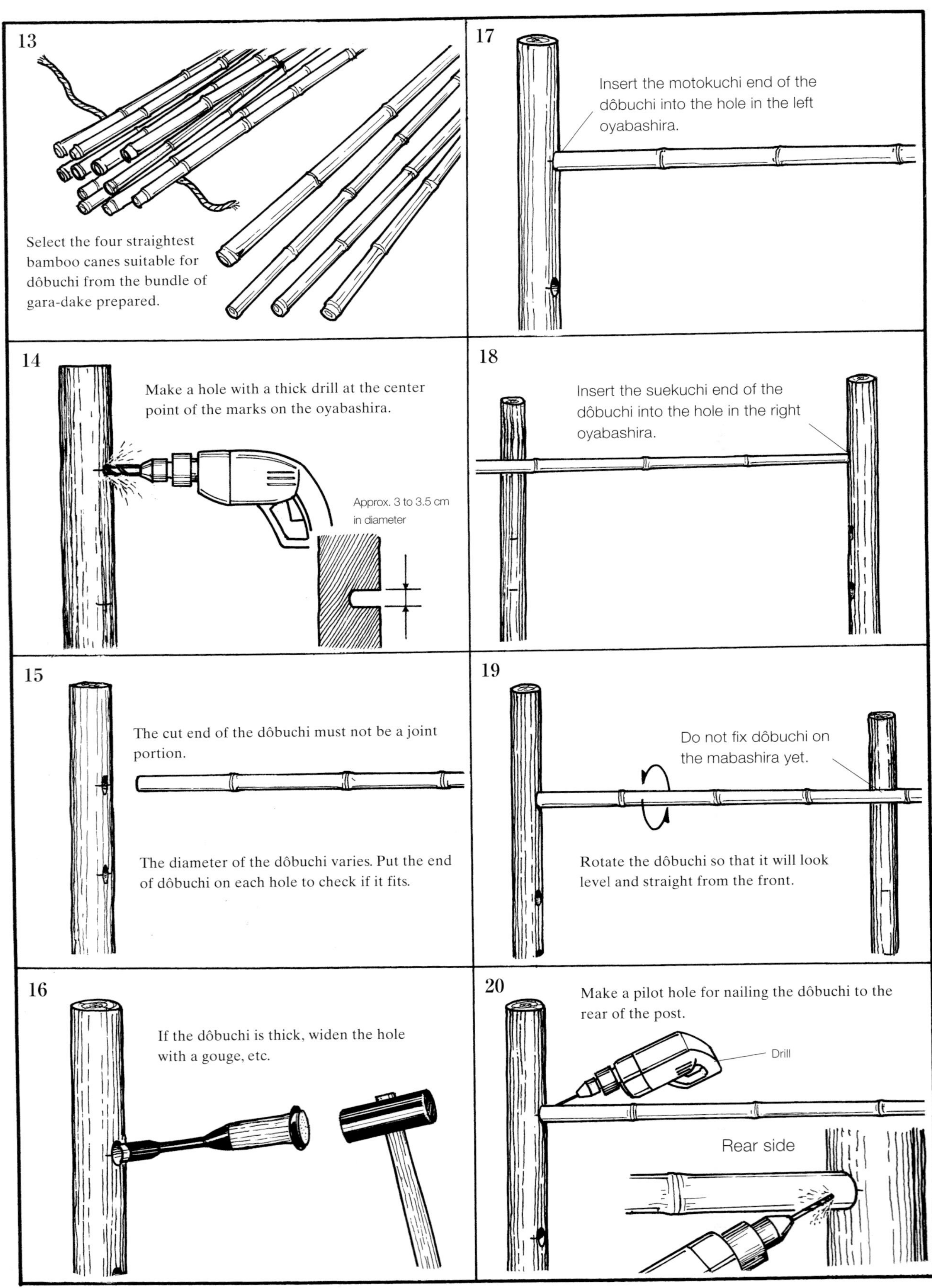
13
Select the four straightest bamboo canes suitable for dôbuchi from the bundle of gara-dake prepared.
17
Insert the motokuchi end of the dôbuchi into the hole in the left oyabashira.
14
Make a hole with a thick drill at the center point of the marks on the oyabashira.
Approx. 3 to 3.5 cm in diameter
18
Insert the suekuchi end of the dôbuchi into the hole in the right oyabashira.
15
The cut end of the dôbuchi must not be a joint portion.
The diameter of the dôbuchi varies. Put the end of dôbuchi on each hole to check if it fits.
19
Do not fix dôbuchi on the mabashira yet.
Rotate the dôbuchi so that it will look level and straight from the front.
16
If the dôbuchi is thick, widen the hole with a gouge, etc.
20
Make a pilot hole for nailing the dôbuchi to the rear of the post.
Drill
Rear side

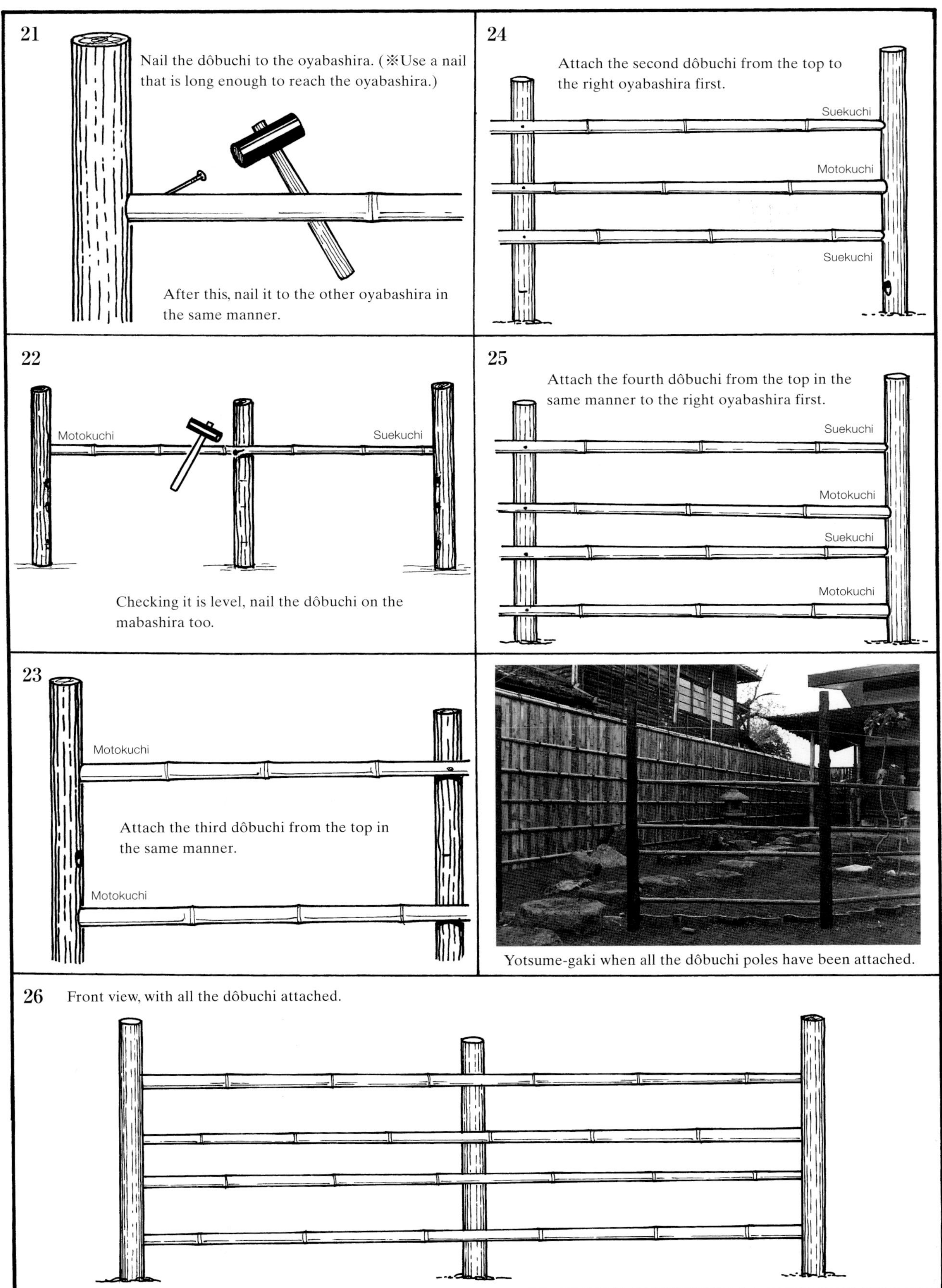
21
Nail the dôbuchi to the oyabashira. (※Use a nail that is long enough to reach the oyabashira.)
After this, nail it to the other oyabashira in the same manner.
24
Attach the second dôbuchi from the top to the right oyabashira first.
Suekuchi
Motokuchi
Suekuchi
22
Motokuchi
Suekuchi
Checking it is level, nail the dôbuchi on the mabashira too.
25
Attach the fourth dôbuchi from the top in the same manner to the right oyabashira first.
Suekuchi
Motokuchi
Suekuchi
Motokuchi
23
Motokuchi
Attach the third dôbuchi from the top in the same manner.
Motokuchi
26
Front view, with all the dôbuchi attached.

Yotsume-gaki when all the dôbuchi poles have been attached.

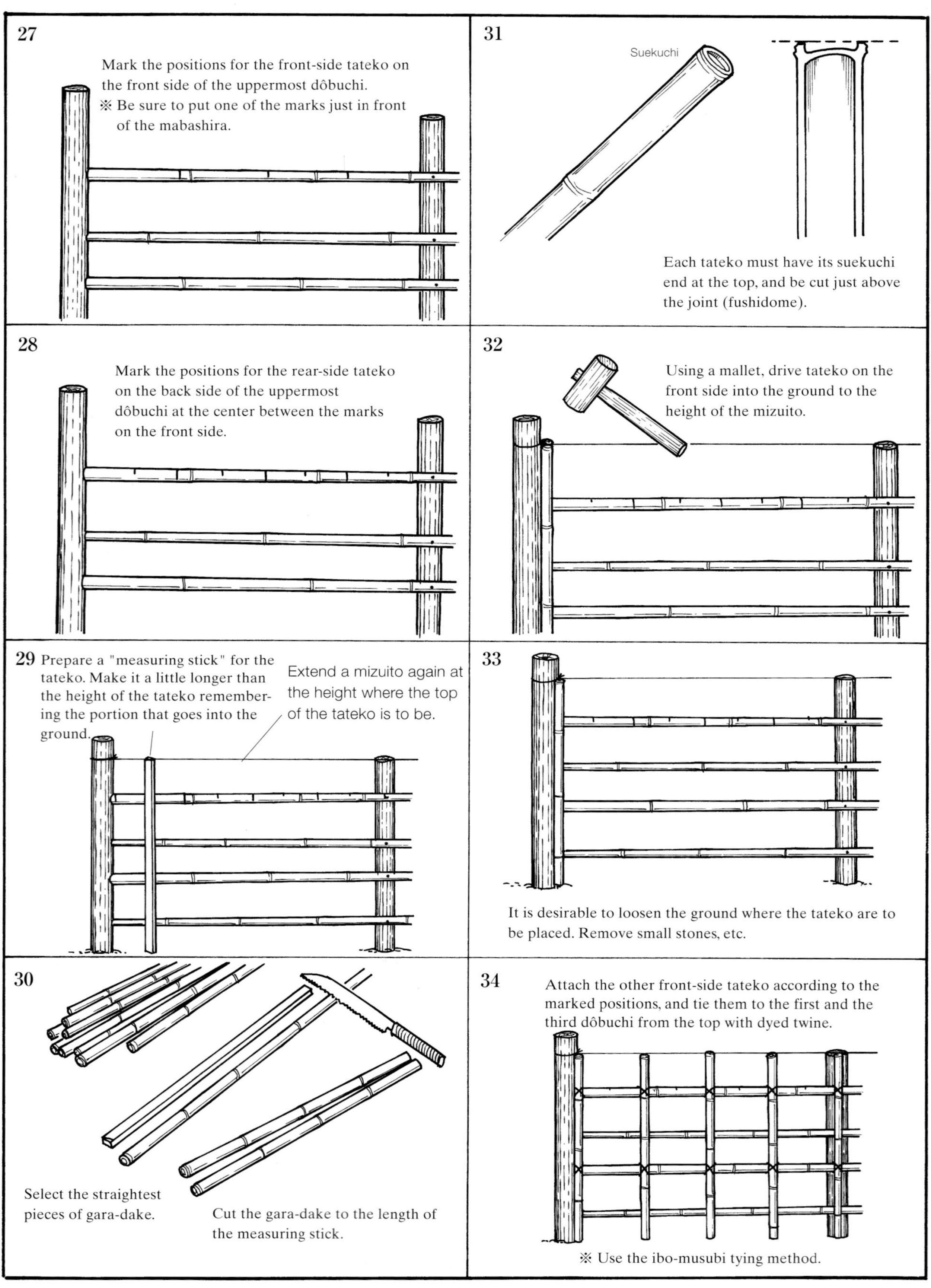
27
Mark the positions for the front-side tateko on the front side of the uppermost dôbuchi.
※ Be sure to put one of the marks just in front of the mabashira.
28
Mark the positions for the rear-side tateko on the back side of the uppermost dôbuchi at the center between the marks on the front side.
29 Prepare a "measuring stick" for the tateko. Make it a little longer than the height of the tateko remembering the portion that goes into the ground.
Extend a mizuito again at the height where the top of the tateko is to be.
30
Select the straightest pieces of gara-dake.
Cut the gara-dake to the length of the measuring stick.
31
Suekuchi
Each tateko must have its suekuchi end at the top, and be cut just above the joint (fushidome).
32
Using a mallet, drive tateko on the front side into the ground to the height of the mizuito.
33
It is desirable to loosen the ground where the tateko are to be placed. Remove small stones, etc.
34
Attach the other front-side tateko according to the marked positions, and tie them to the first and the third dôbuchi from the top with dyed twine.
※ Use the ibo-musubi tying method.

35

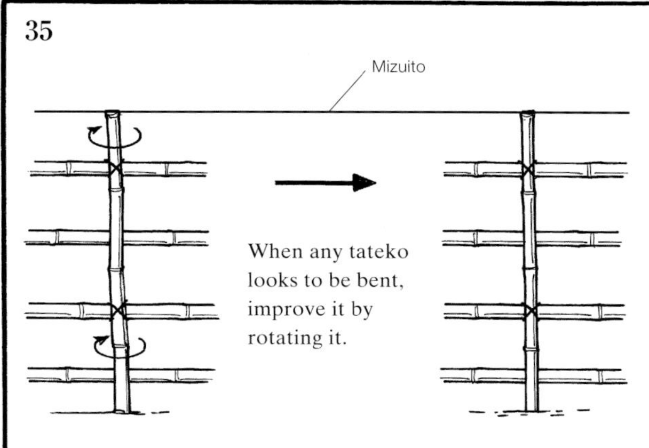

When any tateko looks to be bent, improve it by rotating it.

Note:

- There is brown twine and black twine that is made by dyeing the brown twine with carbon black. Be sure to use the dyed twine for the finishing rope tying.
- The dyed twine must be used after it is soaked in water for a few minutes. This is for the purpose of softening the twine and making it easy to tie as well as removing excessive ink.
- The thickness of the dyed twine varies. Dyed twine with a normal thickness is usually used in two strings together.

36

Process of ibo-musubi tying

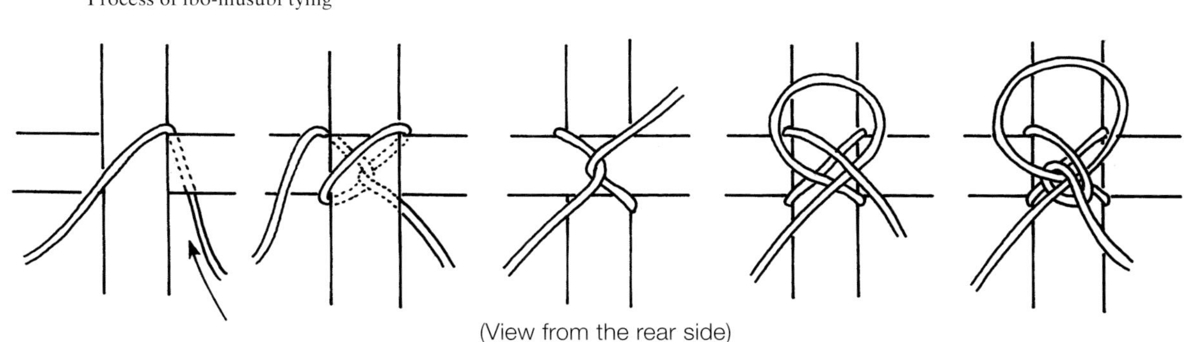

(View from the rear side)

37 Put up and tie the rear-side tateko in the same manner.

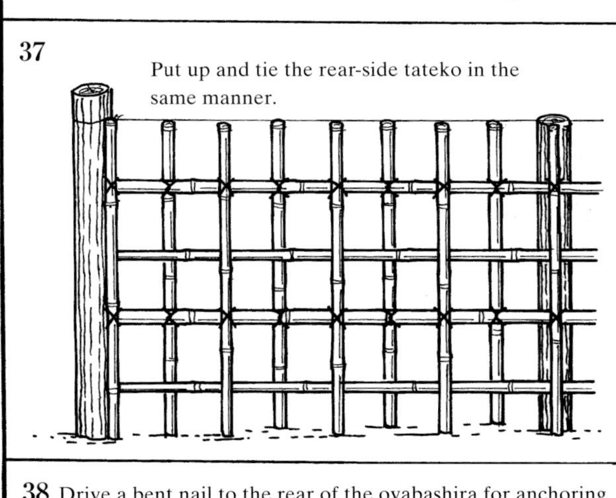

39 Normally, two pieces of dyed twine are strung together.

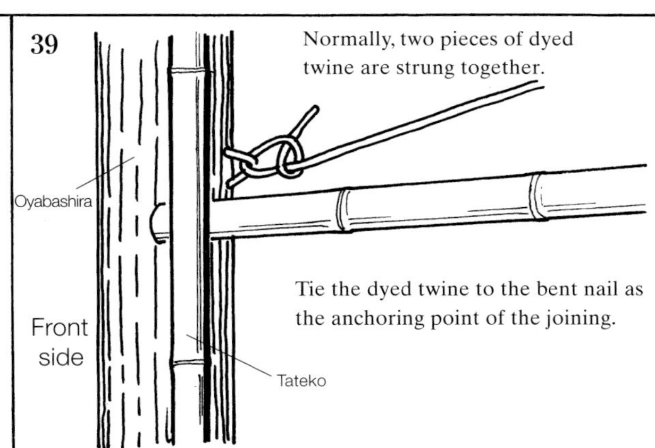

Tie the dyed twine to the bent nail as the anchoring point of the joining.

38 Drive a bent nail to the rear of the oyabashira for anchoring the twine for joining the second and fourth dôbuchi from the top with the tateko.

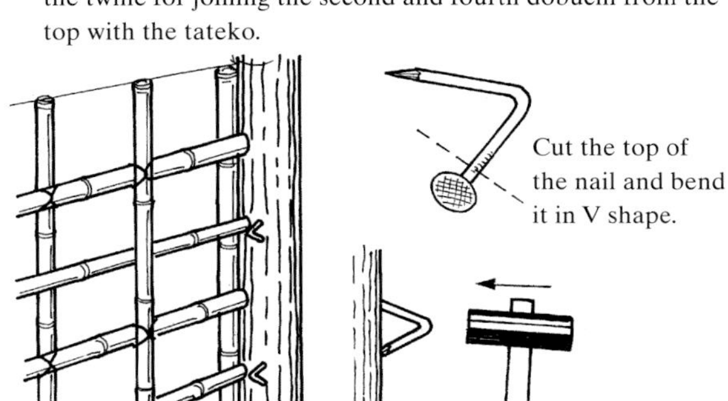

Cut the top of the nail and bend it in V shape.

40

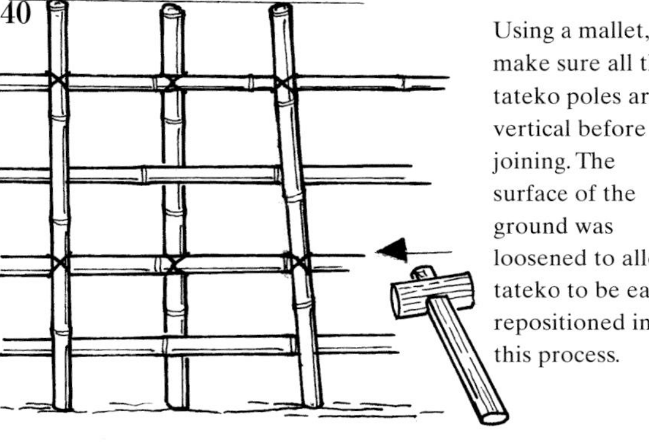

Using a mallet, make sure all the tateko poles are vertical before the joining. The surface of the ground was loosened to allow tateko to be easily repositioned in this process.

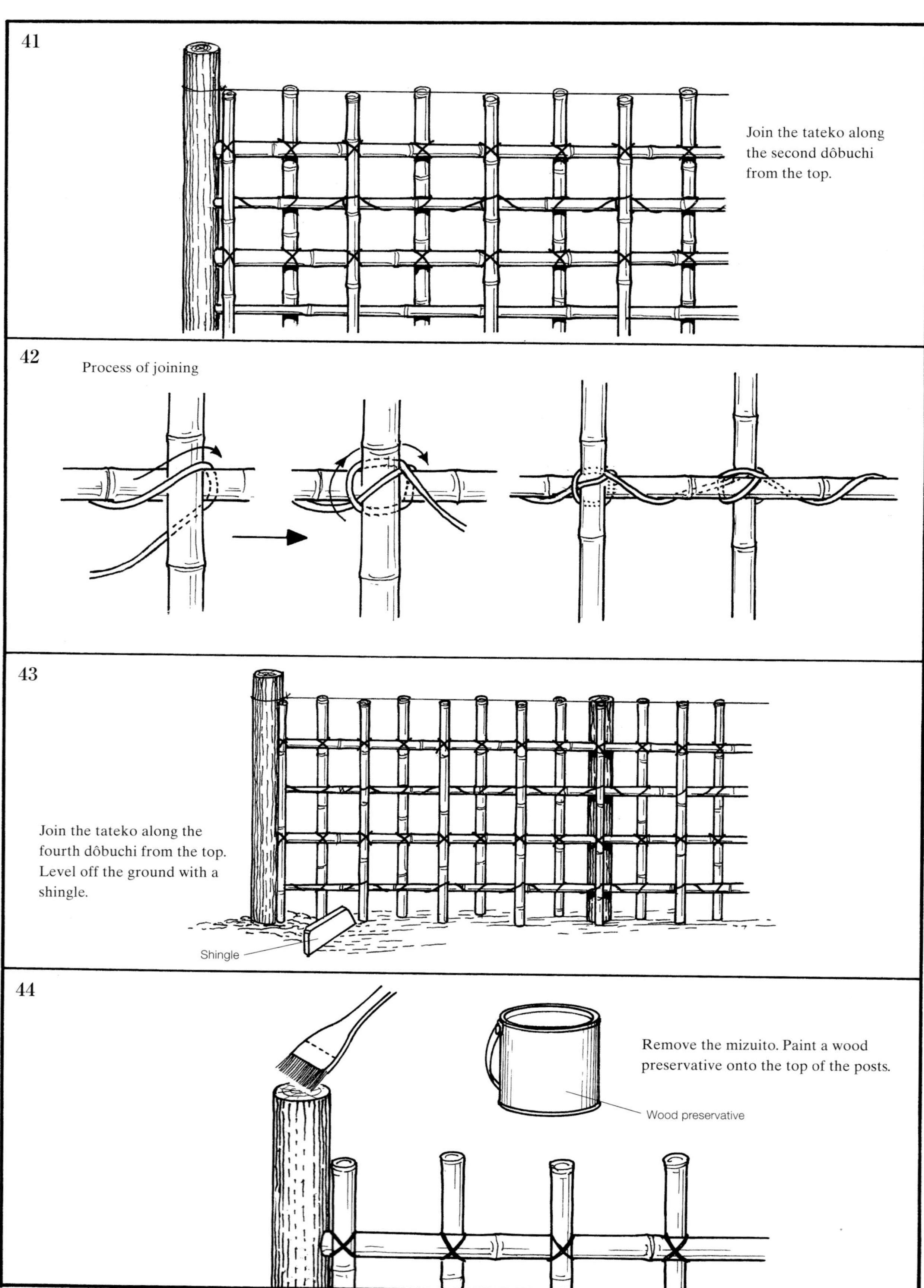
41
Join the tateko along the second dôbuchi from the top.
42
Process of joining
43
Join the tateko along the fourth dôbuchi from the top. Level off the ground with a shingle.
Shingle
44
Remove the mizuito. Paint a wood preservative onto the top of the posts.
Wood preservative

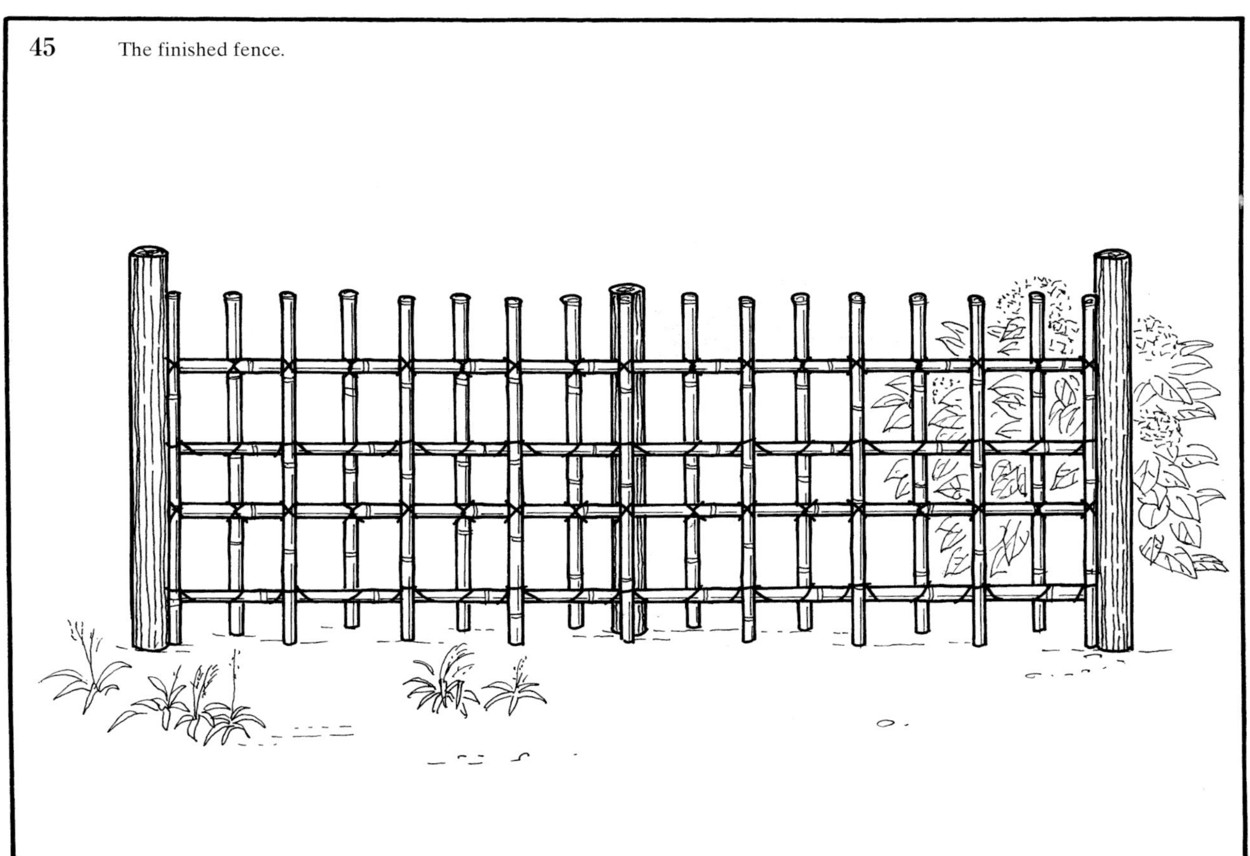

45 The finished fence.

Kinkakuji-gaki

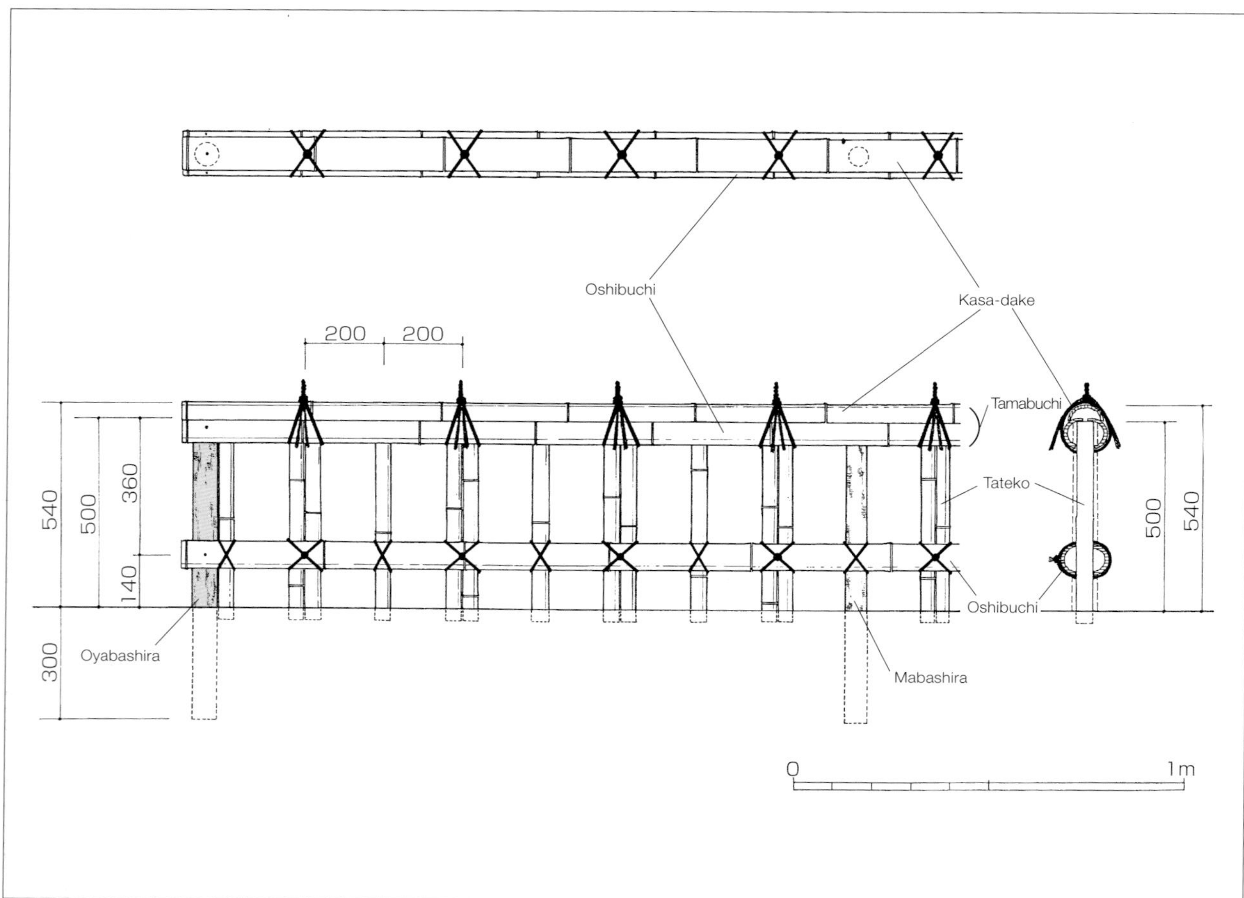

Kinkakuji-gaki is the most popular foot-level fence (ashimoto-gaki) and is known as a very strong fence.

There are several features in kinkakuji-gaki, such as that both oyabashira and mabashira are put up on the same center line of the fence at the same height of tateko, and that oshibuchi are used for a structural component instead of dôbuchi.

Rather thick round bamboo (five to six centimeters in diameter) are used for tateko, and they are put up in the center line of the fence. There are two ways of arranging tateko: one in which only a single tateko is used, and the other in which paired tateko are added for a variation as shown in the above illustration. In addition, there are cases in which the first tateko is put up right next to the oyabashira as illustrated above, and cases in which it is put up at a little distance from the oyabashira.

Tateko in the kinkakuji-gaki are short, so each of them should have the same thickness at the top and bottom ends. When only single tateko are used, they should be put up with the suekuchi end at the top. When tateko are used in pairs, one pole of each pair should be put up with the suekuchi end at the top and the other with the suekuchi end at the bottom for making an even width.

Oshibuchi, which are made by splitting relatively thick bamboo canes in half, are attached relatively near the ground both on the front and rear sides. Oshibuchi should be cut just above a joint (fushidome), and the motokuchi end should be attached to the oyabashira. Oshibuchi on the rear side should be attached in the same manner using the same split bamboo of the oshibuchi on the front side. Oshibuchi are attached with their ends sticking out a little from the oyabashira, and they hold the fence from both sides including the tateko and mabashira. When the oyabashira are thicker than the tateko, there will be a gap between the oshibuchi and the tateko. In order to hold all of the tateko, the inner parts of the oshibuchi are shaved into a curved line, and it is nailed to the oyabashira and the mabashira.

The upper oshibuchi is also attached to the motokuchi end at the oyabashira. At this time, the upper oshibuchi is put somewhat like being hung on the top of the tateko at a slant as shown in the diagram. If there are joints of the oshibuchi that interfere with the top of tateko, the joint portions can be removed. Kasa-dake, which is also of a thick split bamboo, is placed to cover the oshibuchi, forming the tamabuchi of the fence. Rope tying at the crossings of the lower oshibuchi and each tateko should be made by turns on the front and rear sides.

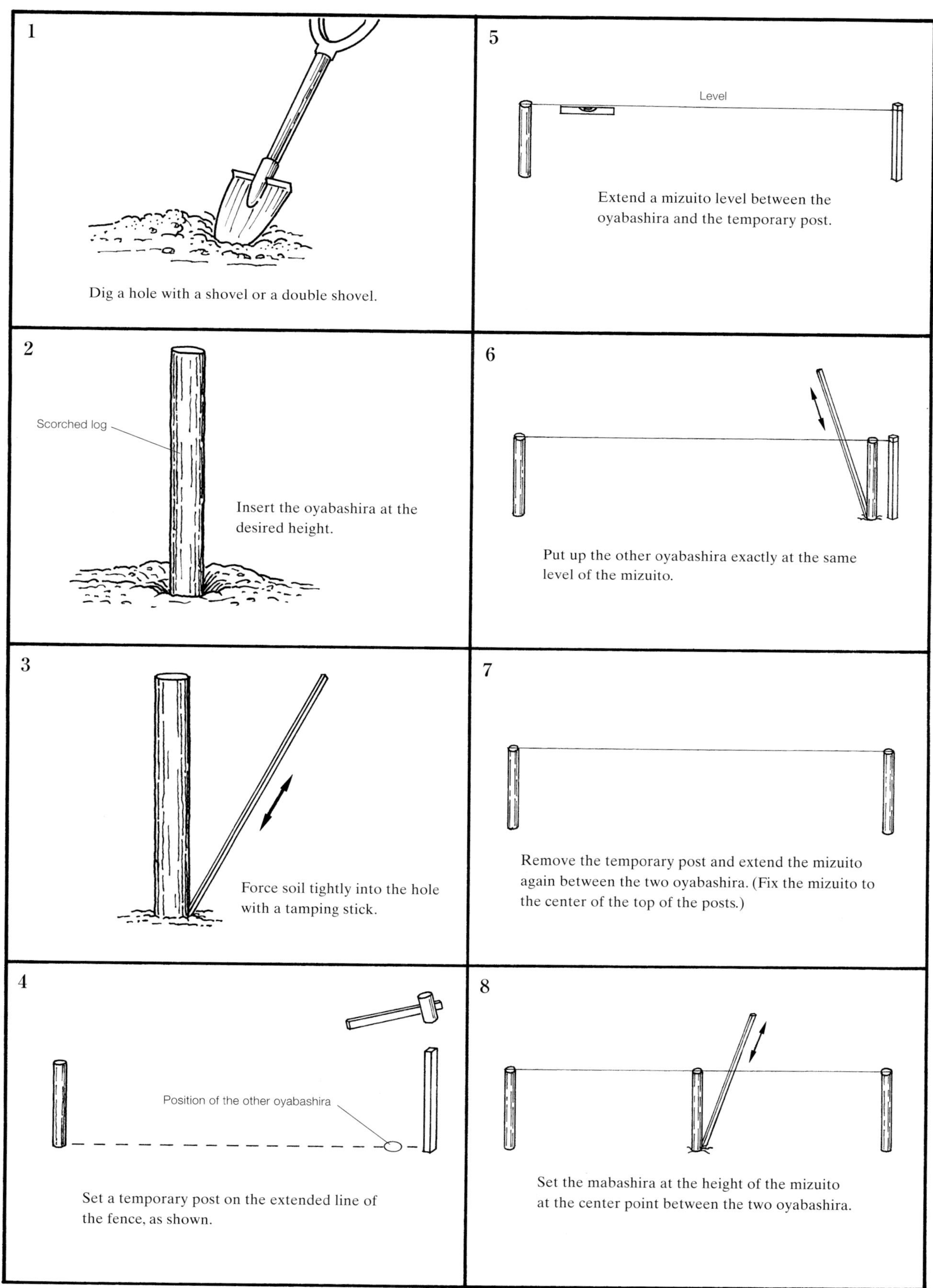

1 Dig a hole with a shovel or a double shovel.

2 Insert the oyabashira at the desired height.

3 Force soil tightly into the hole with a tamping stick.

4 Set a temporary post on the extended line of the fence, as shown.

5 Extend a mizuito level between the oyabashira and the temporary post.

6 Put up the other oyabashira exactly at the same level of the mizuito.

7 Remove the temporary post and extend the mizuito again between the two oyabashira. (Fix the mizuito to the center of the top of the posts.)

8 Set the mabashira at the height of the mizuito at the center point between the two oyabashira.

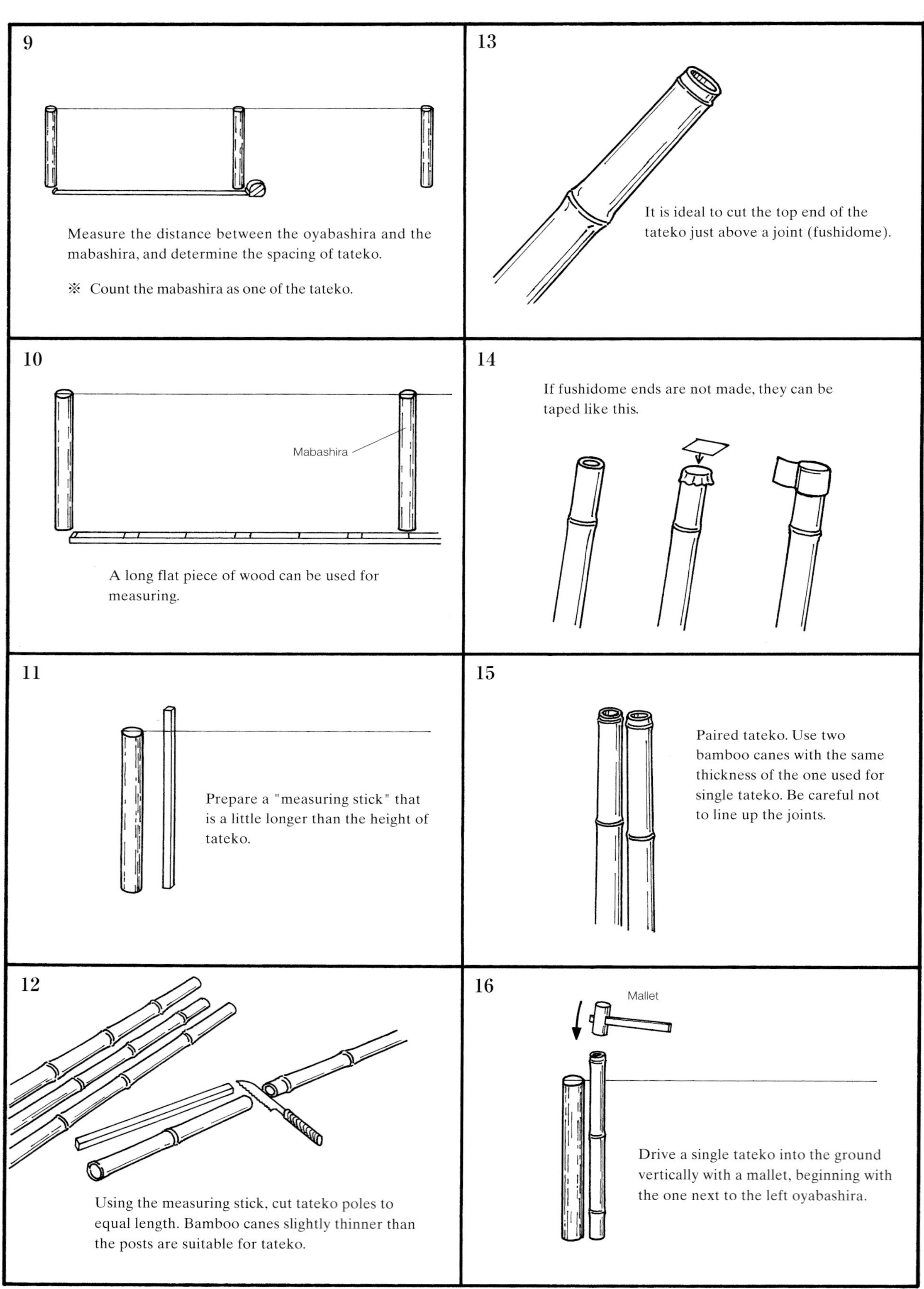
9
Measure the distance between the oyabashira and the mabashira, and determine the spacing of tateko.
※ Count the mabashira as one of the tateko.
10
Mabashira
A long flat piece of wood can be used for measuring.
11
Prepare a "measuring stick" that is a little longer than the height of tateko.
12
Using the measuring stick, cut tateko poles to equal length. Bamboo canes slightly thinner than the posts are suitable for tateko.
13
It is ideal to cut the top end of the tateko just above a joint (fushidome).
14
If fushidome ends are not made, they can be taped like this.
15
Paired tateko. Use two bamboo canes with the same thickness of the one used for single tateko. Be careful not to line up the joints.
16
Mallet
Drive a single tateko into the ground vertically with a mallet, beginning with the one next to the left oyabashira.

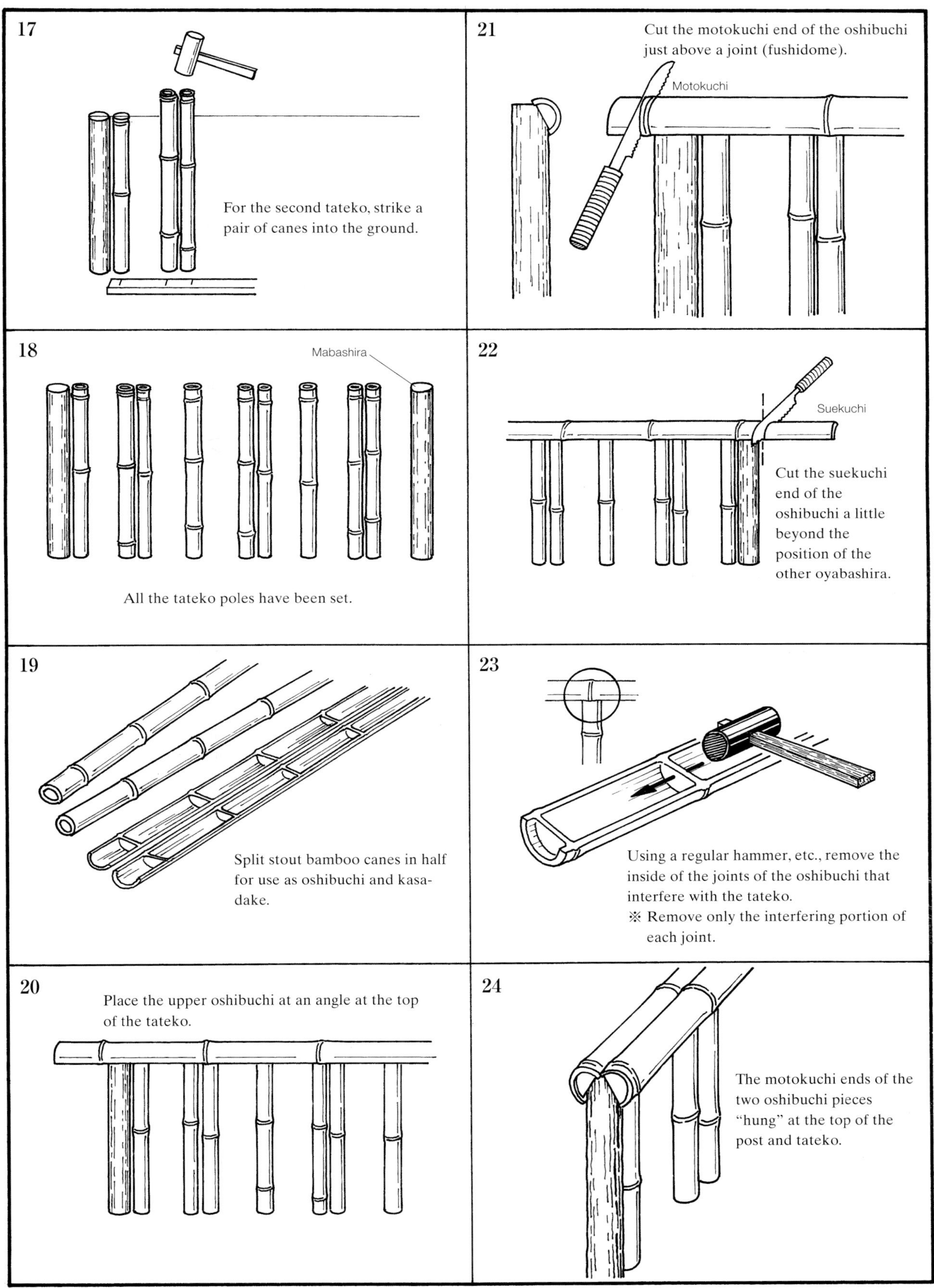
17
For the second tateko, strike a pair of canes into the ground.
18
Mabashira
All the tateko poles have been set.
19
Split stout bamboo canes in half for use as oshibuchi and kasa-dake.
20
Place the upper oshibuchi at an angle at the top of the tateko.
21
Cut the motokuchi end of the oshibuchi just above a joint (fushidome).
Motokuchi
22
Suekuchi
Cut the suekuchi end of the oshibuchi a little beyond the position of the other oyabashira.
23
Using a regular hammer, etc., remove the inside of the joints of the oshibuchi that interfere with the tateko.
※ Remove only the interfering portion of each joint.
24
The motokuchi ends of the two oshibuchi pieces "hung" at the top of the post and tateko.

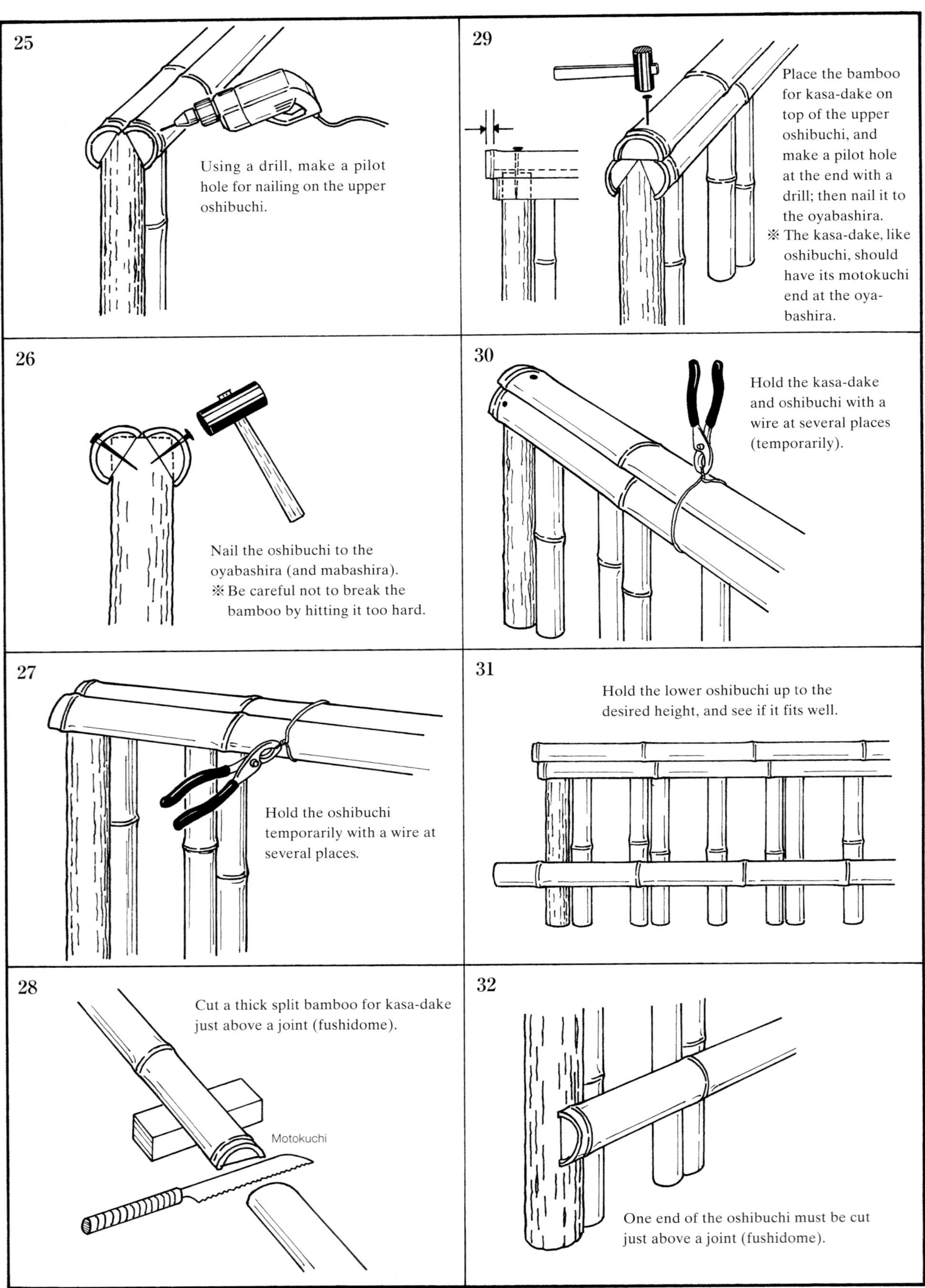
25
Using a drill, make a pilot hole for nailing on the upper oshibuchi.
29
Place the bamboo for kasa-dake on top of the upper oshibuchi, and make a pilot hole at the end with a drill; then nail it to the oyabashira.
※ The kasa-dake, like oshibuchi, should have its motokuchi end at the oya-bashira.
26
Nail the oshibuchi to the oyabashira (and mabashira).
※ Be careful not to break the bamboo by hitting it too hard.
30
Hold the kasa-dake and oshibuchi with a wire at several places (temporarily).
27
Hold the oshibuchi temporarily with a wire at several places.
31
Hold the lower oshibuchi up to the desired height, and see if it fits well.
28
Cut a thick split bamboo for kasa-dake just above a joint (fushidome).
Motokuchi
32
One end of the oshibuchi must be cut just above a joint (fushidome).

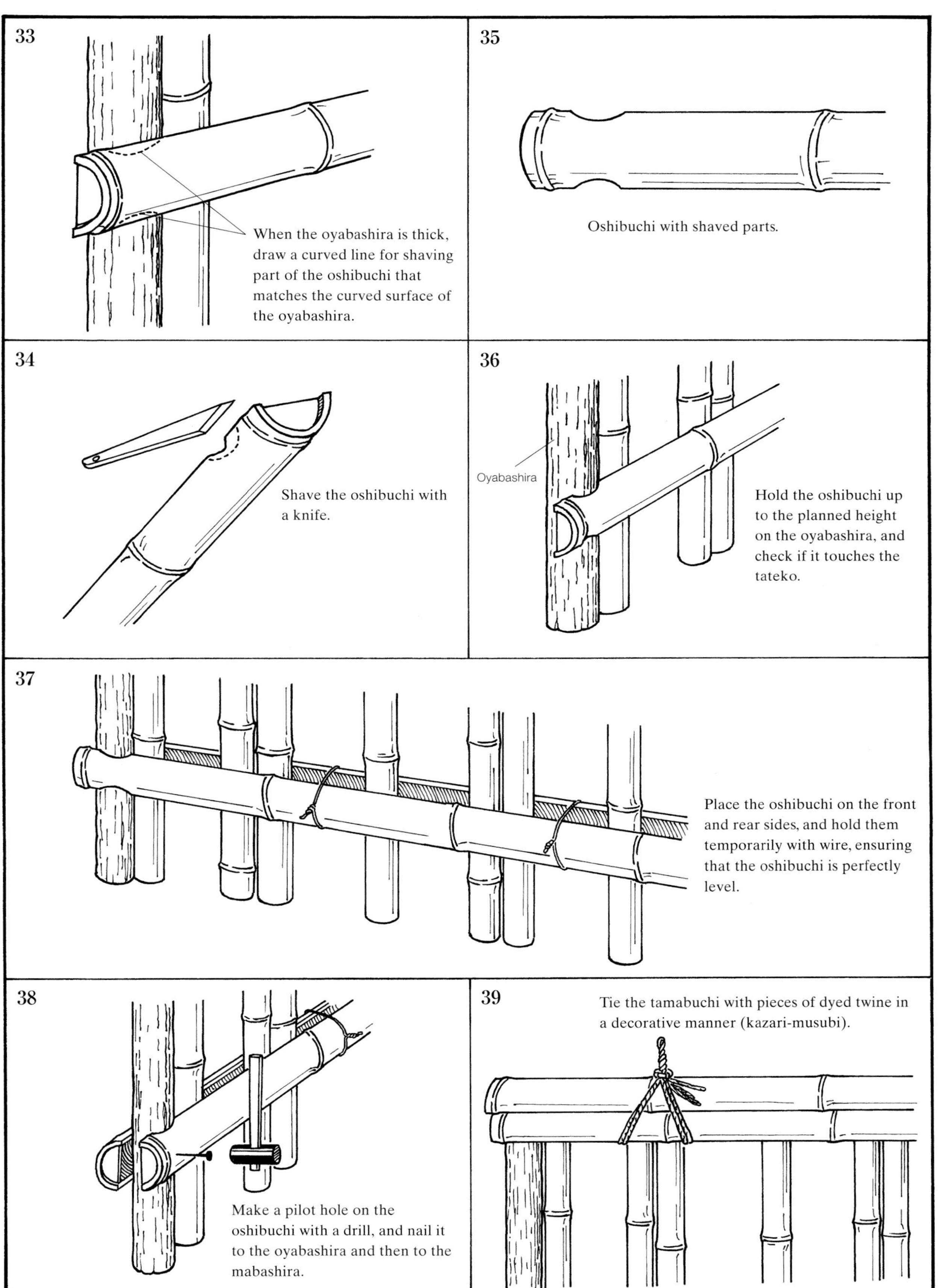
33
When the oyabashira is thick, draw a curved line for shaving part of the oshibuchi that matches the curved surface of the oyabashira.
35
Oshibuchi with shaved parts.
34
Shave the oshibuchi with a knife.
36
Oyabashira
Hold the oshibuchi up to the planned height on the oyabashira, and check if it touches the tateko.
37
Place the oshibuchi on the front and rear sides, and hold them temporarily with wire, ensuring that the oshibuchi is perfectly level.
38
Make a pilot hole on the oshibuchi with a drill, and nail it to the oyabashira and then to the mabashira.
39
Tie the tamabuchi with pieces of dyed twine in a decorative manner (kazari-musubi).

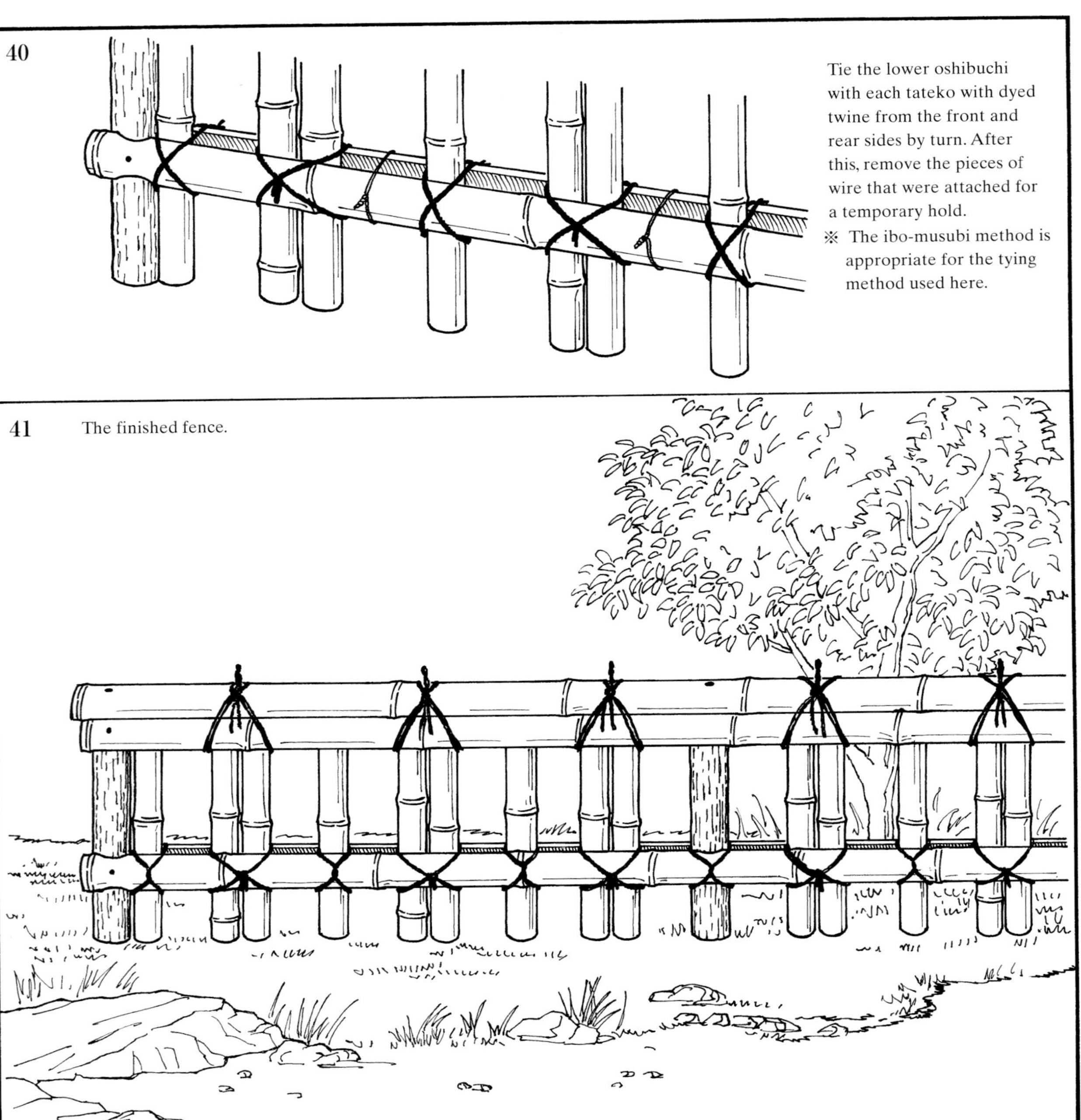

40

Tie the lower oshibuchi with each tateko with dyed twine from the front and rear sides by turn. After this, remove the pieces of wire that were attached for a temporary hold.

※ The ibo-musubi method is appropriate for the tying method used here.

41 The finished fence.

Yarai-gaki (stockade fence)

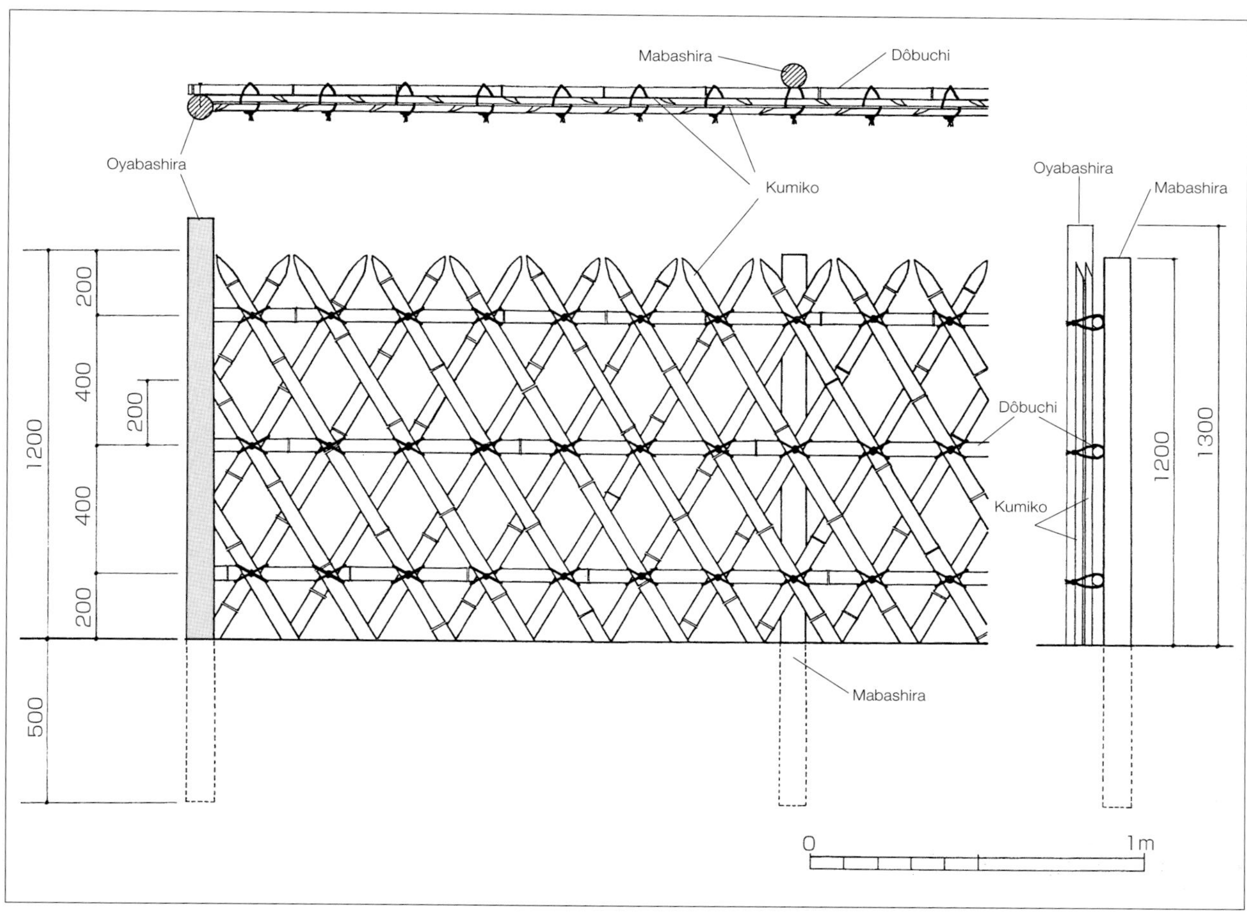

The yarai-gaki (stockade fence) is the oldest type of bamboo fence in Japan. Low yarai-gaki are popular in the Kansai area, and high fences like the one in the above illustration are often seen in the Kantô area. Kumiko of split bamboo are attached to the dôbuchi diagonally. Gara-dake is used for the dôbuchi. Dôbuchi are cut just above a joint (fushidome) and nailed directly to the rear of the oyabashira. The mabashira is put up behind the dôbuchi, and the dôbuchi is nailed to the mabashira on the front side.

There are usually three, or sometimes two levels of dôbuchi. Many of the low yarai-gaki are made with two levels.

Bamboo canes of five to six centimeters in diameter are split in half for kumiko. Kumiko are cut taking their angle into account. The suekuchi end of each kumiko should be cut to be sharp-pointed in the same fashion, but it should not be too acute. The length of kumiko should be a little longer considering the motokuchi end portion that goes into the ground.

The angle of kumiko can be determined by your preference but sixty degrees is considered to be ideal to make a fence seen the most beautiful. A certain numerical formula for the spacing of kumiko with an angel of sixty degrees has been worked out by the author. With this formula, the kumiko can be easily placed by anyone.

Calculating the center-to-center distance of two dôbuchi (the upper and middle dôbuchi, for example) and dividing it in two makes the figure X. With the formula, X × 1.16 = Y, you can obtain the value of Y, which indicates the spacing of kumiko on the dôbuchi.

Please refer to page 120 for specific details about how the formula is used.

There are kumiko attached on the rear side and the front side; here, the kumiko which slant in upper right direction are attached on the rear side and upper left direction on the front side. When they are placed accurately according to the position marks, the kumiko are held tightly with wire at the intersections with dôbuchi. The dôbuchi and two kumiko are tied together at these intersections, so that the intersections along the upper dôbuchi especially must be fastened tightly. The fence is finished with dyed twine tied on the wire.

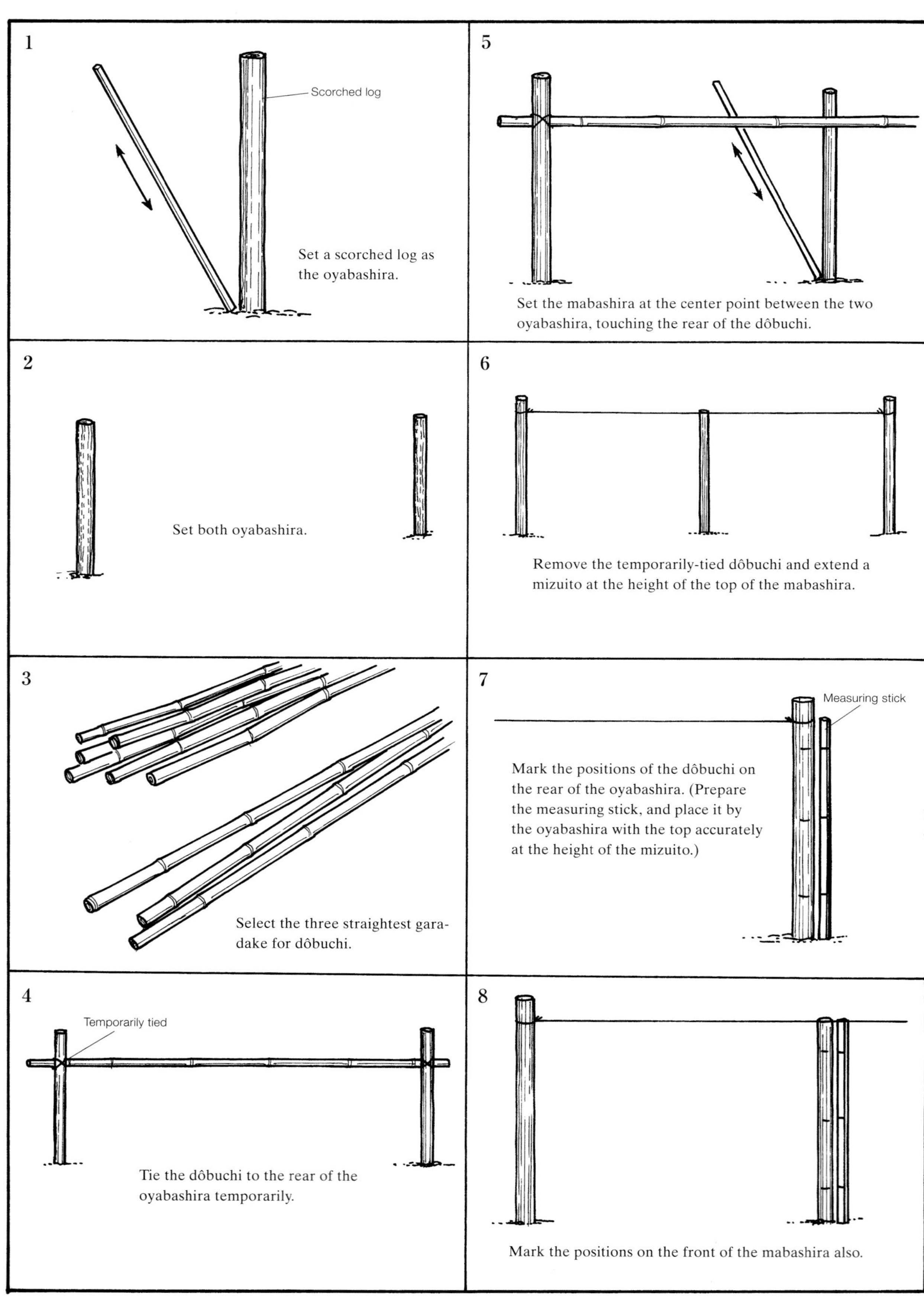
1
Scorched log
Set a scorched log as the oyabashira.
2
Set both oyabashira.
3
Select the three straightest gara-dake for dôbuchi.
4
Temporarily tied
Tie the dôbuchi to the rear of the oyabashira temporarily.
5
Set the mabashira at the center point between the two oyabashira, touching the rear of the dôbuchi.
6
Remove the temporarily-tied dôbuchi and extend a mizuito at the height of the top of the mabashira.
7
Measuring stick
Mark the positions of the dôbuchi on the rear of the oyabashira. (Prepare the measuring stick, and place it by the oyabashira with the top accurately at the height of the mizuito.)
8
Mark the positions on the front of the mabashira also.

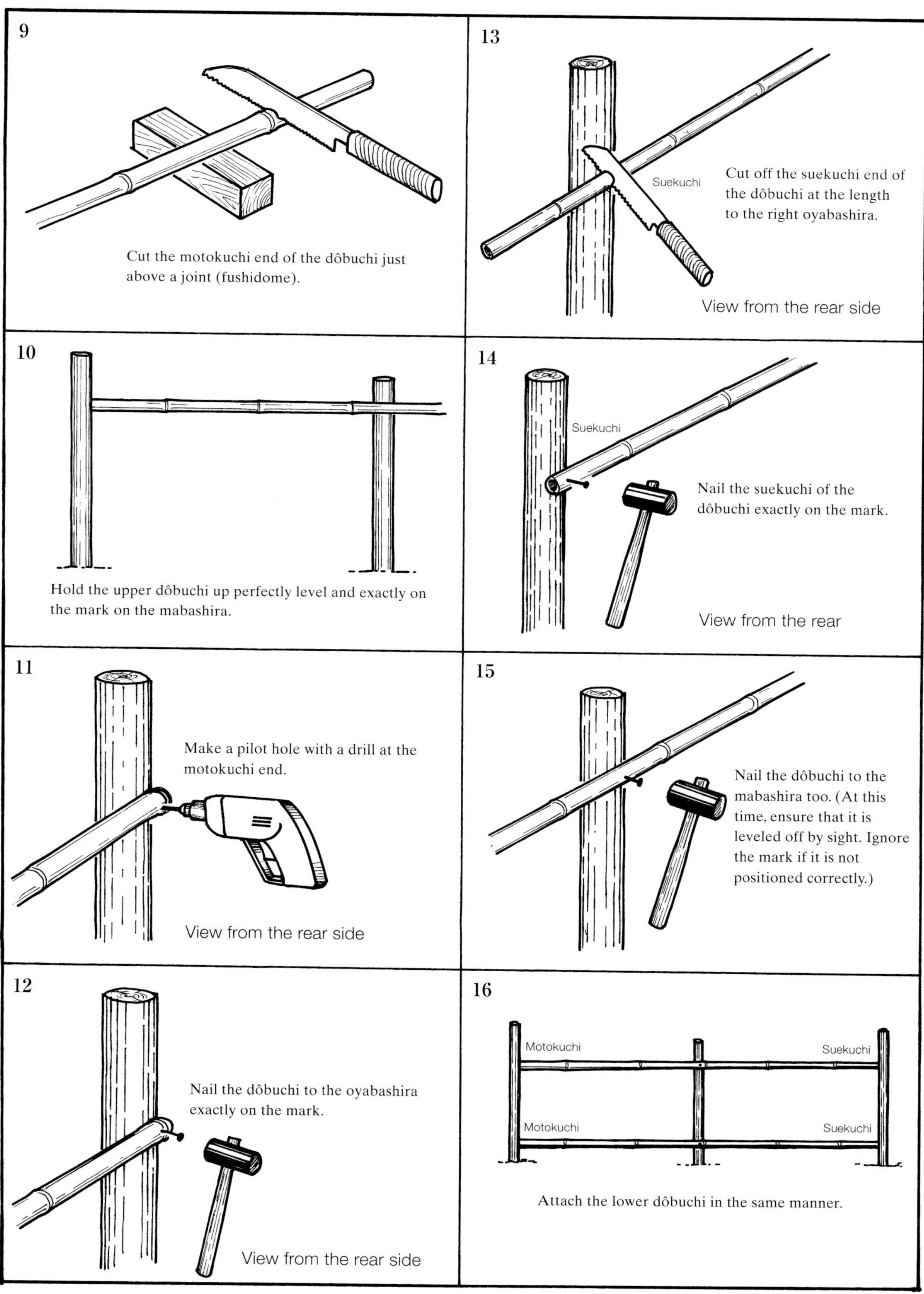

9 Cut the motokuchi end of the dôbuchi just above a joint (fushidome).

10 Hold the upper dôbuchi up perfectly level and exactly on the mark on the mabashira.

11 Make a pilot hole with a drill at the motokuchi end.

12 Nail the dôbuchi to the oyabashira exactly on the mark.

13 Cut off the suekuchi end of the dôbuchi at the length to the right oyabashira.

14 Nail the suekuchi of the dôbuchi exactly on the mark.

15 Nail the dôbuchi to the mabashira too. (At this time, ensure that it is leveled off by sight. Ignore the mark if it is not positioned correctly.)

16 Attach the lower dôbuchi in the same manner.

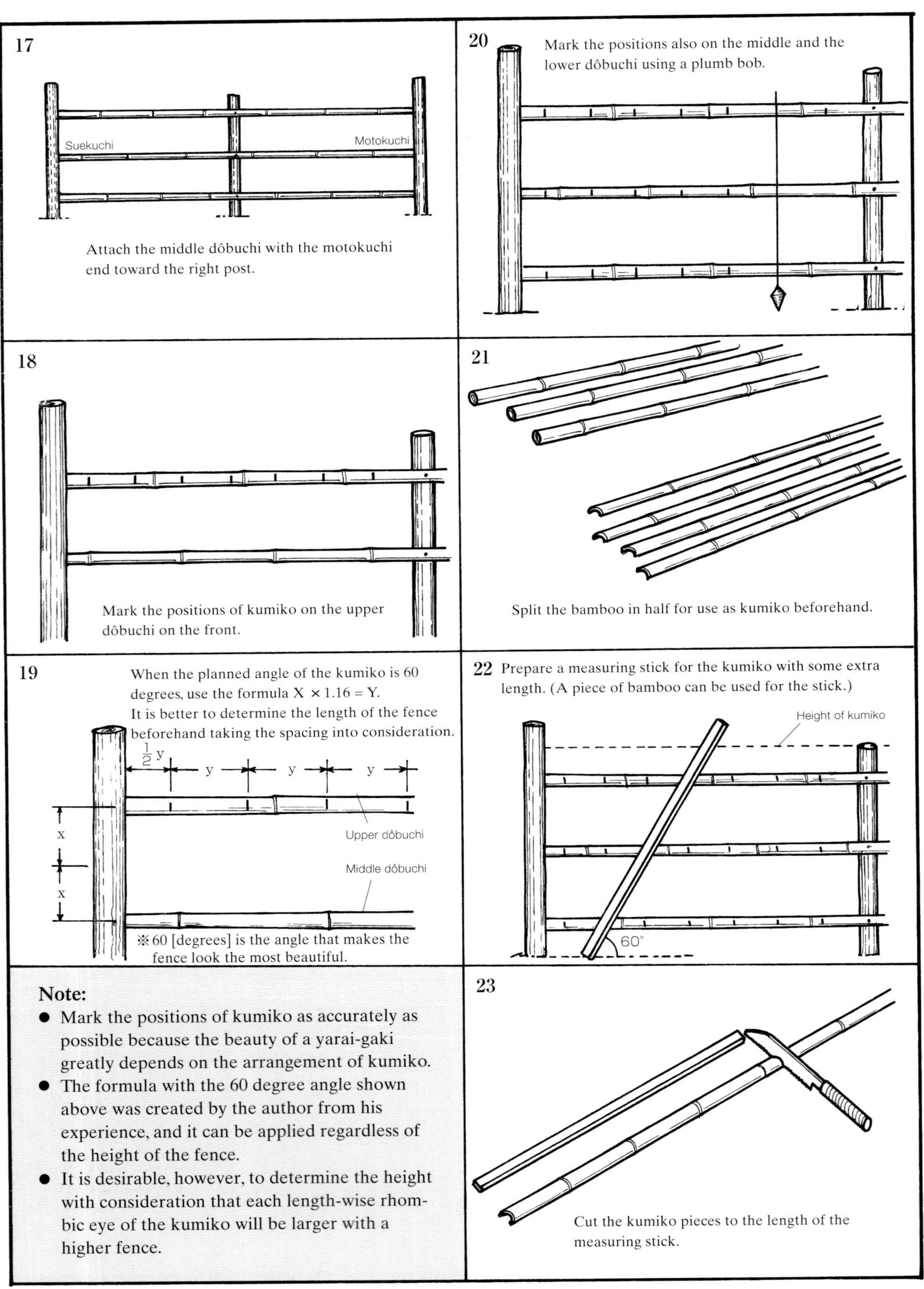
17
Suekuchi
Motokuchi
Attach the middle dôbuchi with the motokuchi end toward the right post.
20
Mark the positions also on the middle and the lower dôbuchi using a plumb bob.
18
Mark the positions of kumiko on the upper dôbuchi on the front.
21
Split the bamboo in half for use as kumiko beforehand.
19
When the planned angle of the kumiko is 60 degrees, use the formula X × 1.16 = Y.
It is better to determine the length of the fence beforehand taking the spacing into consideration.
1/2 y
y
y
y
x
x
Upper dôbuchi
Middle dôbuchi
※60 [degrees] is the angle that makes the fence look the most beautiful.
22
Prepare a measuring stick for the kumiko with some extra length. (A piece of bamboo can be used for the stick.)
Height of kumiko
60°
Note:
● Mark the positions of kumiko as accurately as possible because the beauty of a yarai-gaki greatly depends on the arrangement of kumiko.
● The formula with the 60 degree angle shown above was created by the author from his experience, and it can be applied regardless of the height of the fence.
● It is desirable, however, to determine the height with consideration that each length-wise rhombic eye of the kumiko will be larger with a higher fence.
23
Cut the kumiko pieces to the length of the measuring stick.

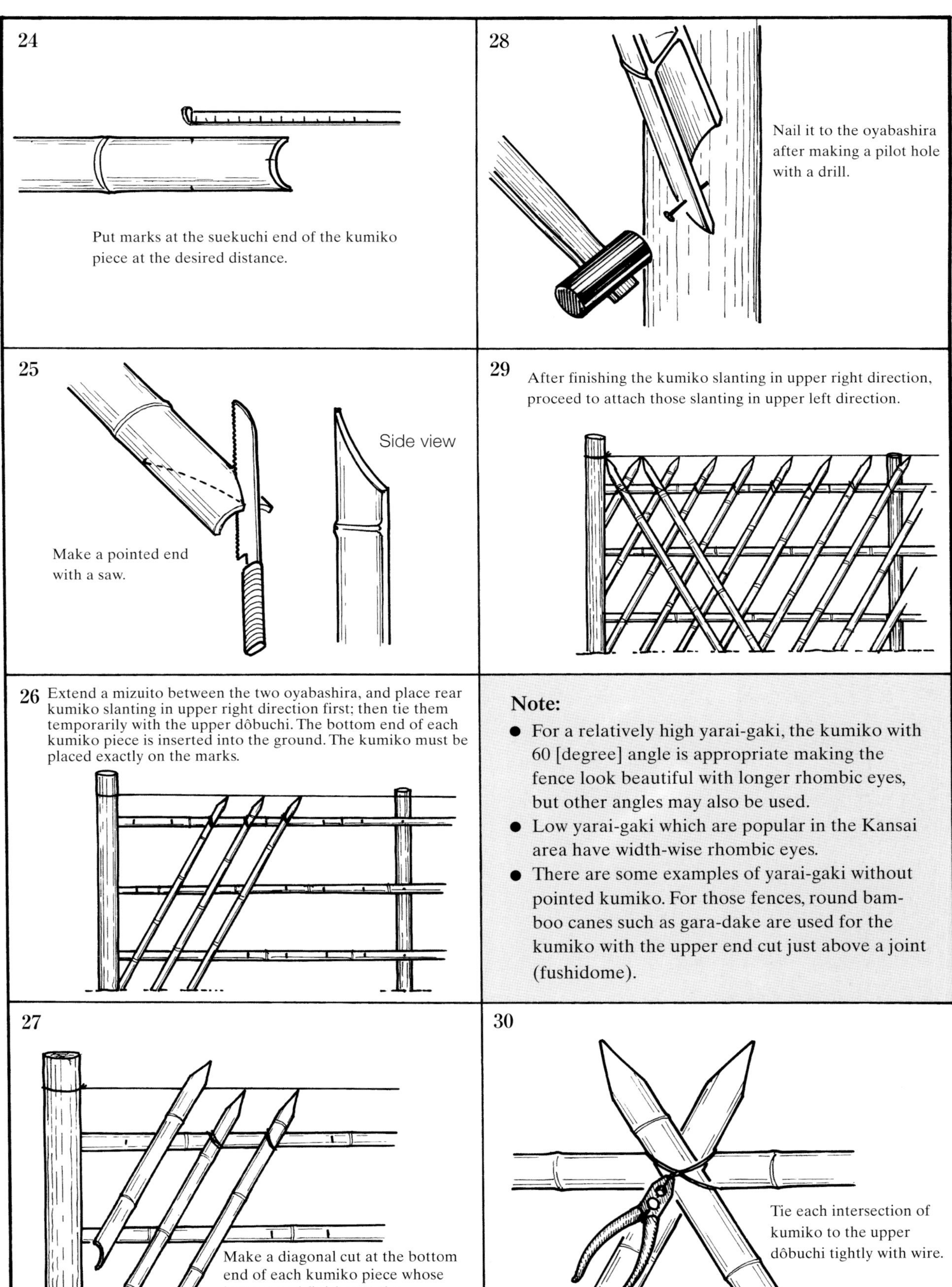

24

Put marks at the suekuchi end of the kumiko piece at the desired distance.

25

Make a pointed end with a saw.

26 Extend a mizuito between the two oyabashira, and place rear kumiko slanting in upper right direction first; then tie them temporarily with the upper dôbuchi. The bottom end of each kumiko piece is inserted into the ground. The kumiko must be placed exactly on the marks.

27

Make a diagonal cut at the bottom end of each kumiko piece whose bottom end finishes at the oyabashira.

28

Nail it to the oyabashira after making a pilot hole with a drill.

29 After finishing the kumiko slanting in upper right direction, proceed to attach those slanting in upper left direction.

Note:

- For a relatively high yarai-gaki, the kumiko with 60 [degree] angle is appropriate making the fence look beautiful with longer rhombic eyes, but other angles may also be used.
- Low yarai-gaki which are popular in the Kansai area have width-wise rhombic eyes.
- There are some examples of yarai-gaki without pointed kumiko. For those fences, round bamboo canes such as gara-dake are used for the kumiko with the upper end cut just above a joint (fushidome).

30

Tie each intersection of kumiko to the upper dôbuchi tightly with wire.

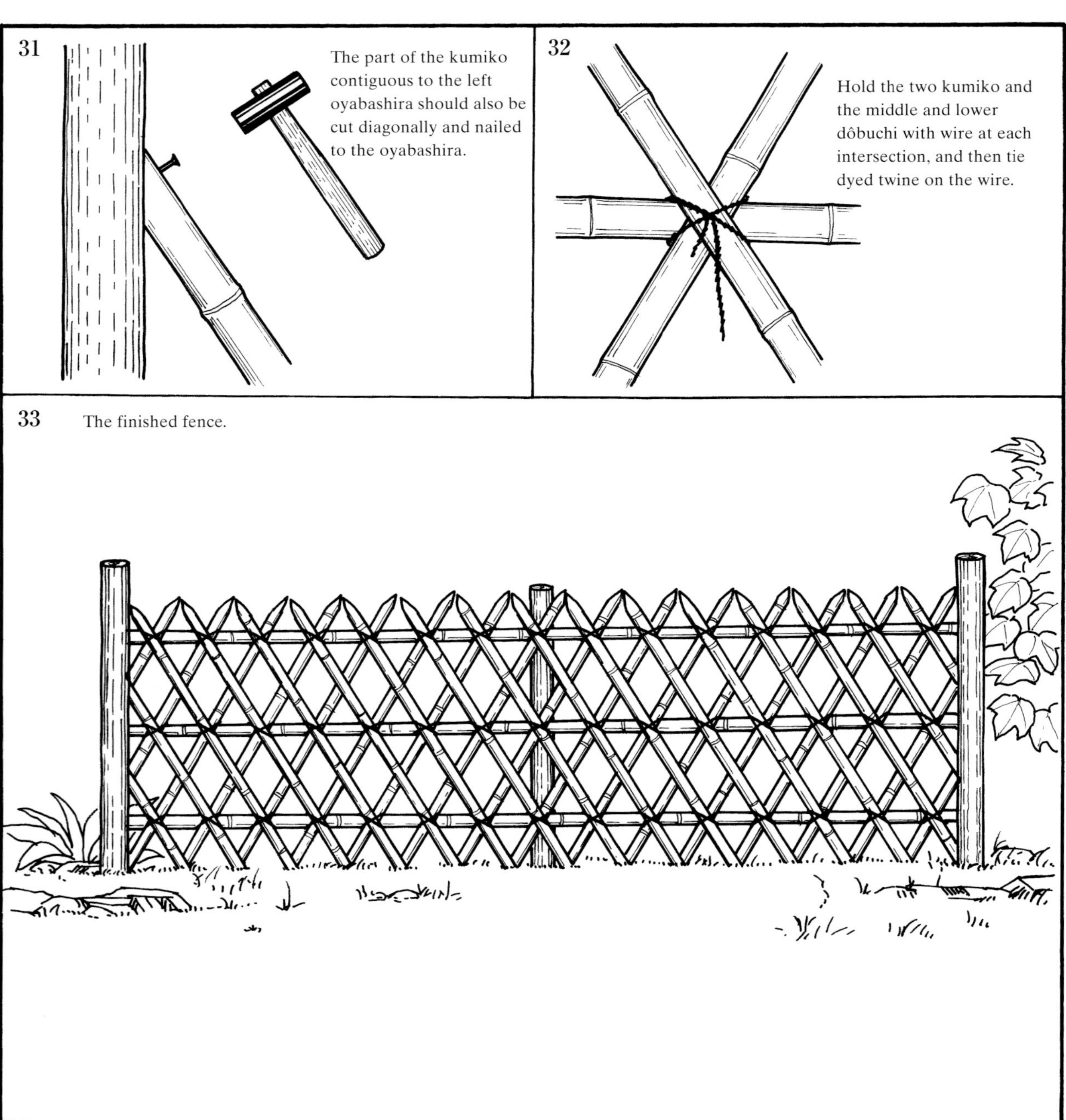
31
The part of the kumiko contiguous to the left oyabashira should also be cut diagonally and nailed to the oyabashira.
32
Hold the two kumiko and the middle and lower dôbuchi with wire at each intersection, and then tie dyed twine on the wire.
33
The finished fence.

Ryôanji-gaki

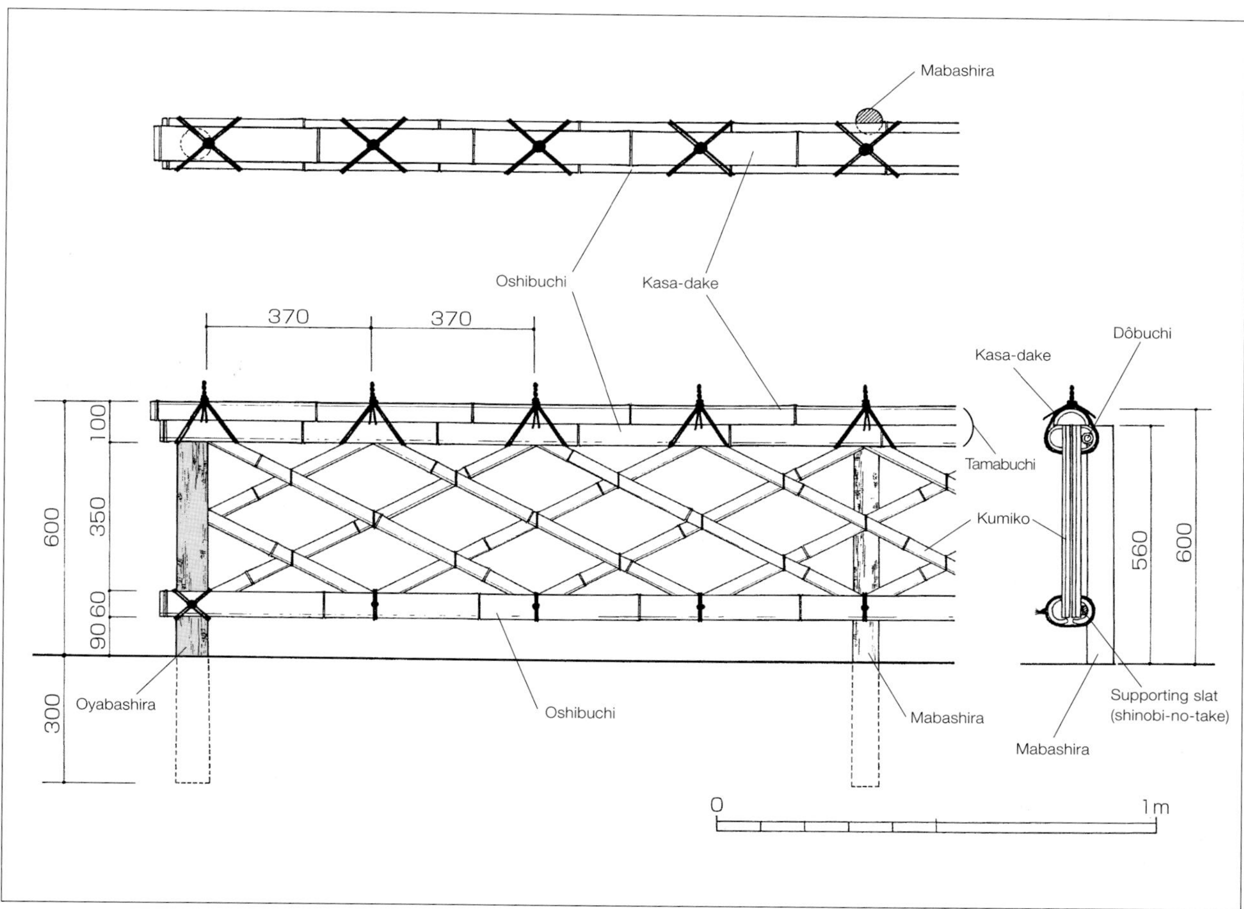

The ryôanji-gaki, like the kinkakuji-gaki, is a common type of foot-level fence (ashimoto-gaki). It appears somewhat like a low yarai-gaki (stockade fence) with a tamabuchi at the top and an oshibuchi near the ground. Placing one dôbuchi of gara-dake at the top is one of the most prominent features of this fence.

In the ryôanji-gaki, the positions of oyabashira, mabashira, and dôbuchi should be carefully considered together. After the oyabashira is put up, the mabashira with the same height is put up at the position shown above, slightly behind the center (about 152 centimeters from the oyabashira, center to center). This delicate positioning of mabashira is determined with respect to the dôbuchi.

The dôbuchi, which is of gara-dake with the motokuchi cut just above a joint (fushidome), is nailed directly to the rear of the left and right oyabashira. The key method is to cut a part of the top of the mabashira to place the dôbuchi on it. The point to notice here is to place the dôbuchi in such a way that it protrudes a little from the front of mabashira in order to have the same vertical plane with the shinobi-no-take (supporting slat of bamboo) running below. It is not easy to understand this kind of delicate work without actually building a fence, but I hope it will be understood to certain extent from the explanations and diagrams in the following pages.

Shinobi-no-take, which is made by splitting long bamboo canes into thin pieces of about two centimeters wide, is placed just like the dôbuchi at about twelve centimeters above the ground. The shinobi-no-take is nailed to the oyabashira with its inner part facing the front. It is important that the shinobi-no-take has the same vertical plane with the upper dôbuchi.

Kumiko should be made by splitting long stout bamboo canes. Ordinary presplit bamboo (1.8 meters long) may be used for kumiko, but the length of kumiko is about one meter, so there will be a lot of waste of bamboo. The kumiko are 2.5 to 3.0 centimeters wide, and two pieces of split bamboo are put together as one kumiko with the inner joints shaved off.

Kumiko are attached as illustrated according to the marks made beforehand on both the dôbuchi and the shinobi-no-take. Finally the oshibuchi will be attached to fix the fence tightly on the front and the rear.

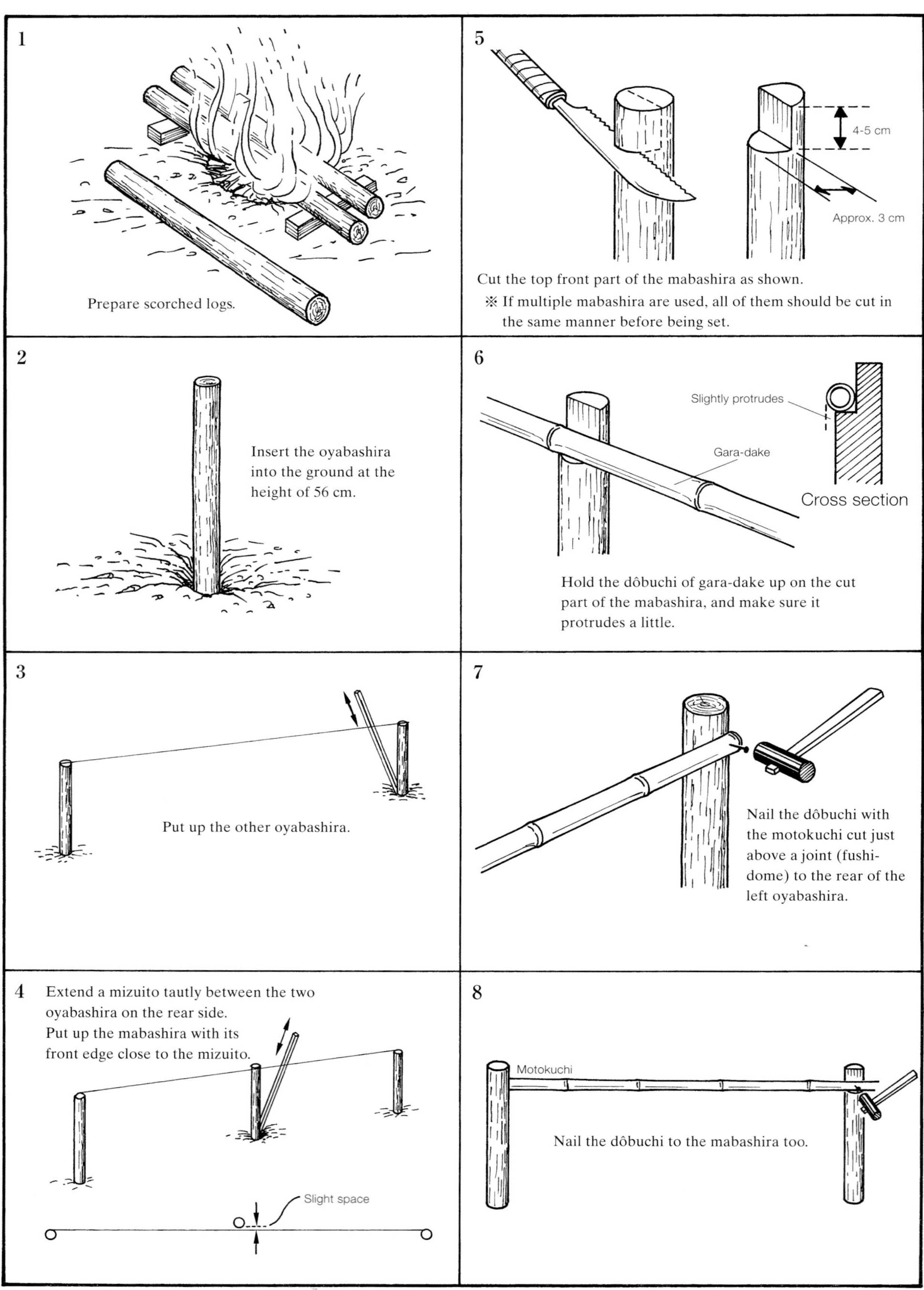
1
Prepare scorched logs.
5
4-5 cm
Approx. 3 cm
Cut the top front part of the mabashira as shown.
※ If multiple mabashira are used, all of them should be cut in the same manner before being set.
2
Insert the oyabashira into the ground at the height of 56 cm.
6
Slightly protrudes
Gara-dake
Cross section
Hold the dôbuchi of gara-dake up on the cut part of the mabashira, and make sure it protrudes a little.
3
Put up the other oyabashira.
7
Nail the dôbuchi with the motokuchi cut just above a joint (fushi-dome) to the rear of the left oyabashira.
4
Extend a mizuito tautly between the two oyabashira on the rear side.
Put up the mabashira with its front edge close to the mizuito.
Slight space
8
Motokuchi
Nail the dôbuchi to the mabashira too.

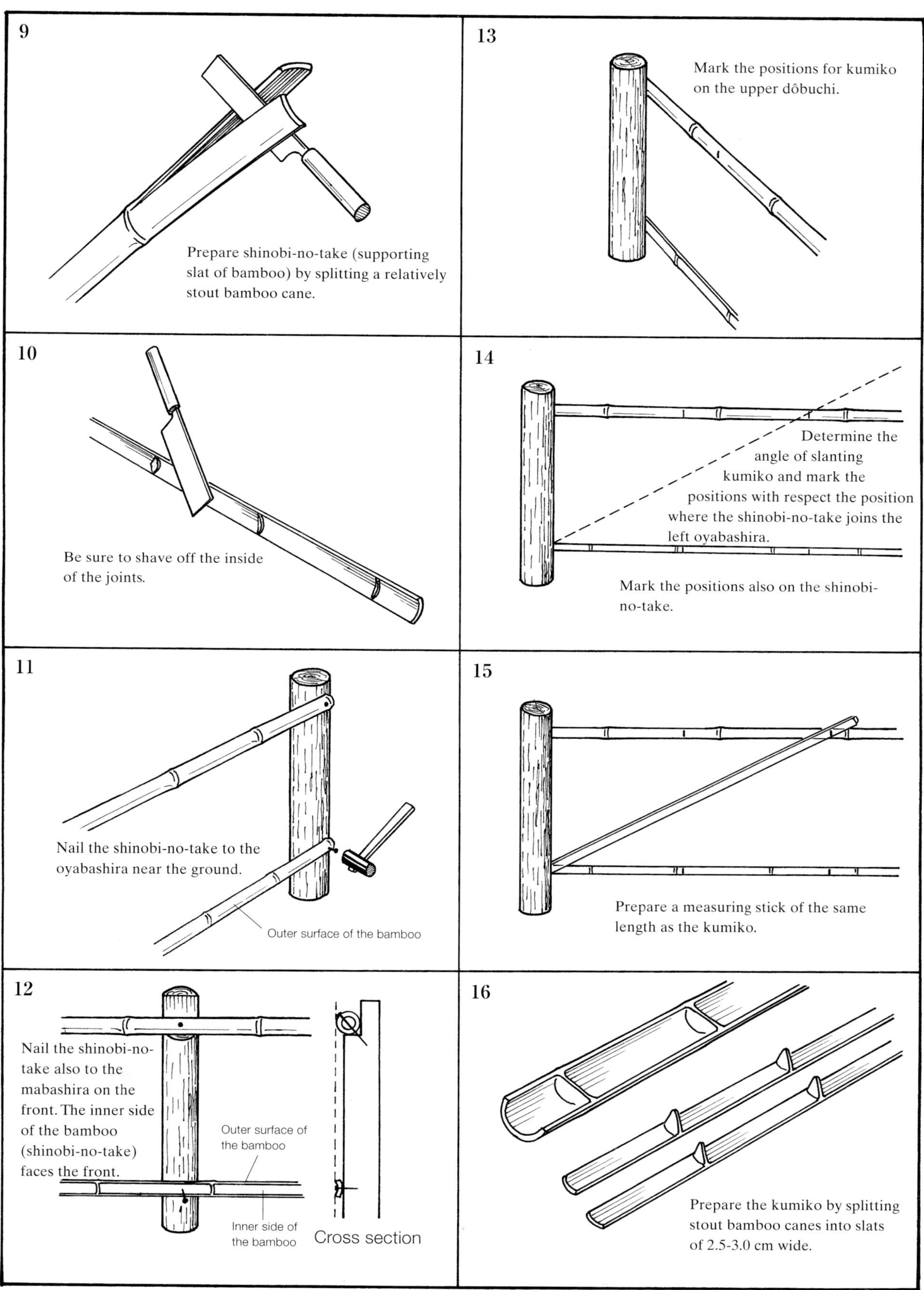
9
Prepare shinobi-no-take (supporting slat of bamboo) by splitting a relatively stout bamboo cane.
10
Be sure to shave off the inside of the joints.
11
Nail the shinobi-no-take to the oyabashira near the ground.
Outer surface of the bamboo
12
Nail the shinobi-no-take also to the mabashira on the front. The inner side of the bamboo (shinobi-no-take) faces the front.
Outer surface of the bamboo
Inner side of the bamboo
Cross section
13
Mark the positions for kumiko on the upper dôbuchi.
14
Determine the angle of slanting kumiko and mark the positions with respect the position where the shinobi-no-take joins the left oyabashira.
Mark the positions also on the shinobi-no-take.
15
Prepare a measuring stick of the same length as the kumiko.
16
Prepare the kumiko by splitting stout bamboo canes into slats of 2.5-3.0 cm wide.

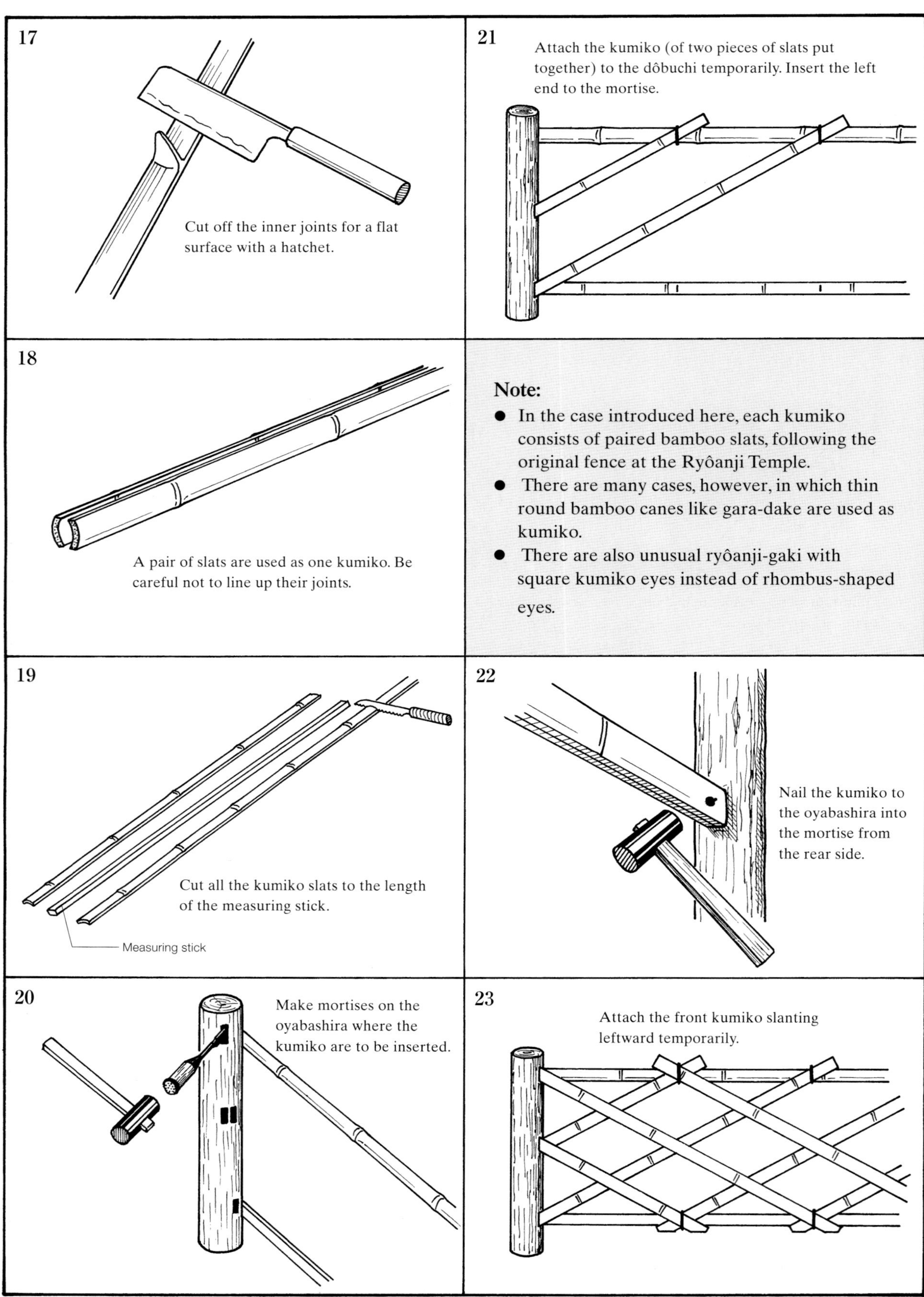

17
Cut off the inner joints for a flat surface with a hatchet.
21
Attach the kumiko (of two pieces of slats put together) to the dôbuchi temporarily. Insert the left end to the mortise.
18
A pair of slats are used as one kumiko. Be careful not to line up their joints.
19
Cut all the kumiko slats to the length of the measuring stick.
Measuring stick
22
Nail the kumiko to the oyabashira into the mortise from the rear side.
20
Make mortises on the oyabashira where the kumiko are to be inserted.
23
Attach the front kumiko slanting leftward temporarily.

Note:

- In the case introduced here, each kumiko consists of paired bamboo slats, following the original fence at the Ryôanji Temple.
- There are many cases, however, in which thin round bamboo canes like gara-dake are used as kumiko.
- There are also unusual ryôanji-gaki with square kumiko eyes instead of rhombus-shaped eyes.

24

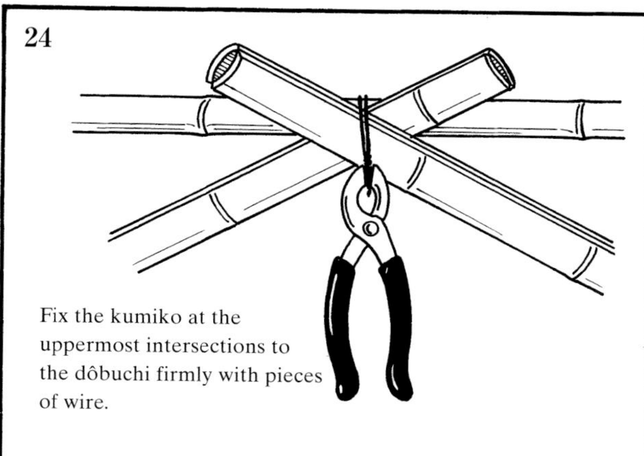

Fix the kumiko at the uppermost intersections to the dôbuchi firmly with pieces of wire.

27

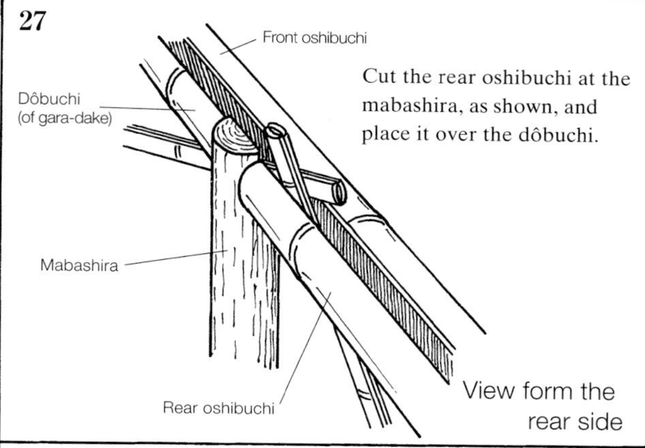

Cut the rear oshibuchi at the mabashira, as shown, and place it over the dôbuchi.

25

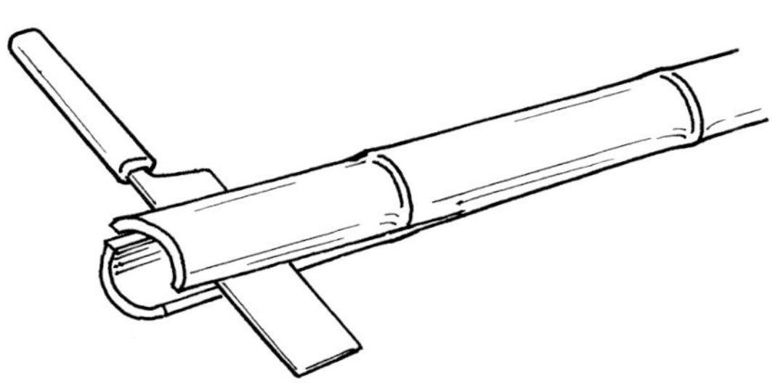

Split stout bamboo canes in half for use as oshibuchi and kasa-dake.

28

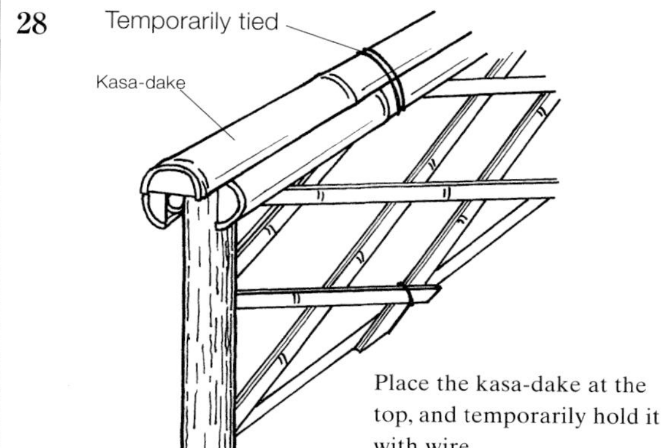

Place the kasa-dake at the top, and temporarily hold it with wire.

26

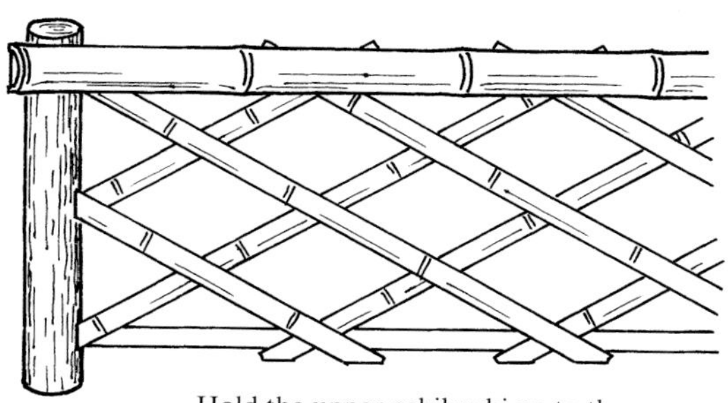

Hold the upper oshibuchi up to the fence on the front to check if it fits.

29

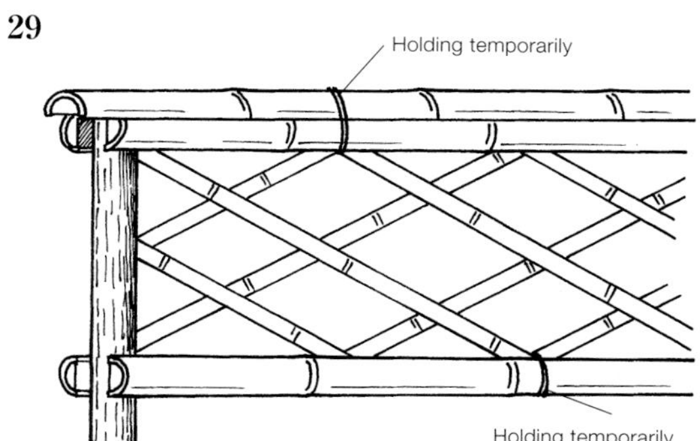

Hold also the lower oshibuchi up to the fence on the front and rear and hold them temporarily.

Note:

- The lower part of kumiko are fixed tightly to the shinobi-no-take (supporting slat) below with wire. Because the shinobi-no-take itself is weak and tends to sway back and fourth, the oshibuchi must be attached over this part firmly from both front and rear sides for a sturdy hold.
- The bottom ends of kumiko go slightly past the shinobi-no-take. The ends should be cut horizontally in order not to be seen sticking out from behind the oshibuchi.

30

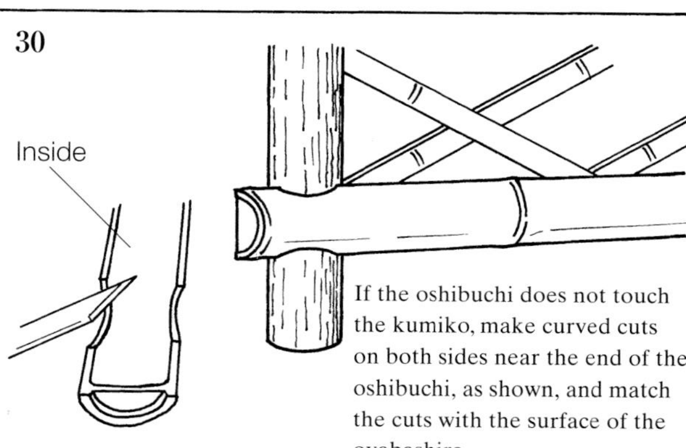

If the oshibuchi does not touch the kumiko, make curved cuts on both sides near the end of the oshibuchi, as shown, and match the cuts with the surface of the oyabashira.

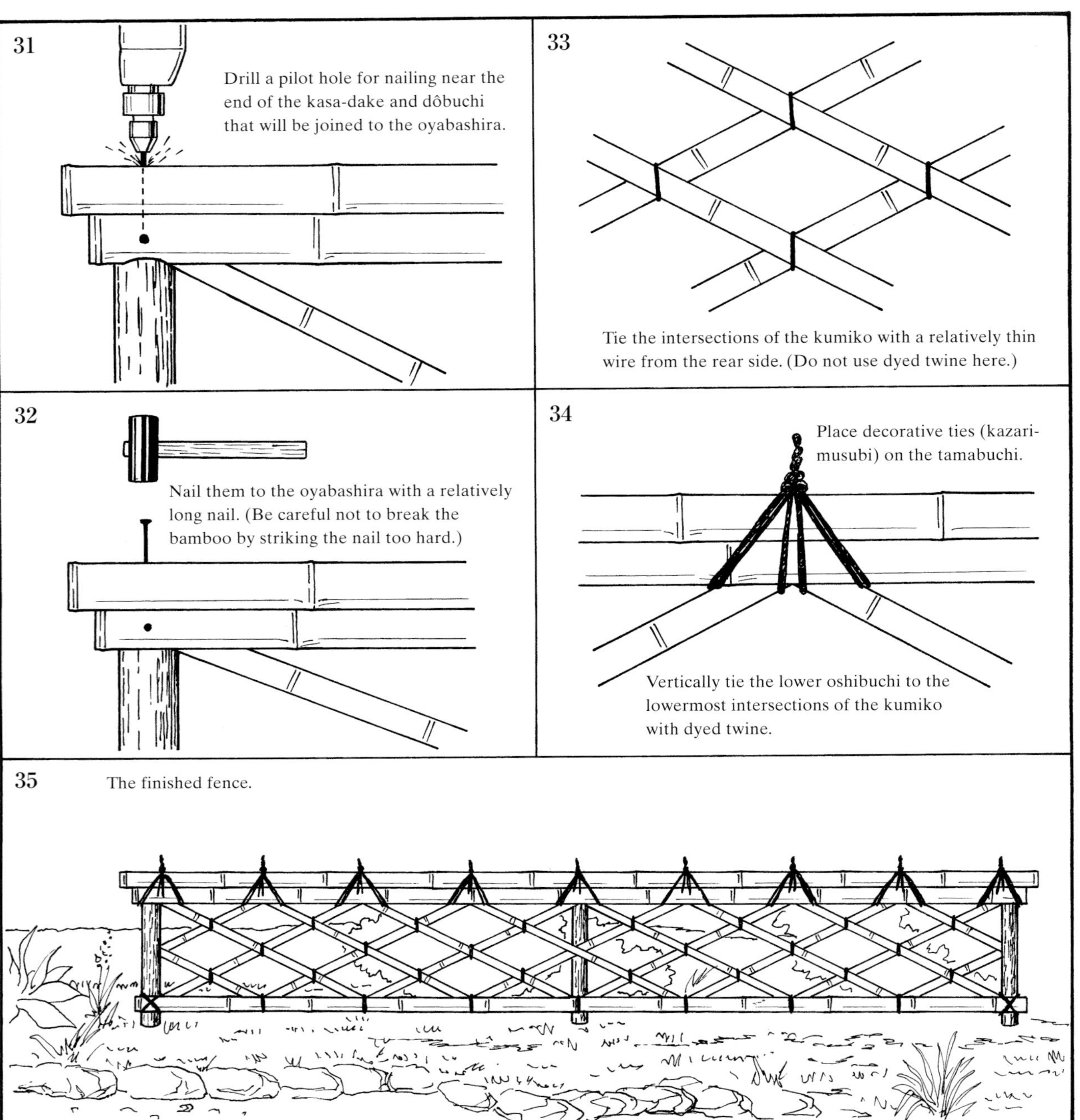
31
Drill a pilot hole for nailing near the end of the kasa-dake and dôbuchi that will be joined to the oyabashira.
32
Nail them to the oyabashira with a relatively long nail. (Be careful not to break the bamboo by striking the nail too hard.)
33
Tie the intersections of the kumiko with a relatively thin wire from the rear side. (Do not use dyed twine here.)
34
Place decorative ties (kazari-musubi) on the tamabuchi.
Vertically tie the lower oshibuchi to the lowermost intersections of the kumiko with dyed twine.
35
The finished fence.

Kôetsu-gaki

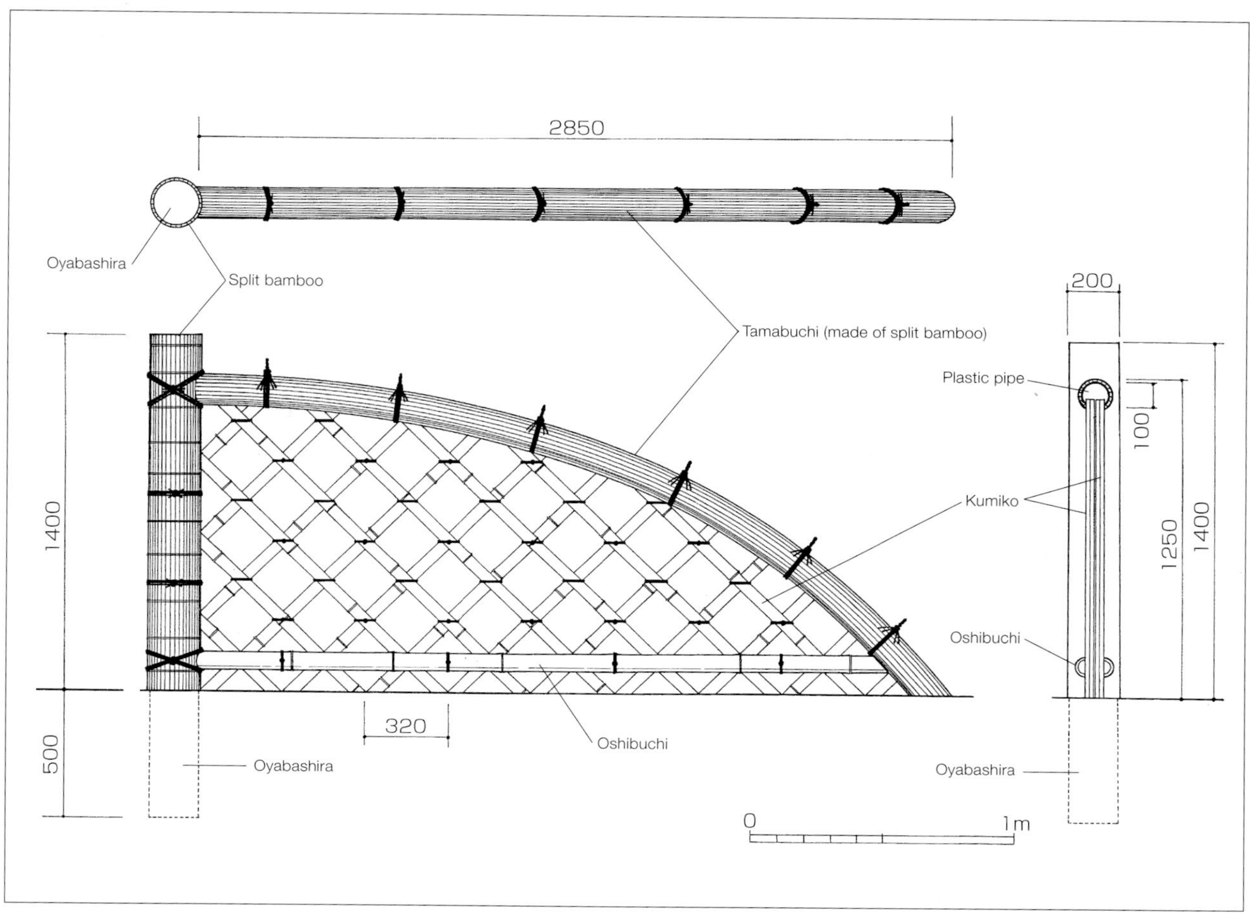

Although the kumiko are arranged in a manner similar to that of the yarai-gaki, the kôetsu-gaki has its prominent feature in using only one oyabashira and placing a tamabuchi at the top, the end of which curves downward, reaching the ground.

A thick log is used for the oyabashira, into which tamabuchi and slats are inserted. Whether the tamabuchi is placed before or after attaching kumiko depends on the structure and material of the tamabuchi. The fence shown here has a plastic pipe for the core of the tamabuchi, and this pipe is placed before attaching kumiko and after the oyabashira have been set.

In other cases, i.e. when a tamabuchi is wrapped with bamboo branches, the fence is built by first setting up a reinforcing steel rod in the shape of the planned curve. The kumiko are attached to the steel rod, and then a tamabuchi is placed.

Slats of presplit bamboo (yamawari-dake) are used in pairs for kumiko arranged at an angle of forty-five degrees, so the eyes of the kumiko will be square. The size of the eyes is a matter of choice, but the size shown in the illustration above is thought to be the best balanced. With the height of the oyabashira being approximately 1.4 meters or less, the number of the square eyes in the vertical direction should be about three and a half at oyabashira end.

Following this basic rule, with even lower fences than this example, the eyes of the kumiko become smaller in proportion to the fence height; thus good balance can be secured.

Mortises into which the kumiko are inserted are made on the oyabashira and the bottom side of the plastic pipe. A mizuito should be used so that the intersections of the kumiko are precisely aligned in the horizontal direction.

After attaching the kumiko, thin split bamboo will be wound around the tamabuchi and the oyabashira. Relatively long thin pieces of bamboo are used for this covering. Very thinly split bamboo should be used for the curved pipe portion of the tamabuchi to prevent them from twisting. After covering the tamabuchi and oyabashira with the thinly split bamboo, the oshibuchi is placed near the bottom of the kumiko from both the front and rear sides; the fence is now completed.

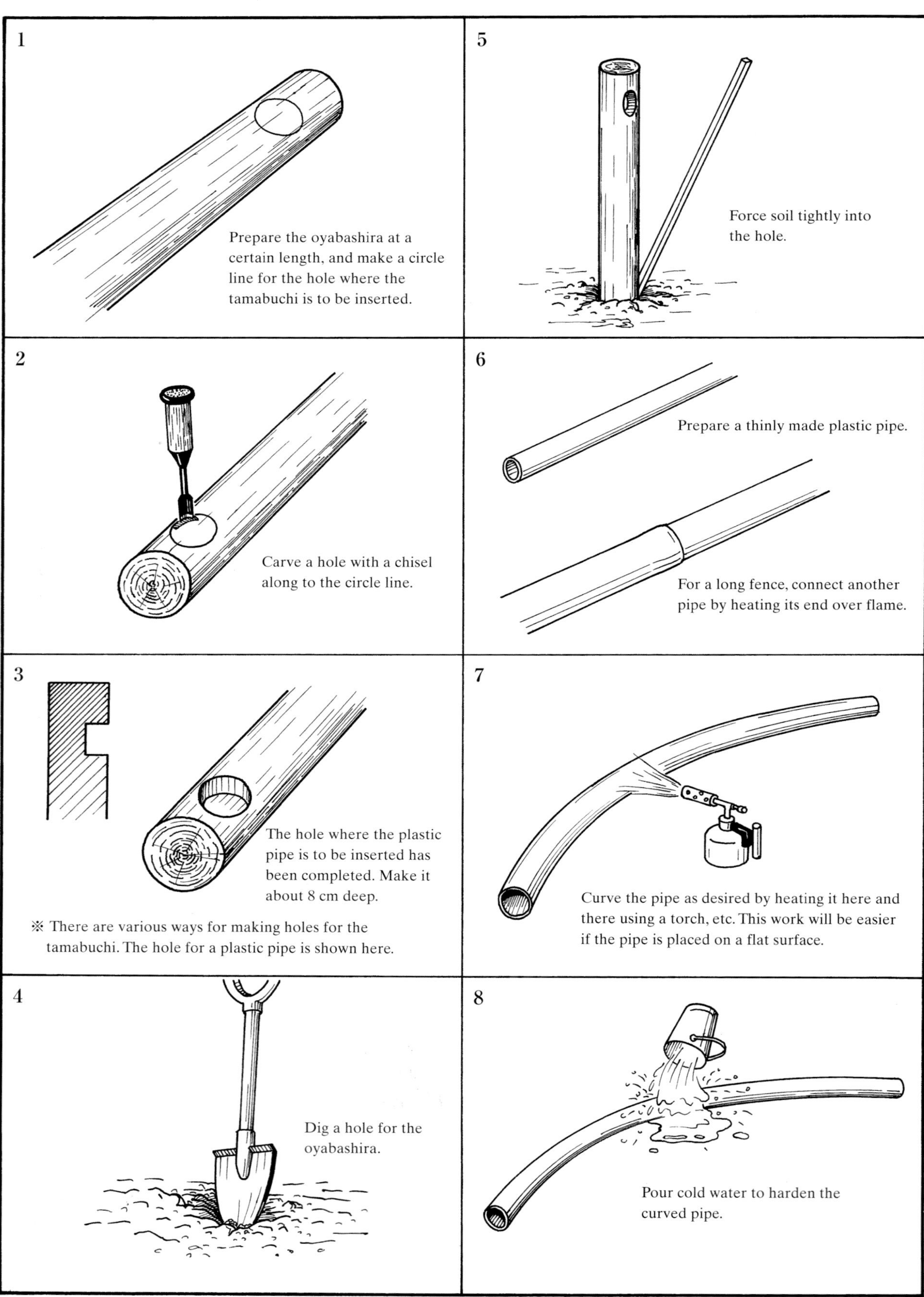
1
Prepare the oyabashira at a certain length, and make a circle line for the hole where the tamabuchi is to be inserted.
2
Carve a hole with a chisel along to the circle line.
3
The hole where the plastic pipe is to be inserted has been completed. Make it about 8 cm deep.
※ There are various ways for making holes for the tamabuchi. The hole for a plastic pipe is shown here.
4
Dig a hole for the oyabashira.
5
Force soil tightly into the hole.
6
Prepare a thinly made plastic pipe.
For a long fence, connect another pipe by heating its end over flame.
7
Curve the pipe as desired by heating it here and there using a torch, etc. This work will be easier if the pipe is placed on a flat surface.
8
Pour cold water to harden the curved pipe.

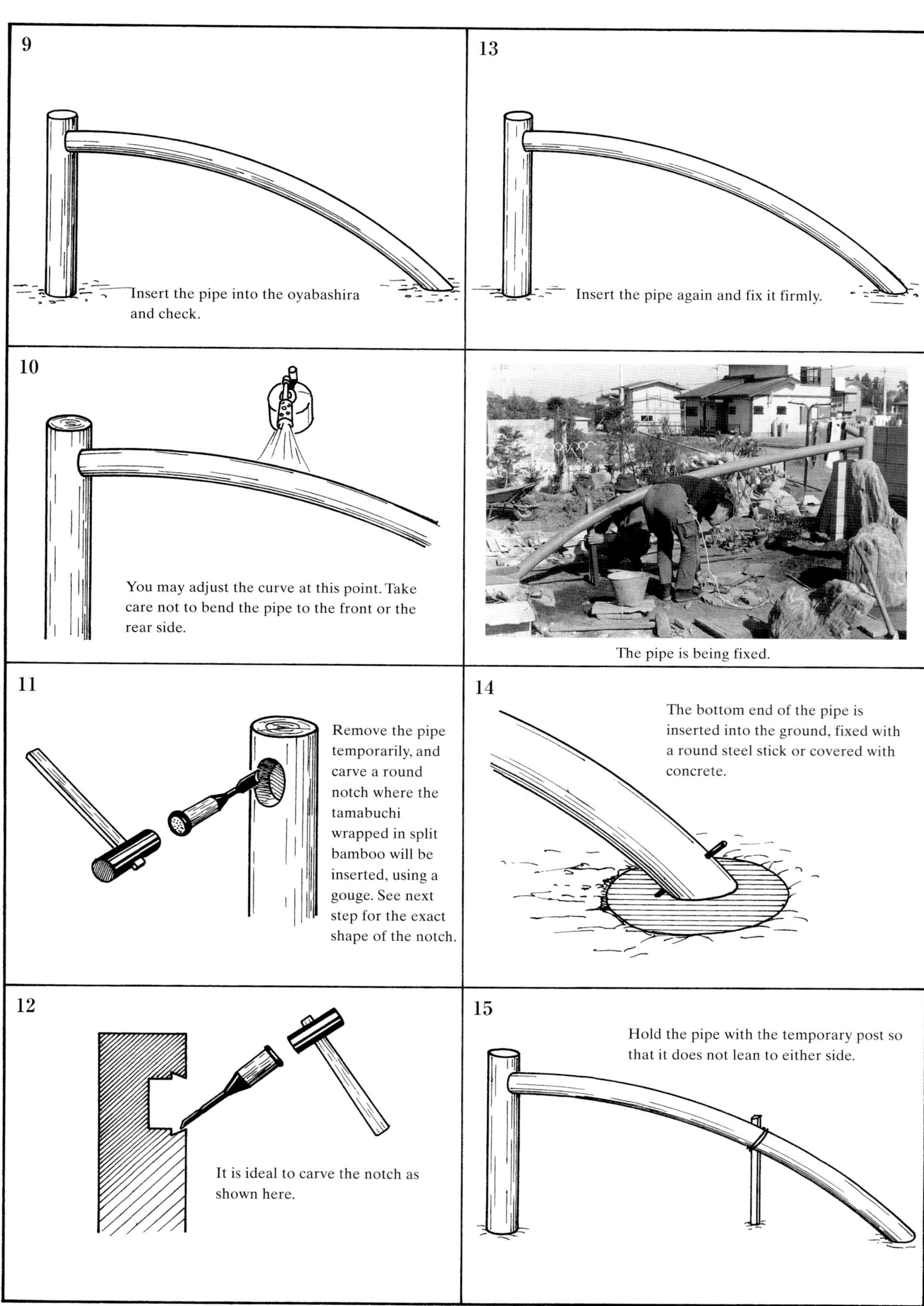
9
Insert the pipe into the oyabashira and check.
10
You may adjust the curve at this point. Take care not to bend the pipe to the front or the rear side.
11
Remove the pipe temporarily, and carve a round notch where the tamabuchi wrapped in split bamboo will be inserted, using a gouge. See next step for the exact shape of the notch.
12
It is ideal to carve the notch as shown here.
13
Insert the pipe again and fix it firmly.
The pipe is being fixed.
14
The bottom end of the pipe is inserted into the ground, fixed with a round steel stick or covered with concrete.
15
Hold the pipe with the temporary post so that it does not lean to either side.

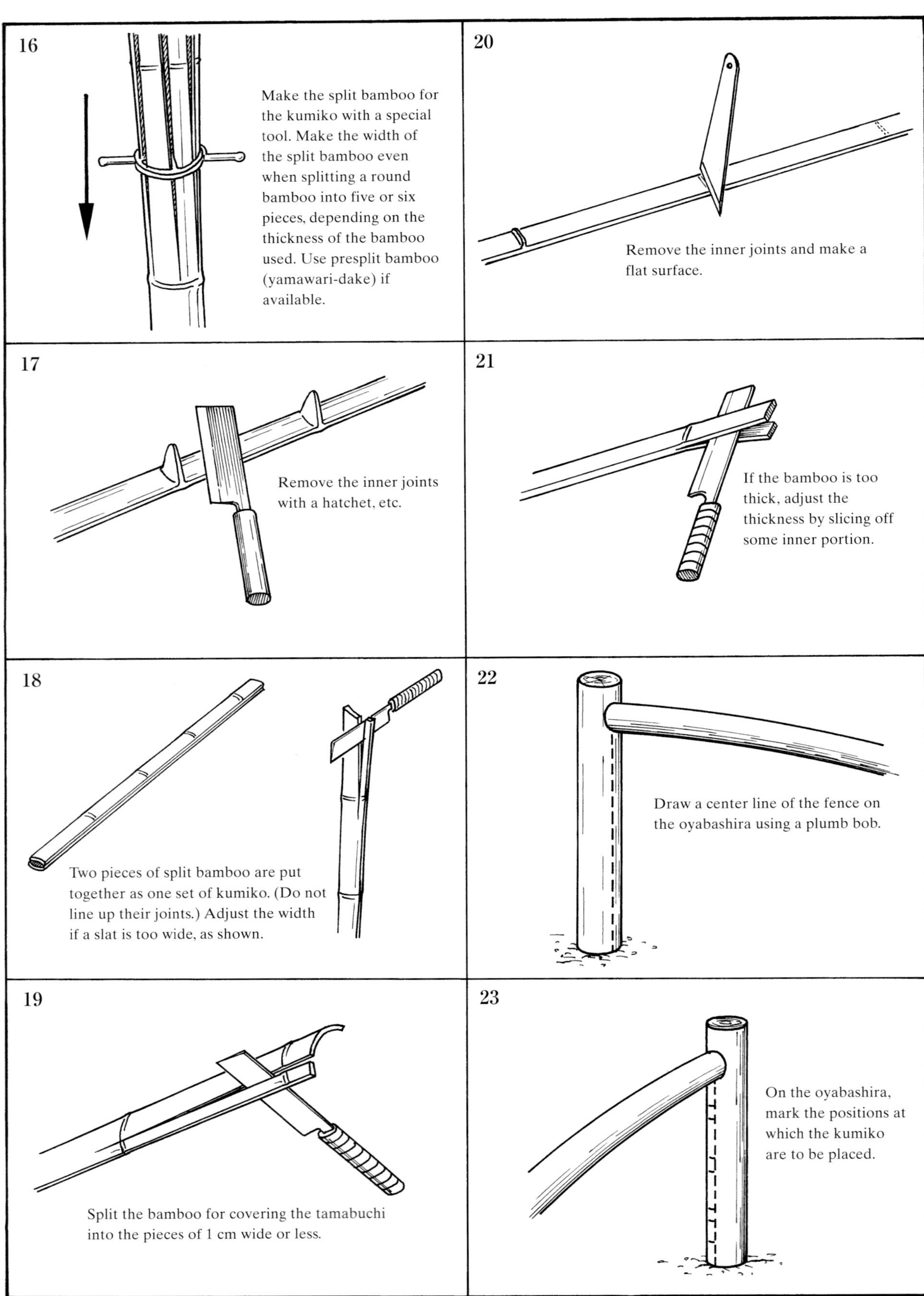
16
Make the split bamboo for the kumiko with a special tool. Make the width of the split bamboo even when splitting a round bamboo into five or six pieces, depending on the thickness of the bamboo used. Use presplit bamboo (yamawari-dake) if available.
17
Remove the inner joints with a hatchet, etc.
18
Two pieces of split bamboo are put together as one set of kumiko. (Do not line up their joints.) Adjust the width if a slat is too wide, as shown.
19
Split the bamboo for covering the tamabuchi into the pieces of 1 cm wide or less.
20
Remove the inner joints and make a flat surface.
21
If the bamboo is too thick, adjust the thickness by slicing off some inner portion.
22
Draw a center line of the fence on the oyabashira using a plumb bob.
23
On the oyabashira, mark the positions at which the kumiko are to be placed.

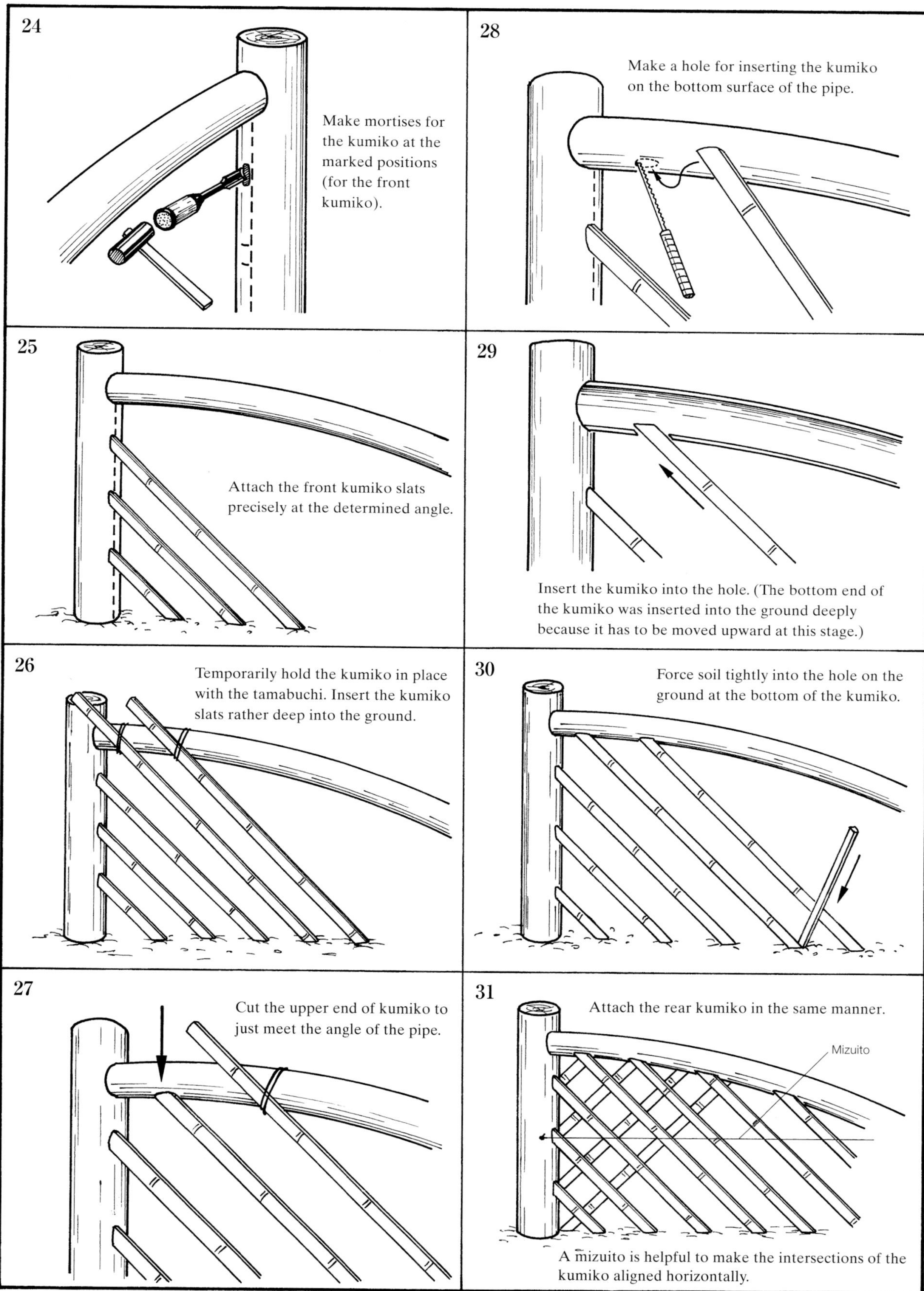
24
Make mortises for the kumiko at the marked positions (for the front kumiko).
25
Attach the front kumiko slats precisely at the determined angle.
26
Temporarily hold the kumiko in place with the tamabuchi. Insert the kumiko slats rather deep into the ground.
27
Cut the upper end of kumiko to just meet the angle of the pipe.
28
Make a hole for inserting the kumiko on the bottom surface of the pipe.
29
Insert the kumiko into the hole. (The bottom end of the kumiko was inserted into the ground deeply because it has to be moved upward at this stage.)
30
Force soil tightly into the hole on the ground at the bottom of the kumiko.
31
Attach the rear kumiko in the same manner.
Mizuito
A mizuito is helpful to make the intersections of the kumiko aligned horizontally.

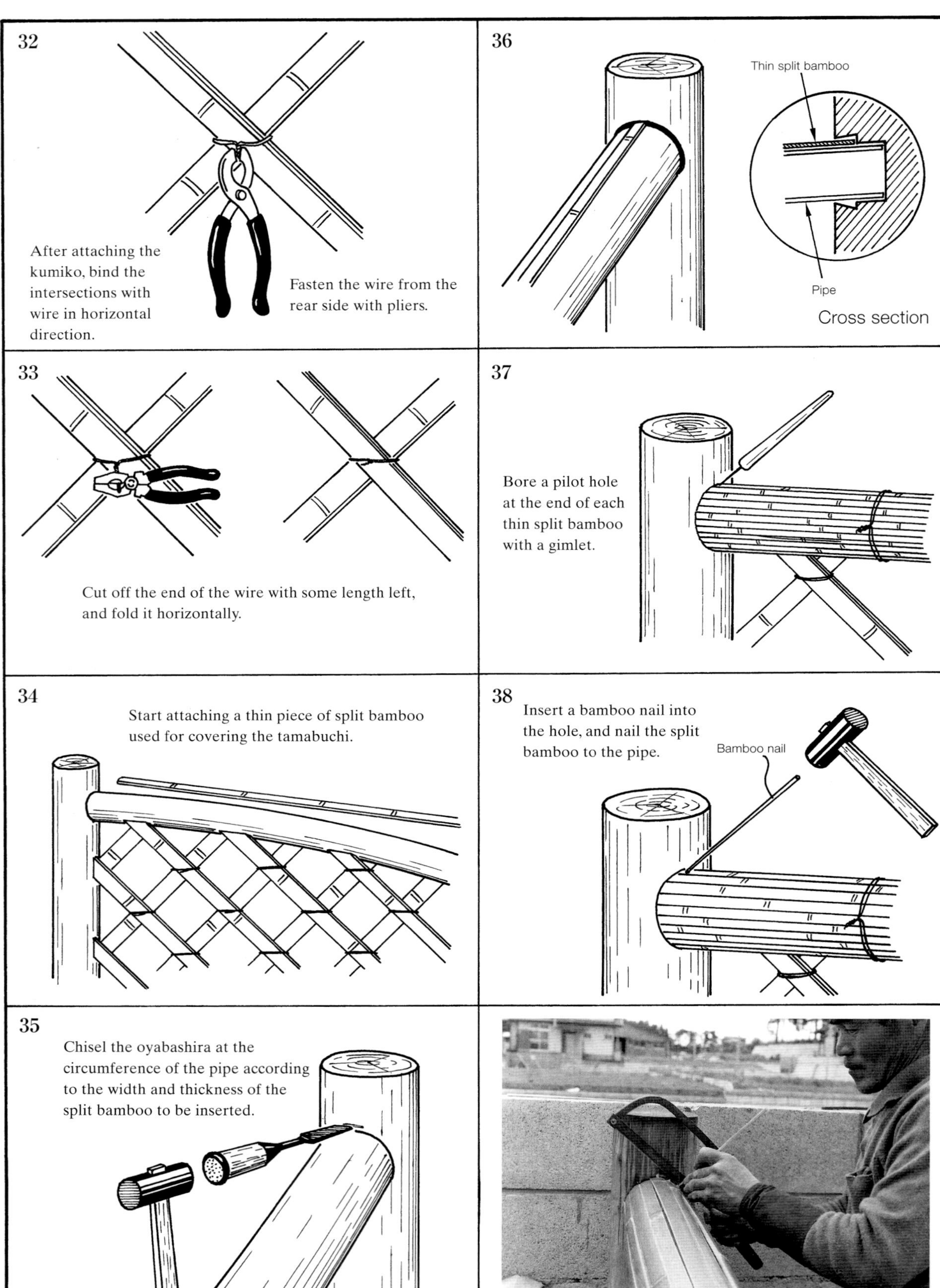

32
After attaching the kumiko, bind the intersections with wire in horizontal direction.
Fasten the wire from the rear side with pliers.
33
Cut off the end of the wire with some length left, and fold it horizontally.
34
Start attaching a thin piece of split bamboo used for covering the tamabuchi.
35
Chisel the oyabashira at the circumference of the pipe according to the width and thickness of the split bamboo to be inserted.
36
Thin split bamboo
Pipe
Cross section
37
Bore a pilot hole at the end of each thin split bamboo with a gimlet.
38
Insert a bamboo nail into the hole, and nail the split bamboo to the pipe.
Bamboo nail

Cut off the remaining part of the bamboo nail with a saw.

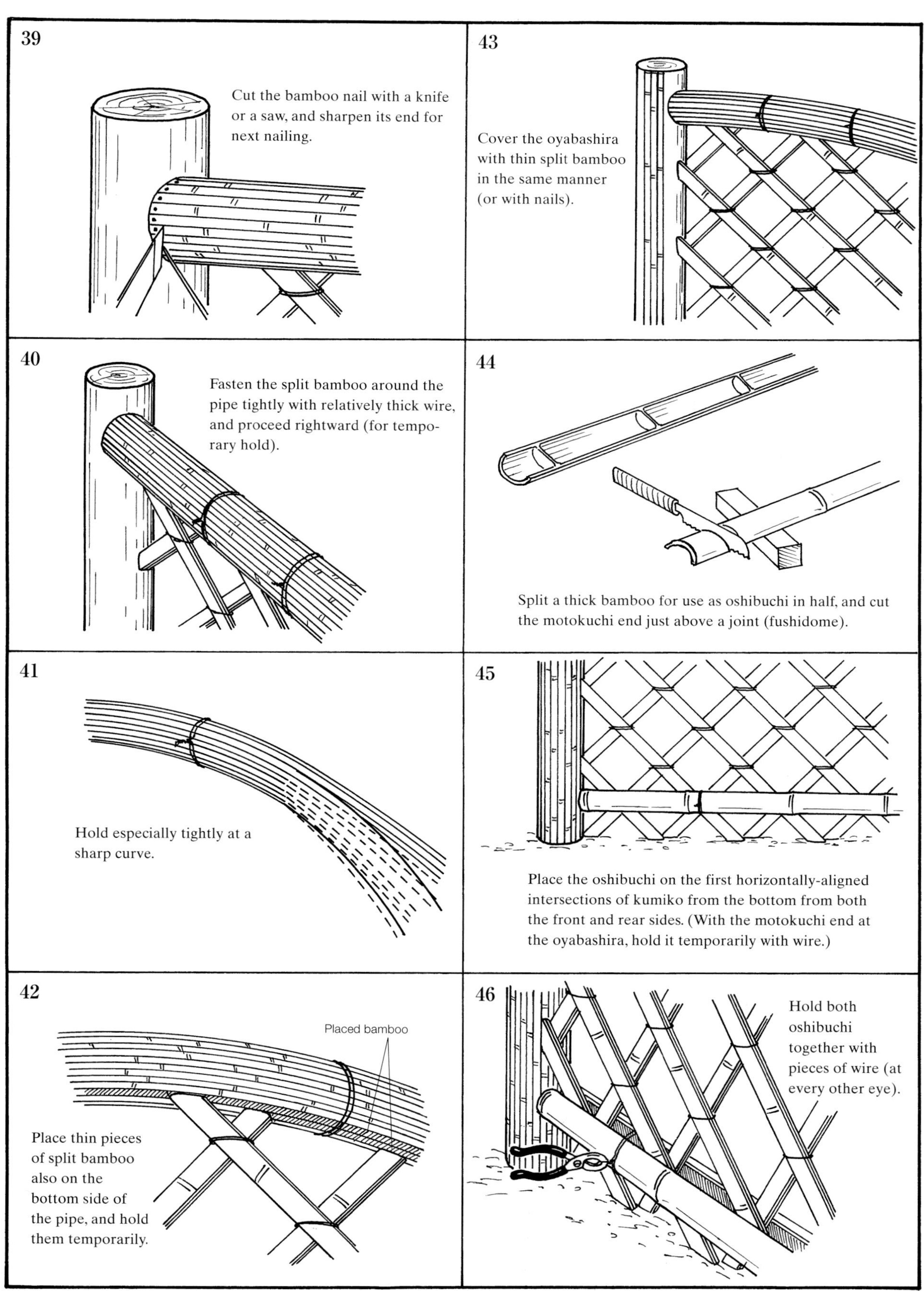
39
Cut the bamboo nail with a knife or a saw, and sharpen its end for next nailing.
43
Cover the oyabashira with thin split bamboo in the same manner (or with nails).
40
Fasten the split bamboo around the pipe tightly with relatively thick wire, and proceed rightward (for temporary hold).
44
Split a thick bamboo for use as oshibuchi in half, and cut the motokuchi end just above a joint (fushidome).
41
Hold especially tightly at a sharp curve.
45
Place the oshibuchi on the first horizontally-aligned intersections of kumiko from the bottom from both the front and rear sides. (With the motokuchi end at the oyabashira, hold it temporarily with wire.)
42
Placed bamboo
Place thin pieces of split bamboo also on the bottom side of the pipe, and hold them temporarily.
46
Hold both oshibuchi together with pieces of wire (at every other eye).

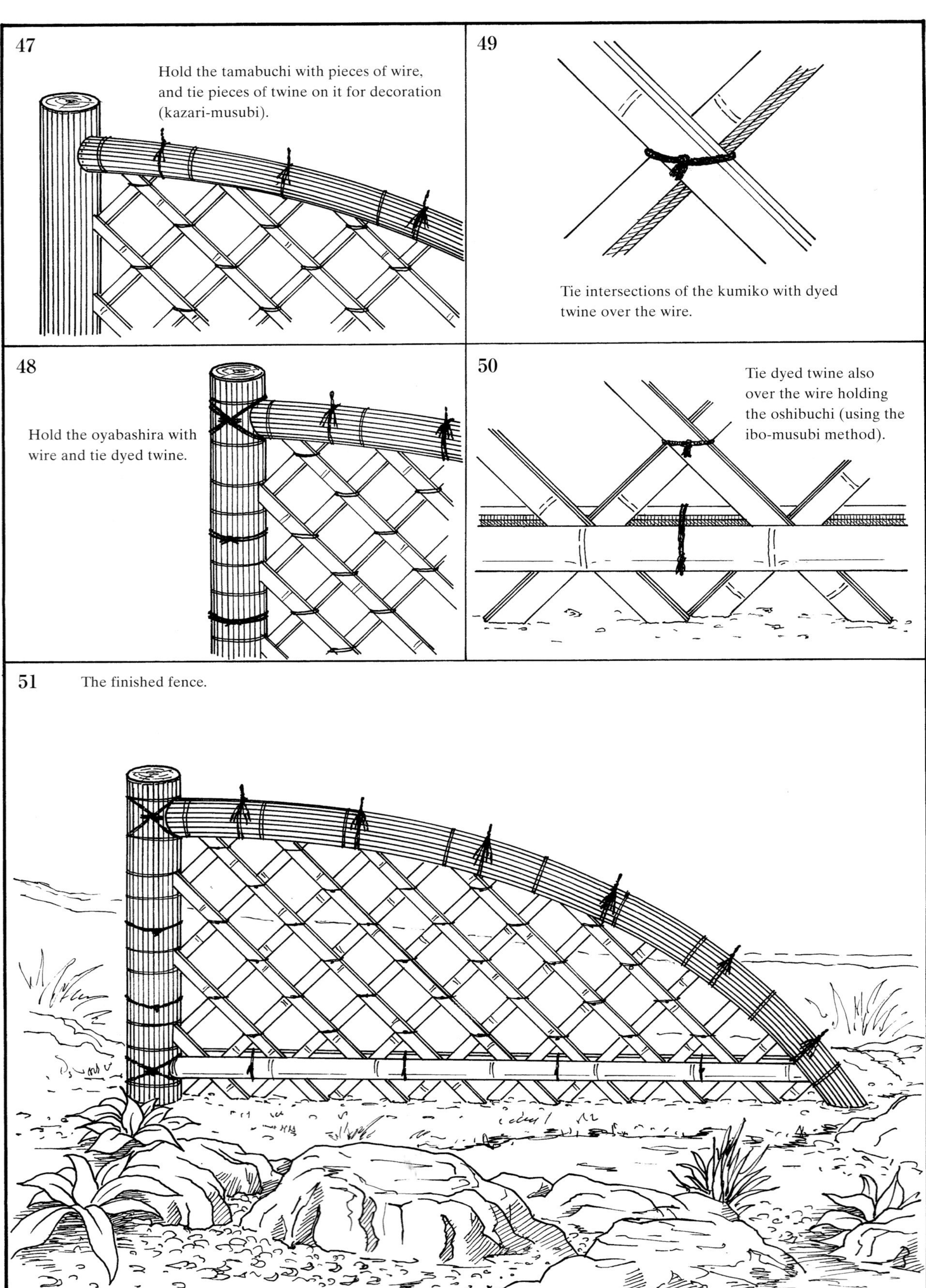
47
Hold the tamabuchi with pieces of wire, and tie pieces of twine on it for decoration (kazari-musubi).
49
Tie intersections of the kumiko with dyed twine over the wire.
48
Hold the oyabashira with wire and tie dyed twine.
50
Tie dyed twine also over the wire holding the oshibuchi (using the ibo-musubi method).
51
The finished fence.

Glossary

- **aboshi pattern:**
a pattern stressing its diagonal lines inspired by a fisherman's net spread to dry on a beach. The aboshi-pattern balustrade on the verandah of the tea ceremony room in the Shûgakuin Imperial Villa in Kyoto is well known. The fence that uses this design is the "aboshi-gaki".
- **ashimoto-gaki (foot-level fence):**
a special low-lying fence, which is built along pathways, usually at one's knee level or lower. Common ashimoto-gaki are the kinkakuji, ryôanji, nison'in, and nanako-gaki; yotsume-gaki are also made as ashimoto-gaki.
- **awase:**
a style of attaching tateko on both sides of a fence. If the fence has tateko of split bamboo on the front side only, the inner part of the split bamboo is seen from the rear side. In order to avoid this, the tateko are attached on both sides, front and rear.
- **bakabô:**
a name used among landscape architects for a measuring stick.
- **bussaki:**
undesirable status of the split bamboo which the wedge-shaped cut made for mending bending becomes wider when the bamboo is straightened. Opposite of "nemuri".
- **chikarabashira:**
another name of oyabashira
- **chirashi:**
a method of using something in an irregular way. One of the example is to give some variety by tying tokusa-gaki (Dutch rush fences) with dyed twine.
- **dôbuchi:**
a main horizontal supporting piece extending between the oyabashira of a fence at several levels. In screening fences (shahei-gaki), the dôbuchi are usually hidden, so they can be of ordinary pieces of wood other than bamboo. In see-through fences, however, they are usually visible, so round bamboo is often used. Some fences are made without dôbuchi.
- **double shovel:**
a kind of scoop designed to dig a small and deep hole on the ground, especially suitable for digging a hole for inserting oyabashira and mabashira of bamboo fences.
- **fujizuru-musubi:**
tying a fence with a wisteria vine instead of dyed twine; mainly used for sode-gaki, etc.
- **fukiyose:**
an arrangement in which two long pieces of bamboo, such as oshibuchi, are brought nearer to each other than usual (but not made to touch).
- **furedome:**
a long thin piece of round or split bamboo attached horizontally near the top of a fence which does not have tamabuchi to hold the tateko in place. Used for screening fences (shahei-gaki), notably bamboo branch fences (takeho-gaki) and brushwood fences (shiba-gaki).
- **fushibiki:**
making a cut on a joint part to make the cut not so noticeable. Sometimes it is called fushikiri.
- **fushidome:**
cutting bamboo just above the joints (fushi). This method gives stronger pieces and hides the inside of them, thus making them more sightly and resistant to rain.
- **gagyû-gaki (gagyû fence):**
another name for the kôetsu-gaki (kôetsu fence)
- **gara-dake:**
a name used among landscape architects for thin madake bamboo, which is used mainly for the yotsume-gaki. The name probably came from "kara-take", another name for madake.
- **hari:**
a flat needle used for rope tying. There are kuribari (a type of hook) and a straight needle.
- **hi-gaki:**
a type of ajiro-gaki (wickerwork fences), which was once popular in the old days. Hinoki board is sliced thinly and woven like a wickerwork to build a fence. The hi-gaki fence was the most popular ajiro-gaki fence.
- **hikime:**
a cut on a part of bamboo by a saw, mainly for mending bent tateko of split bamboo
- **hishigi-dake:**
"hishigi" means "crush", so hishigi-dake refers to the split round bamboo which is crushed flat. Split pieces of the same bamboo provide the aligned position of joints in group. The "hishigi-dake" fences use this characteristic. There are some examples of using this for a wall.
- **hishime:**
a diamond space made by kumiko attached diagonally and crossed. The yarai-gaki and the ryôanji-gaki are typical fences with diamond space.
- **ho:**
same as "takeho"
- **ho-gaki:**
another name for "takeho-gaki"

- **honka:**
translated here as "the original fence"; the first fence of a given type. The originals of most bamboo fence types have not been determined; some of those that have known honka are the kinkakuji, the ryôanji, and the kôetsu-gaki.
- **ibo-musubi:**
one of the most basic rope tying methods for bamboo fences. It is also simply called ibo, or yuibo, otoko-musubi (male knot), or yotsume-no-otoko-musubi; as the last variant indicates, one of the main uses of ibo-musubi is for yotsume-gaki.
- **kaizuka-karage:**
one of the karage shuhô (karage methods)
- **kakitsuke:**
a method of joining the tateko with dôbuchi with a rope one by one without tying them; seen in the kenninji-gaki, etc.
- **kanna:**
a plane, a tool mainly used for smoothing wood; one-blade plane is suitable for smoothing bamboo canes.
- **karage shuhô (karage methods):**
joining methods using rope, but not involving tying. A single piece of rope is wound around tateko or tamabuchi. Used mostly for the yotsume-gaki, the karage methods have such variations as yotsume karage and kaizuka karage.
- **kari-musubi (temporary tying):**
one of the rope tying methods having the same procedure with ibo-musubi but not tying completely at last so that it comes apart when one of the ends is pulled.
- **kasa-dake:**
a bamboo cap; the split bamboo covering at the top in case of using the tamabuchi in the kenninji-gaki.
- **kazari-musubi:**
decorative rope tying. The main purpose of tying is to hold the fence tightly but it is also one of the important features of the fence to tie the rope as a decoration to make the fence look beautiful. Kazari-musubi is often used for the tamabuchi with various tying methods including "ishidatami".
- **kekkai:**
partitioning an area by running a piece of round bamboo as a simple bamboo fence forbidding entry to the area.
- **kiri:**
a drill, a tool to bore a hole in the wood; A triangular drill is often used for bamboo canes.
- **kizuchi:**
a mallet or wooden hammer used to strike parts of a fence that may be damaged if a metal hammer is used. Most of them are made from hard wood such as oak.
- **kuigake:**
tying dôbuchi, etc. and the mabashira so that they do not come off after nailing.
- **kumiko:**
a piece of bamboo or a branch of tree which is used at the surface of bamboo fences as their main feature; usually refers to the diagonally and horizontally placed ones rather than the vertically placed ones, which are called tateko. Kumiko are mainly used for the numazu-gaki and bamboo screen fences (misu-gaki), etc. among screening fences (shahei-gaki), and the yarai-gaki, the ryôanji-gaki and the kôetsu-gaki , etc. among see-through fences (sukashi-gaki).
- **kuri-bari:**
a type of hook; used for a rope tying work for yourself for the kenninji-gaki, etc. by inserting between tateko at the positions that you can not reach behind the fence.
- **kuroho:**
the black branches of kurochiku (a black variety of sturdy species of bamboo); used for the takeho-gaki (bamboo branch fences). Kuroho have a unique texture of dark black color and are popular in the Kantô region. They are widely used as a material for the mino-gaki (raincoat fences) and the yoroi-gaki (armor fences).
- **mabashira:**
Most bamboo fences have oyabashira at both ends as the main supporting structure. Relatively thin mabashira of a long fence, spaced about 1.8 meters apart, are put up between the oyabashira.
- **makibashira:**
log posts wound with fine round or split bamboo, bamboo branches, spicebush (kuromoji), or bush clover (hagi); used mainly for the kôetsu-gaki and teppô-gaki (rifle barrel fence) and for the oyabashira for sode-gaki (sleeve fence).
- **maki-tatego:**
tateko which are of branches of bamboo, spicebush (kuromoji), bush clover (hagi), etc., wound and bundled together; they are used mainly for teppô-gaki (rifle barrel fences).
- **maru-nomi:**
a gouge. a chisel having a partly cylindrical blade; used for making a hole on oyabashira, and so on.
- **mawari:**
determining the size of a bamboo fence. Also called warima.
- **mewari:**
a method to split round bamboo at its branch bud. This splitting method is for tamabuchi. For

oshibuchi, on the contrary, the bamboo is split so that the branch bud is seen from the front.

- **midare shuhô (midare method):**
purposely making the length of the tateko different so that the top of a fence is uneven. This gives the subdued image. When the method is used for the kenninji-gaki and yotsume-gaki, the result is a sô-style fence.
- **mizuito:**
a thin strong string for seeing the level of the top of tateko.
- **moji-gaki:**
a kind of creative fences which has certain letters to give abstract design on the surface of a fence.
- **motokuchi:**
motokuchi of round and split bamboo; opposite to "suekuchi"(small end).
- **mumeita:**
a piece of wood running between two oyabashira. By making a cut on the inner part of the oyabashira mumeita is connected horizontally near ground level. Tateko resting on mumeita do not rot as easily as they otherwise would.
- **neko:**
kumiko that are used horizontally are sometimes called "neko".
- **nemuri:**
a technique to mend a bending spilt bamboo. After making a wedge-shaped cut on the bamboo with a saw, the cutting part will not be so invisible when the cane is straightened.
- **orekugi:**
hooked nail; a nail whose top is cut off and nailed to the oyabashira for anchoring the twine when joining tateko (kumiko).
- **oshibuchi:**
pieces of bamboo placed tightly over tateko or kumiko to hold them in place. Oshibuchi is important in the design as well as the structure of the fence and the arrangement of oshibuchi influences greatly the overall beauty of fence. Stout bamboo split in half is usually used, although thin round bamboo are sometimes seen. Oshibuchi are usually placed horizontally, but in such fences as the katsura-gaki and the bamboo screen fence (misu-gaki), they are arranged vertically.
- **otoko-musubi (male knot):**
see ibo-musubi
- **oyabashira:**
relatively thick log post inserted into the ground as the main structure to support the fence. In most cases, oyabashira are put up at both ends of the fence, so it is also called "tomebashira" (fixing post), or "chikarabashira"(strengthening post). However, in the sode-gaki (lit. sleeve fences), a single post is often used.
- **sarashi-dake:**
a processed form of ma-dake or hachiku (sturdy pieces of bamboo). Thin pieces of bamboo are heated over a flame to remove the oils (today, chemicals are often used instead of fire) to be straightened and they are used for tateko. Used often for kumiko of bamboo screen fences (misu-gaki).
- **sashi-ishi:**
small and flat stones upon which tateko or kumiko rest. The part of the tateko (kumiko) inserted into the ground will rot after a long time and the sashi-ishi prevent this.
- **shahei-gaki (screening fence):**
general term for bamboo fences that can not be seen through for screening purpose. Even if it is of low height, the fence with such a structure is classified as a shahei-gaki. Typical varieties are the kenninji-gaki and the bamboo screen fence (takeho-gaki).
- **shimizu-dake:**
a product name of a processed bamboo, mainly of shino-dake (shino bamboo). Polished at the surface, straightened and oils removed from them. Pieces are of fixed length and used to make shimizu-gaki.
- **shin-gyô-sô:**
refers to three forms of style in many fields. Shin is the most formal, proper style; the sô form breaks down the shin in a beautiful but subdued way; and the gyô is a form between the other two. In bamboo fence making, the kenninji-gaki, yotsume-gaki and others exhibit the three forms.
- **shinobi-no-take (lit. hidden bamboo rail):**
thin split bamboo used temporarily to hold bamboo branches in place during the process of constructing a bamboo fence; also called simply shinobi. Sometimes the shinobi-no-take that is invisible is left as a part of the fence; in some processes it is removed before the fence is completed.
- **shino-dake:**
a small, thin kind of bamboo; a general term for a variety of bamboo such as ya-dake, me-dake and hakone-dake. Shino-gaki is the fence made of shino-dake.
- **shinshin (center-to-center):**
the distance between the centers of the two oyabashira.

- **shiori:**
  the process of severely bending bamboo or wood. In bamboo fences, a shiori-do (shiori door) is made by bending a thinly sliced outer surface of bamboo.
- **shiroho:**
  light-colored bamboo branches of such varieties as môsôchiku, hachiku, and ma-dake bamboo. It was named from its whitish color as compared with the black bamboo branches of kurochiku bamboo. Originally it was referred to the branches of hachiku bamboo. There is also an opinion that it refers to as the branches of hoteichiku bamboo.
- **sode-gaki (lit. sleeve fence; also wing fence):**
  a small bamboo fence with a single oyabashira just beside a building; named because they resemble the sleeve (sode) of a kimono. Most of the fences are screening fences on the purpose of screening and composing scenery alongside a gate, but some examples of see-through fences are also seen. Elaborate design in general can be seen because of its strong decorative factor. In addition, having many kinds and names is another characteristic of sode-gaki.
- **somenawa (dyed twine):**
  a hemp palm rope dyed black for tying bamboo fences. Today the rope made from real hemp palm is rarely used, and most of them are made from a coconut palm. Dyed twine should be soaked in water and softened before tying.
- **suekuchi:**
  the small end of a round bamboo cane. Opposite to motokuchi (motokuchi).
- **sugikawa:**
  cedar bark thinly peered off the surface of a trunk of cedar. The fence made by putting up the cedar bark is the sugikawa-gaki.
- **sui-gai:**
  a kind of panel fence that was used as a partition between buildings in the Heian and the Kamakura periods. The fence is made with gaps to be seen through. A fence with woven sliced bamboo pieces is also said to have existed.
- **suihei-ki (spirit level):**
  an instrument for the determining the horizontal by a bubble in water.
- **sukashi-gaki (see-through fence):**
  a bamboo fence that can be seen through, used widely for fences serving as inner partitions in gardens but still making it possible for the beautiful design of a garden to be seen. The yotsume-gaki and the kôetsu-gaki are typical examples.
- **takehiki noko:**
  a special saw for cutting bamboo: has a different angle of teeth from the saw for cutting wood.
- **takeho:**
  bamboo branches other than trunks. So takeho fences (takeho-gaki) vary from the one that uses thick bamboo branches to the one which uses flexible end at the top of bamboo. Takeho is distinguished between shiroho (light-colored bamboo branch) and kuroho (black bamboo branch).
- **take-no-kawa:**
  outer surface of round bamboo.
- **take-no-niku:**
  whitish inner part (pith) of split bamboo.
- **take-wari:**
  a special hatchet for splitting bamboo. Its edge must be wedge-shaped.
- **take-yarai:**
  bamboo stockade. Yarai originally meant stockade in a broad meaning, not limited to a bamboo stockade. However, bamboo grows fast and is easy to obtain anywhere. So the bamboo stockade were made so often that the name take-yarai arose. Originally all bamboo stockade were referred to as take-yarai, but today it is understood as another name of the yarai-gaki (yarai fences), with diagonally bamboo (kumiko) .
- **tamabuchi:**
  bamboo or other molding placed along the top of a fence as decoration and to protect the fence from the rain. When split bamboo is used, oshibuchi may be placed to both sides of the top of the fence and a kasa-dake placed on the top. Tamabuchi of bundled bamboo or bush clover (hagi) branches, and bamboo branches covered with thin split bamboo also exist. Fences of a given type may have varieties with or without tamabuchi.
- **tamabuchi-musubi:**
  a general term for the tying made on tamabuchi; mostly referred to the decorative tying on the tamabuchi of split bamboo of the kenninji-gaki, etc. The tying procedure is illustrated by a picture in the manual.
- **tatejitomi:**
  a kind of fence like tsuitate (portable screen), which was made mainly in the Heian and the Kamakura periods; most of them are portable. Some are made as an ajiro-gaki (wickerwork fence).
- **tateko:**
  a kind of kumiko that is used on the surface of the bamboo fence. Vertically placed kumiko are

seen most often and they are called tateko. They are called tateko whether they are of round bamboo, split bamboo, bamboo branches, or wood, etc.

- **teppô-zuke:**
  a method of tying tateko with dôbuchi (oshibuchi) between the oyabashira on the front and rear sides by turns. Several tateko in group may be attached by turns. This style is used for the yotsume-gaki and the teppô-gaki.
- **tokkuri-musubi:**
  one of the basic methods of nawa musubi (rope tying); the tying method by which the rope will not loosen without making a knot. The procedure is illustrated in the manual.
- **tokusa bari:**
  a general term for an appearance of split bamboo of the tateko put up like an appearance of tokusa (scouring rush). The fences with this appearance are tokusa-gaki (Dutch rush fences) and tokusa-bei (Dutch rush wall).
- **tomebashira:**
  another name for oyabashira
- **tori:**
  a status of looking straight. The bamboo cane that has almost a straight line is called "a bamboo with a good tori".
- **tsuitate-gaki (portable screen fence):**
  a general term for bamboo fences that are made portable like tsuitate (portable screen).
- **tsukibô:**
  a long tamping stick to force soil tightly into the hole on the ground into which the oyabashira or mabashira of a bamboo fence are inserted.
- **unokubi-musubi:**
  see tokkuri-musubi
- **warabi-nawa:**
  a kind of rope used for bamboo fences, which is made by twisting a bracken fiber. Warabi-nawa is much stronger than dyed twine, and lasts even longer than a bamboo fence itself. However it is expensive with extremely limited production, so it is used only for a small sode-gaki (sleeve fences) today.
- **warima:**
  determining the spacing of horizontal and vertical elements such as the number of dôbuchi with respect to the height of a fence, and the number of tateko with respect to the distance between the oyabashira. The spacing influences the feature of the fence greatly so that the spacing must be carefully examined in the design stage. Warima has almost the same meaning as "mawari".
- **yamawari-dake:**
  standard (1.8 meters) lengths of stout split bamboo; sold in a bundle; used mainly for the tateko of the kenninji-gaki.
- **yarai (stockade):**
  see "take-yarai".
- **yotsume karage:**
  one of the karage methods
- **yotsume no otoko-musubi:**
  another name for "ibo-musubi"
- **yuibo:**
  another name for "ibo-musubi"

● Illustrations by Makio Suzuki — P53~59, P61~67, P69~73, P75~79, P87~93, P95~100, P102~109, P118~122

Kazuaki Kometani — P81~85, P11~116, P124~128, P130~136

● Designed by Kenichi Kametani

Isao Yoshikawa

Born in Tokyo in 1940. Graduated from the Architecture Department of Shibaura Technical University. He established the Japan Garden Research Association in 1963. Presently chairperson of the Association. The honorary president of the Suzhou Society for study of Landscape & Gandens, China. The honorary president of the Hangzhou Society for study of Landscape & Gardens, China. He plays an active part as a scholar of Japanese gardens, a garden architect, a designer of stone art objects, etc.

Major books he has authored include "Bamboo fences" (Ariake Shobo, 1977), "Style of Famous Garden in Japan" (Kenchiku Shiryo Kenkyusha, 1978),"Details of Garden Design" (Kenchiku Shiryo Kenkyusha, 1978), "Paving Stones and Stepping Stones" (Ariake Shobo, 1979), "Gardens in Kyoto" (Kodansha, 1981), "An Illustrated Dictionary of Bamboo Fence and Rock Arrangement" (Kenchiku Shiryo Kenkyusha, 1984), "Japanese Garden Architects" (Japan Garden Research Associaton, 1993) and "Making a Small Garden" (Boutique-sha Co., 1996).

The publication by GRAPHIC-SHA PUBLISHING CO,. LTD. include "The Bamboo Fences of Japan" (1988, co-authored), "Stone Basins" (1989), "Chinese Gardens " (1990), "Element of Japanese Garden" (1990), "Zen Garden" (1991), "Japanese Stone Garden" (1992) and "Creat your Own Japanese Garden" (1995, co-authored).

Address: 2-30-4 Akatsutsumi, Setagaya-ku, Tokyo 156 Japan
Tel/Fax: 81-3-3322-7407